YOUTH MINISTRY FROM THE OUTSIDE IN

HOW RELATIONSHIPS AND STORIES SHAPE IDENTITY

BRANDON K. McKOY

IVP Books

An imprint of InterVarsity Press
Downers Grove, Illinois

InterVarsity Press
P.O. Box 1400, Downers Grove, IL 60515-1426
World Wide Web: www.ivpress.com
Email: email@ivpress.com

InterVarsity Press® is the book-publishing division of InterVarsity Christian Fellowship/USA®, a movement of students and faculty active on campus at hundreds of universities, colleges and schools of nursing in the United States of America, and a member movement of the International Fellowship of Evangelical Students. For information about local and regional activities, write Public Relations Dept., InterVarsity Christian Fellowship/USA, 6400 Schroeder Rd., P.O. Box 7895, Madison, WI 53707-7895, or visit the IVCF website at www.intervarsity.org.

Scripture quotations, unless otherwise noted, are from the New Revised Standard Version of the Bible, copyright 1989 by the Division of Christian Education of the National Council of the Churches of Christ in the USA. Used by permission. All rights reserved.

While all stories in this book are true, some names and identifying information in this book have been changed to protect the privacy of the individuals involved.

Design: Cindy Kiple
Interior design: Beth Hagenberg
Images: Black and white minority drawing: B & W minority, 2007 Diana Ong (b. 1940/Chinese-American)
    Computer Graphics Stock Photos/Glow Images
    cardboard surface: © Bill Noll/iStockphoto

ISBN 978-0-8308-4106-6 (paper)
ISBN 978-0-8308-9579-3 (digital)

Printed in the United States of America ∞

Library of Congress Cataloging-in-Publication Data
A catalog record for this book is available from the Library of Congress.

P	23	22	21	20	19	18	17	16	15	14	13	12	11	10	9	8	7	6	5	4	3	2	1
Y	33	32	31	30	29	28	27	26	25	24	23	22	21	20	19	18	17	16	15	14	13		

To my family

Contents

Foreword

Brandon McKoy is one of those students a professor never forgets. Smart. Intense. Committed. Never shy or withholding of his perspective, even if no one else in the room quite understood what he was getting at. Brandon McKoy is a one-of-a-kind deep thinker and passionate servant of Jesus Christ and the kingdom of God.

For professors, especially of doctoral students, we love it when students have their own opinions and perspectives—but, frankly, only to a point. When Brandon came into the first year of a multi-year cohort armed with a way of thinking that no one else had ever heard of, much less personally encountered, I admit to being a little thrown off. His depth of knowledge of "narrative" thinking, especially "narrative theology," forced the entire cohort, including me, to rethink long held assumptions about the nature of the self, identity and spiritual formation.

For the next three years, Brandon allowed himself to integrate that which he had brought to the cohort with the new information and perspective of the program. His desire to explore how the structure of practical theology could intersect with the social constructionism championed by theorists like Kenneth J. Gergen became his scholarly and pastoral quest. The outcome of Brandon's work is masterfully presented here, and I fully and enthusiastically endorse what he offers us, not only for those in youth ministry but in any missional leadership setting.

For those who are well versed in Dr. Gergen's contributions or the basic tenets of narrative as a framework, this book will be an inspiring next step to providing relationship leadership in any ministry context. For the rest— which is likely most of the readers of this book—I invite you to not allow yourself to be thrown off by language that may be challenging or unfamiliar. I believe that because most of us have been so saturated with a cultural predisposition toward "me-centeredness," whenever we are forced to think outside of that framework we become uncomfortable and possibly confused. Brandon freely takes on many such *a priori* assumptions common in our society, and he does not attempt to hide that his understanding of the way so many of us view life—primarily through the lens of individualism— is not only a philosophical premise to be dethroned, it is flat out unbiblical.

Brandon's rhetoric at times may be intimidating to the uninitiated, but his starting point is the same as anyone in youth ministry: helping young people discover and trust the God who has created them and called them into reconciled relationship. The deeper question he asks is important for any believer: How can I/we encourage a theologically sound understanding of identity that is rooted in relationships and story?

That is the driving question in this book. It is important—no, it is vital. The notion of "me and Jesus" and "me in the mirror" is simply not how God has wired us to live. As Brandon makes clear, I find my true self within the context of relationships and story. I distort God's image when I see life and faith as simply looking in the mirror.

This book is now a staple of the Youth, Family and Culture department curriculum. It is a perspective we may not all buy, especially initially, but it is nonetheless something we all must first understand, and second, wrestle with together. I am glad you have joined in the conversation.

Chap Clark
Chair, Youth, Family, and Culture Department
Fuller Theological Seminary

Acknowledgments

It takes a village to raise an author—especially this author.

Writing scared me. I never had confidence in writing or thought about writing for publication until Chap Clark encouraged me to do so. I trusted Chap, and I met with Tabitha Plueddemann (a freelance editor) to see if I had anything worth publishing. She was more excited about this book than I was, and she connected me with Julie Cramer (another freelance editor), who became my writing therapist and friend, counseling me into a whole new way of writing and engaging my audience. Without the encouragement and support of Chap, Tabitha and Julie, I would have never attempted to write, and this book would not exist.

Thanks to Chap Clark and Kenneth J. Gergen for writing the foreword and afterword. Their positioning as bookends to this book are significant. Chap represents practical theology to youth; Ken is the Dalai Lama of social constructionism. This book is a blending and integration of the two.

Thanks to Rachelle P. McKoy, my wife, friend and coauthor of many amazing life stories. You have been my greatest inspiration concerning the depth and value of relationships. Our struggles, accomplishments and many dialogues are laced throughout this book.

Kaden and Makenzie McKoy, you call me into being as "daddy." Although you are both young at the completion of this book (Kaden, age eight, and Makenzie, age five), you have taught me more about the power and influence of stories and language during infancy and childhood than anyone else. I look forward to all of the stories we will create in our future.

Mom and Dad McKoy, and Mom and Dad Pettit: Thank you for your encouragement, love and support. The process was made easier knowing that I have two loving families who supported me every step of the way.

Ned Buckner, my former pastor and friend: Your support and encouragement throughout writing this book was a constant source of strength. You truly exhibit the love of God in all that you do. You taught me how to relationally engage people by looking into their eyes and valuing them as God's precious creation—especially those who do not value love.

New Hope Baptist Church in Gastonia, North Carolina—my church family—thank you for embracing me and sharing God's love with our surrounding area.

My youth (current and previous): Thank you for teaching me how to be a minister. I have changed your names in the book and, due to confidentiality, I have split some of the stories. You will recognize many of our stories, and I consider it a great privilege to journey with you through many dangers, toils and snares in becoming more like Christ.

Gardner-Webb University (faculty and students): Thank you for inviting me to teach and implement much of this book in my youth discipleship classes. The conversations with my students were vital in the formation of this book. You all rock!

Fuller Theological Seminary: Thank you for providing a doctorate program in youth, family and culture that supported the integration and exploration of cutting-edge ministry practices. Much love to Chap and my cohort family that tolerated my obsession with narrative and my incessant comments and questions.

Thanks to the many conversation partners who have been a valuable resource in the completion of this book: Todd Bolin, Kent Blevins, Andy Smith, Mike Sears, Steve Knight, Josh Berryhill, Dennis Teal-Flemming, Jonathan Hale and my theologically diverse and lively Sunday morning class.

I would also like to thank the InterVarsity Press staff and Dave Zimmerman. Taking on a first-time author is risky business. Dave patiently walked me through my first book, and the IVP staff worked cohesively as a team to offer the reader the best work possible.

Finally, I would like to thank the reader. You may be someone I know, someone I will meet or someone I will never know personally. Regardless of our relationship, the words in this book and my role as an author come into existence because of you. Thank you for keeping this work alive.

Introduction

This is not the end of the story. It is not the beginning either. I used to think that stories, like this book, begin with the first sentence. To the contrary, stories do not appear from nowhere and neither do the relationships that mold them. Even when a story reaches its last sentence, its impact continues in the lives of those who have participated in its reading, telling and living.

I did not always have this understanding of story. I had simplified stories to a literary genre or more casual categories, such as "whispered around campfires," "as told through movies" and "heard at bedtime." Never had I thought of my life, including the decisions I have made, as a multifaceted story comprised of the stories I have read, seen, told and heard. I was introduced to this concept through a diverse reading of anthropologists, therapists, psychologists, sociologists, philosophers, literary theorists and theologians.

Through the stories of these authors and my relationships with them, the word *story* morphed into a metaphorical understanding of experience. I began to understand my life as a storied reality through relationships and language (verbal and nonverbal). Stories constitute our identity and saturate our lives with significance. Without stories, I would not be able to write this book; you would not be able to read it; and there would be no history from which we could learn, build on or apply to our lives.

As the word *story* began to take on a new meaning for me, I began to examine and research how youth understand, tell and hear stories. I knew that my four-year-old heard and told stories differently than the sixthgraders in my youth ministry, and I knew the sixth-graders heard and told stories differently than my high school juniors and seniors. I was driven to learn exactly what constituted those differences and how stories shape youth and their understanding of identity into adulthood.

Because of this quest, I entered a doctoral program at Fuller Theological Seminary to study with Chap Clark. As evident in his groundbreaking book, *Hurt,* Chap was one of the few in youth ministry who engaged youth culture from a sociological perspective. I had limited story and storytelling to being within the mind of individual students, and Chap encouraged me to take a closer look at the relational dynamics and social structures of youth.

Over four years, I read anything and everything that mentioned the word *narrative.* Many authors quoted Kenneth J. Gergen, and I noticed that his work in social constructionism was vital in the formation of narrative therapy, appreciative inquiry, positive aging, solution-focused therapy, collaborative therapy, relational learning, qualitative research and many more. His work seemed to influence just about every field that provided cutting-edge opportunities for ministry and social practices. When a friend called and offered me the opportunity to take a workshop with Ken and his wife, Mary, I made reservations in Swarthmore, Pennsylvania, where Ken works as the senior research professor of psychology at Swarthmore College.

My weekend encounter with the Gergens initiated a dance between social constructionist theory and practice, and my background in practical theology—a dance that had already taken place a few years earlier among a scholarly group of practical theologians.[1] Like this group, I found enormous possibilities in placing social constructionism in dialogue with practical theology.

However, I was a little uneasy with this dance partner. I had been warned that she was seductive, and not long after the dance, she would surely have me in the bedroom of relativism. After all, social constructionism is also known by other labels such as post-enlightenment, post-foundational, post-structural and postmodern. These were posts that some of my ministerial friends were using for attaching their "keep away" signs.

Nevertheless, I decided to dance, and the dance changed my rhythm of life and of ministry to youth. I encountered a paradigm shift—not one that took me away from Christian practices and principles, but that deepened them. I began to savor the importance of relationships, the biblical story, our relationship with God and the church's role within God's relational reign.

With my background in practical theology and my new lenses of social constructionism, I was able to see things differently. Youth ministry as it is generally practiced has not been particularly fruitful in its exploration and proclamation of the biblical story. With the current loss of biblical narratives in many youth ministry settings, youth ministry has become captive to the grand cultural narrative of individualism. Meaning, communication and responsibility have been considered individual matters ascertained through individual choices. The problems youth experience—and the responsibility for those problems—are located intrinsically within individual youth.

Youth Ministry from the Outside In attempts to provide new spaces of understanding from which more promising youth ministry practices may emerge. I hope to move beyond traditional youth ministry models to a more holistic and integrative approach to youth, Scripture and church.

Although there has been a rise in youth ministry literature about stories and relationships, no one has written about the dynamics between the two. Throughout this book, I will attempt to articulate stories, relationships and human development through a relational perspective that will advance youth ministry beyond individualistic practices and assumptions.

Youth Ministry from the Outside In is divided into three parts. In part one, I demonstrate the way we currently see the world and relationships through individualism, and I introduce a theological and social constructionist view of relationships and stories. Chapter one begins with an emphasis on perspective and on how slight shifts may change everything. I explain how changing to a relational understanding of youth altered both my life and how I ministered to them. I challenge the concept that we are separate and autonomous individuals and propose a relational vision. One of the major issues in recovering biblical narratives in youth ministry is the way the grand cultural narrative of individualism shapes Western society's view of human action and development. Chapter one chisels away this perspective with the hammers of social constructionism and practical theology.

Chapter two explores the inadequacies of individualism. When we consider the uniqueness of youth to be solely internal, we view failure as an internal, individual problem. Through a story of a teenager, I illustrate how her feelings of inadequacy and failure were a result of her relationships and stories—not of individual personal failure. I conclude the chapter with a biblical perspective on relationships that focuses more on our interconnectedness than on our individuality.

Chapter three magnifies how we are relational beings. A youth becomes a particular person and plays specific roles within each relationship. His relational interactions provide material for the stories he tells. The chapter concludes with an emphasis on how a youth and youth pastor shape each other and their future through language.

Our life stories are not "reality," but they are "*our* reality." Chapter four unpacks this and emphasizes how we approach our youth's stories as being real, while keeping in mind that we can help them rewrite their life stories. I conclude the chapter with an example of how we can help our youth revise pieces of their story.

Part two examines the importance of our coordination of our life story, how our relationships from infancy into adolescence shape our identity. Chapter five introduces the life story, and it challenges our understandings of identity as something that is in the mind rather than the outcome of interactions with people. It shows how identity is shaped through the stories we coordinate with others, detailing the four coordinations present in every life story.

The framework for how youth approach the world and construct stories of the world with others is heavily influenced by their interactions with adults and the narratives of those adults during their childhood. Chapter six introduces four foundational elements needed in childhood for adolescents to be able to share their life story. It begins with how care and support in early childhood establish the narrative tone for how children relate to others and tell their own stories. Our primary Western understanding of language as a word picture is challenged through examining how we learn language through our use of it.

The importance of temporal coordination with children illustrates how a sense of time locates events, establishes a sense of self and affords youth the opportunity to structure their present story with God's future reality. The chapter concludes by focusing on evaluative narratives as central to how children reflect on and evaluate their lives and tell their life stories in adolescence.

Chapter seven illustrates the transformative power of stories and relationships in early adolescence, and it highlights the increase in relational encounters among youth. The differences between understanding youth from an individualistic tradition and understanding them from a relational narrative perspective are discussed, and dominant paradigms from the developmental sciences are called into question—namely, that the adolescent journey is about independence.

The chapter also centers on how early adolescents begin their first attempts at a life story through personal fables, which are partial life stories. They include cultural and temporal coordination, but early adolescents do not have thematic or causal coordination. Without these, they construct stories of themselves without recognizing the many contradictions that may be present, or they organize them according to certain themes.

Through midadolescence (high school age), personal fables are rewritten as youth begin their first drafts of their life story. Through social interactions and relational narrative development, youth gain thematic and causal coordination. With this new understanding of stories, youth are able to structure their life stories intentionally around particular themes and to causally connect various stories from their life history. However, the ability to develop thematic and causal coordination largely depends on their interactions with adults. Chapter eight reveals the life story of a senior in high school and emphasizes the importance of youth pastors knowing their youth's emerging life stories, rather than just the stories they tell.

Chapter nine raises issues concerning biblical interpretation, the importance of reading Scripture as story and the interpretive maneuvers we use when the text is not read as story. When Christians read the Bible as a narrative whole, hermeneutical biases are limited to the story's progression and overarching themes. This chapter questions how youth ministers read their Bible and highlights basic assumptions that people inherit from academic training and church experiences. It explores how those assumptions configure their view of God and their approach to Scripture. The chapter concludes with the importance of reading the Bible as story and of reading Scripture through the lenses of the multifaceted life story of Jesus.

Chapter ten examines the current trend toward the loss of the biblical story in youth ministry. When I recognized the phenomenon of increasing unfamiliarity with the biblical narratives among teenagers, college students and adults, coupled with a lack of meaning in their faith, I began exploring alternative means to understand and communicate the biblical story to the youth I encounter. This chapter articulates how the life and ministry of

Jesus makes his birth, death and resurrection meaningful and how neglecting the life story of Jesus does not offer a context in which to situate the
significance of his death and resurrection. Seven popular youth ministry
practices complicit in the loss of biblical story are discussed, and movements that aim to thicken the presentation of the biblical story and reclaim
Jesus' life story in youth ministry practices are suggested.

The stories youth ministers incorporate matter, because they become
fundamental to how youth understand, communicate and take responsibility in the world. Chapter eleven is an invitation to rediscover what it
means to structure the life story of youth with Jesus' life story. When development is understood through a relational narrative perspective—coupled
with a relational narrative understanding of Scripture—new youth ministry
practices emerge as the life story of Jesus becomes the central narrative for
shaping future stories of youth ministry practices.

Jesus' life story also becomes the narrative that confronts and stands
against our society's individualistic stories. The centrality of his story reveals the centrality of the kingdom of God in youth ministry practices.
Chapter eleven presents the life story of Christ as the ultimate guiding story
that thematically and causally structures youth's life stories.

Restructuring our life story with the life story of Jesus calls us into being
as the body of Christ. Being the body of Christ means being responsible in
God's relational reign. Chapter twelve addresses our understanding of responsibility and places it within the context of relationships and the
kingdom of God. Responsibility in the West has rested primarily on the
shoulders of the individual, with dire consequences. I address these consequences and offer an alternative way of viewing responsibility and action in
youth ministry. This chapter exposes the problem-saturated stories that
dominate, objectify and cripple youth and takes a closer look at implementing Christ's life story over and against such stories.

At the end of each chapter I have included questions. The questions are
not designed for you simply to provide an answer, but to encourage you to
implement some of the resources provided in this book. I also include a
critic's voice in each chapter. In these sections I try to engage concerns
about the material discussed. I do not intend for my response to be the final
word to the critic, but I hope to open dialogue and space where the critic
can feel welcome.

I assigned a social constructionist book to my youth discipleship class at Gardner-Webb University. One student told me that he kept throwing the book across the room because it was unraveling his faith; he said he simply couldn't believe certain tenets of social constructionism. But he felt better about the book and our class when I told him that social constructionism is not a belief system. It requires nothing from anyone. It is a tool.

I have been a brick mason since I was thirteen, and I carry tools in my mason's bag: a trowel, line blocks, a mason's line, a level, a plumb line, a laser level, a trig and so on. None of my tools require anything from me. Yet they allow me to build and construct in ways I couldn't without them. You will never hear me talking about how I believe in my brick hammer or how people should submit their life to it. To say I believe in social constructionism or that I try to convince others to believe in it would defeat the use of the tool itself. I am no more a social constructionist than I am a brick hammer. Therefore, I'm inviting you to pick up the tool of social constructionism and imagine with me a new way of doing youth ministry.

Youth Ministry from the Outside In is not concerned with a right or wrong way—or liberal or conservative way—of doing youth ministry. It offers an alternative way that takes the life stories of youth seriously and integrates them with the transformative power of the life story of Jesus.

I have watched friends burn out in youth ministry because the individualistic approaches left them and their ministries relationally and spiritually bankrupt. I hope this book sparks imagination, curiosity and excitement about your youth ministry practices. I pray that God will use this book to speak new life and energy into your life and how you minister to our youth.

Part One

BEYOND SELF AND
INDIVIDUAL IDENTITY

1

The Way We See It

Social Constructionism
and Practical Theology

I asked my youth to draw pictures of their families. With markers in hand and blank sheets of paper before them, they began drawing their family portraits. Round circles for heads, straight lines for the arms and body, each separated by space. Unique physical attributes delineated each figure, and objects signified parents' jobs. All of my youth's drawings pictured families made up of individuals—except for one.

Tony's family picture was horrendous. It had one body, four heads, eight arms and eight legs. And the pairs of legs and arms were all different. Several youth laughed at his picture and called it ridiculous. I imagine the apostle Paul experienced similar ridicule from members of the church in Corinth when he suggested viewing Jesus as a head and his followers as feet, ears, hands and so on. Tony's perspective was different, but profound.

"Why are you laughing?" Tony asked, holding the paper protectively to his chest.

"Because it's not real," Heather hissed.

"Is your picture *real*?" I asked.

Heather looked down at the lines and circles that represented her family. "No," she said, shrugging.

"Whose picture is real? If I gathered your family and took a picture with my phone, would that be real?" I asked.

My youth stared at me, shaking their heads.

"Who taught you how to draw? Talk? Write?" I went on.

"Our parents," they said in unison.

"Do you think your drawing is just 'your drawing'? Or do you think your families have influenced the way you hold your pencil, how you talk to others, how you view others? So even in the act of drawing, your family presses firmly on your pencil."

For my youth, Tony's drawing did not represent a "real" family because our Western reality teaches us that we are fundamentally separated and distinct people. But to pretend that my familial relationships do not exist while they are not physically present is an illusion. Dominican priest Albert Nolan stated this well:

> We remain one flesh all our lives, no matter what illusions of independence and separateness we may develop in our minds. In reality we are intertwined, interconnected, and interdependent. None of us could survive without others. We would have no language and no knowledge. We belong together. We are one.[1]

In an episode of the TV reality show *Undercover Boss,* Steve Choice, CEO of Choice Hotels, said in a choked voice, as he let the tears come, "I know my mom was proud of me, but I know she would be really proud of me today." Steve's relationship with his mother, which no longer existed physically, continues to shape him. Are we really as separated as what we see with our own eyes? Or are we as connected as Tony's picture illustrates?

My youth's diverse pictures were not right or wrong; they each presented a portrait of their family. If I wanted to know what role each family member played and their occupation, Heather's portrait would have provided me with more information. I am emphasizing Tony's family portrait here because the interconnectedness that he sees is absent in most of our youth ministry practices.

Tony's perspective is a simple shift in the way of seeing his family. He sees the interconnectedness of his family—even when they are not physically available. How do you view your family? Church? Ministry?

I presented figure 1.1 to my youth, and said, "Don't tell me what you see. Reflect on what you would add to the picture. What's missing? What kind of environment would you draw if you were the artist?"

"A pond," Jon shouted.

"A pond? Do you want to drown it?" Paige asked, wrinkling her brow.

"Why?" Jon asked. "What would you add?"

Paige let out a frustrated sigh. "A forest, briar patch and some carrots. Duh!"

"Why would you feed a duck carrots?" Jon asked, staring at her.

"Because I'm not feeding a duck; it's a rabbit!"

"It's both a duck *and* a rabbit," said Stephan, who had seen the picture before.

Figure 1.1.

Jon and Paige looked at the drawing a second time and laughed when they finally saw the other's duck, the other's rabbit.

The picture illustrates how our perspectives change how we see and understand the same object. Why is it that Jon, Paige and Stephan couldn't help but see it in certain ways? A simple shift in perspective can reveal entirely different animals.

A CHANGE IN PERSPECTIVE

Perhaps you have had shifts in perspective that have changed the way you view people, situations and yourself. I've had my share of those too. As mentioned in the introduction, my encounter with the Gergens and social constructionism shifted my view of self, family, youth and youth ministry practices.

In the initial research for my dissertation, I studied individual youth. I believed I could better understand my youth and how to minister to them if I began with each individual. As the motto goes, I attempted to meet youth at their point of need. I would observe Cassie and try to understand what made her tick. I thought that if I could figure out Cassie's outward influences, I would know what affected her mental processes. Or if I could figure out her mental processes (and deficits), I could discover what caused her actions—or lack of action.

Instead of pitting the outer and inner against each another (psyche versus social and nature versus nurture), I attempted to place them in a relationship. It was no longer either/or but both/and. Therefore, I understood Cassie as a product of the relationship between her psyche and social influences, and I adopted the term *psychosocial*. I wrote more than two hundred pages on ministering to youth from a narrative psychosocial perspective. Here's the issue, though: in both her outward influences and her mental processes, Cassie was never alone. Social constructionism helped me see there's no *I* in *psychosocial*.

Through the lenses of social constructionism, I began to see that my view of human action was limited to the individual, causing me to miss a fuller understanding of my youth. Within the framework of social construction, I had room to shift my perspective of Cassie's individual action to her *co-action* in relationships.[2] The focus and attention was no longer on the individual, but on the person *in relationships*.

At first, this concept seems like it removes the internal in favor of the external—namely, Cassie is solely determined by her relationships. Though she is not determined by her relationships, she mutually constructs her world with her mom, dad, sister, brother, teacher, friends and so on. In the context of youth ministry, I would ask, "Who does Cassie become through her relationships with her youth pastor, mom, dad, sister, brother, friends and teachers?" She is a different person in each of these relationships. Therefore, the focus is not on her internal workings or how the external changes the internal, but on the collaboration that occurs differently in each of her relationships. The shift to the coordination of the relationship moves us beyond several age-old arguments that divide nature versus nurture, social versus psyche and outside versus inside.

SOCIAL CONSTRUCTIONISM

Social constructionism is not a singular and unified theory; it is better understood as an unfolding dialogue among a wide variety of scholars and practitioners. The pivotal idea of social constructionism is that we create our world through our relationships and through the language we use and the stories we share.[3] This description appears simple and straightforward, but as we unpack its implications, we will see its complexity—and the richness it offers the youth in our ministries.

As Westerners, we view the world from an individualistic perspective—a view that many practical theologians share when engaging in theological reflection and praxis. Yet social constructionism illuminates our relational formations that are eclipsed by individualism. Our tendency to begin with the individual shapes how we see God, read Scripture, communicate, interact with others, understand youth development, minister and so on. Social constructionism is a tool that we can use to remove the lenses of individualism so that we can recapture the ministry of Jesus in our relationships and in the stories we share with our youth.

Individualism blinds us to how connected we are. Our choices and decisions really do affect those around us. If we do not see our connectedness, we are like the man who went fishing with two friends. In the middle of the lake, he decided to drill a hole under his seat in the bottom of the boat. The other two men began to panic and scream, "What are you doing?" With calm detachment, he said with a sneer, "What is it to you? I am only making the hole under *my* seat."[4] Social construction helps us to see that we are all in the same boat. Living as if we are not is like drilling a hole under our seat and thinking that we are affecting no one but ourselves.

LANGUAGE: THE LENS THROUGH WHICH WE SEE AND CREATE THE WORLD

Relationships come before all that is intelligible. This idea is central to social constructionism. We wouldn't see a duck or a rabbit if no one had ever taught us the terms for those animals. Of course, the animals exist, but as we describe and explain them, they become real for us in particular ways.

A cow to many Western children means milk. A farmer sees a cow as income. A meat lover sees a steak. A Hindu bows and worships. How do you see a cow? What we deem a cow, calf, bull, cattle and so on depends on the relationships we have established with others and the language we have learned to label and classify such beings. A cattle breeder would laugh at our oversimplification of cows, because there are over eight hundred breeds of cattle. Not until we are introduced to the language of the cattle breeder can we see the complex world of cattle the way he does.

You probably don't see brick buildings the same way that I see them. I have been a brick mason most of my life. I try to show people rowlocks, sailors, soldiers, stretchers, quoin corners, head joints, bed joints, Flemish bonds, herringbones and Spanish bonds, but they see only bricks and patterns. Introducing brick masonry terminology allows people not only to see but also to appreciate brick buildings in completely different ways. At first people have a difficult time understanding what they're seeing, but the more they use the brick mason's language, the more their perception and their experiences change. So it really does make a difference what kind of language we use in youth ministry and how we talk and share stories—particularly biblical stories—with our youth.

Relationships and language are vital to who we are and who we become. This emphasis on the coordination of relationships and language (in particular narratives) in human action was a natural segue for me to get back into the basics of practical theology.[5]

Social constructionism became a tool that grounded my practical theology within the context of relationships. Seeing the world through the relationships and stories that form us—and seeing our actions through them—leads us into a deeper, thicker and richer understanding of youth ministry. For Christians, it invigorates two of the most prominent forms of ministry: relationships (to God and people) and stories (biblical stories and shared stories).

Social construction coupled with practical theology equipped me to ask questions concerning the relational co-action between youth and youth pastor, youth and church, youth and adults. How well are we as youth pastors doing with our "God language" in everyday ministry? Our words do not just state information, but construct a world with our youth. What kind of vocabulary is our youth ministry providing so that they can talk about God?

Youth can't articulate, understand and have a meaningful experience of God without God language. "The lone individual might have an experience of God, but without any theological language [stories of God] he would have no way of knowing what the experience was," philosopher and theologian Nancey Murphy said.[6] The more stories—shaped and framed by the biblical story—youth ministers provide, the more opportunities youth have to "story"—frame and reframe—their experiences of God in more nuanced ways. Proclaiming the biblical story equips students with the language to interpret and share their experiences of God.

When the cultural language of *Holy Spirit, sin, savior, everlasting life* and *God* are no longer used in communal gatherings and in society in general, religious institutions die out.[7] As Kenneth Gergen states, "If we do not continue to speak the way we do, then our long-standing traditions of cultural life are under threat. . . . Sustaining one's traditions requires a continuous process of regenerating meaning together."[8] The more limited youth and youth ministers are in framing and telling the biblical stories, the more limited they will be in articulating and sharing their experiences with others.

Without the appropriate narratives, youth will inevitably develop "thin" stories—stories that do not provide them with much meaning or a deep articulation of their faith. This neglect of developing thicker narratives through meaningful communication is evident in current research.[9] Youth could not articulate matters of faith, not because they were incapable, but because they were not provided the language and/or the opportunity to learn how to speak it.[10] Could this be the direct result of our Western focus on ministry to the individual? Why would youth pastors be concerned with the co-action of our language and stories with youth if we don't see them as the central aspect of youth's identity formation? To address this issue, we must begin shifting our perspective on how we see youth.

THE WAY I SEE IT

If you open a high school yearbook and look at the individual portraits, what do you see? A child maturing into an independent adult? A child of God? A person who is free to make his or her own choices? If you know one of the students, perhaps you could give a list according to what you know and see: Fred Swaynee, sixteen, brown hair, brown eyes, dark complexion, athletic, fun, loving, caring and humorous. What's *not* pictured? Relationships.

If your yearbook is like mine, each student's picture is separated by a space: Fred's at the top left, Marjorie's beside him, Janice below and a host of other students surrounding them. They are clearly delineated as individuals. To see relationships, we flip to a different section of the yearbook and find a picture of Fred with some of his peers. Social construction helps us recognize that the lone individual we see blurs our vision to the relational matrix that is present. Fred without relationships is only one way of viewing the world.

Fred's picture doesn't require us to view him in the ways listed above. The relationships we have with others shape our perspective. A photographer sees a photogenic smile. A hairstylist sees last year's hairstyle. An orthodontist sees a potential client. A fashion designer sees a stylish teenager. A high school girl sees a prospective prom date.

Just as each of these views emerges from particular relationships and language descriptions, so does our view that Fred is an individual, with no signs of relationships present. From a social constructionist perspective, I see Fred as a rich, deep, multifaceted young man who has constructed his life in the ebb and flow of relationships. On a surface level, if we look at the hairstyles and clothing of our youth in yearbooks as a whole and compare it to another yearbook from ten to twenty years earlier, we see the cultural constraints of relationships.

On a deeper level, Fred has constructed ways of acting, being and doing in his relationships. And although the picture of Fred does not show us relationships, they are present and more real than what our eyes capture. Fred is smiling, facing a certain direction, wearing particular clothes and maintaining an upright posture precisely because of his relationships.

SEEING THE WE IN ME

How we understand relationships shapes how we minister. And our understanding of relationships governs how we view stories. We tend to view the world in terms of fundamental separation: me here, you there. And we do not have a relationship until we come together. Yet nothing *requires* us to view people and relationships in this manner. This is not how it is or how it has to be.

This is Western culture, and our culture accounts for only a sliver of the global cultural pie. In fact, most cultures around the world find it peculiar that we regard ourselves as unique, singular and separate individuals who act consciously on our own.[11] A multitude of scholars are echoing this befuddlement and sounding an alarm that our individualistic view of the world is undermining our communities, families, relationships and churches. What will happen if we do not teach our children and youth another way of seeing?

What would occur if, instead, we framed our speech, descriptions and explorations about self and youth ministry in relational rather than individual terms? How might we talk about, describe and explore our understandings of God, Scripture, youth, church, ministry and education? The shift may seem as simple as changing our view to see a duck or a rabbit. In the end, as with the duck-rabbit, we will have an altogether different perspective.

Focusing solely on individuals as entering into and out of relationships results in a failure to appreciate the importance of the relational self and how meaning and communication exist through coordinated action between

---

THE CRITIC'S VOICE

Criticism

It seems to me you are taking away the individual and replacing him with relationships. This removes the individual's voice in favor of the relationship and neglects the freedom of the individual to do or say on his own. This notion reminds me too much of George Orwell's novel 1984, where it becomes so much about the community that they can't break free of the abusive group think.

Response

A social constructionist view of human development and action is sometimes criticized as ignoring the individual and therefore removing the personal in favor of the social. This is not the case. I do not cease being Brandon K. McKoy and lose my identity. Instead, I have a deeper, healthier, broader, richer view of identity when I realize how relationships form and shape me and how my relationships have shaped and formed others. How do I view and understand myself after I have considered the matrix of relational formations? Doesn't this allow me to have a fuller picture of me?

If I think I can make my own choices and decisions apart from the constraints of my relationships, I have no freedom, because I am bound by the illusion of individualism. However, when I recognize that meaning—and even our notion of freedom—exists in the context of relationships, I create with others this space of belief and sustainability. My relationships do not control me. In one sense they do constrain me, but in another they offer the freedom to create new realities and new forms of action through them. We do not fall into relational oblivion and become one among many. Even Paul used metaphors of being free from sin and enslaved to others and Christ (Rom 6:22; 1 Cor 7:22; 2 Cor 4:5; Gal 5:13).

---

people.[12] When we begin with an individual view of the world, relationships are understood as the outcome of individual action. But relationships are much broader and more complex than this Western view implies. I believe a better way to understand youth is to change our perception entirely.

The illusion of isolation (it is just me and my individual self when I withdraw from others) keeps us from recognizing that our relationships continue to shift and shape us when others are not physically present. We are a lot more connected than we may ever realize.

The individualist perspective prevents the exploration of broader circumstances and actions, and it becomes a demeaning and simplistic way of understanding others. If I approach youth merely as their own unique individuals making their own unique choices and decisions, then I neglect their relational formations, which would provide me with not only a reservoir of better understanding but also a source for healing. A teen's negative actions at church, for example, may have more to do with her relationships within the church, and how she has been treated in those relationships, than simply her individual action. When deeper aspects of relationships are overlooked, communal growth and genuine connectivity are hindered. As Gergen states, "When the self is the essential atom of society, we find invitations to isolation, distrust, narcissism, and competition; we find relationships reduced to manipulation and artifice; and we find a stunting simplification of the problems we confront."[13]

CONCLUSION

Recognizing the shaping power of relationships and stories—that we literally form pieces of each other through our interactions and stories—will transform the way we live everyday life. For us—or Fred and Tony—to "mean" anything in society, we must be engaged in relationships.

My goal with the remainder of this book is to invite you into the dialogue as you explore social constructionist ideas and practical theology in your life and ministry. I will sketch out basic aspects of social constructionist theory that have shifted my youth ministry practices in the hope that it will generate the same curiosity, excitement and transformation for you as it has for me.

I believe the combination of social constructionism and practical theology plows the soil for a paradigm shift in youth ministry. My hope is that the seeds planted in this book will produce theological fruit that will sustain and nourish your ministry—and your youth—for ages to come.

REFLECTION QUESTIONS

1. Describe those around you from an individualistic perspective. Emphasize how you see them as separate, autonomous agents of their own actions and choices. After you have completed your description, focus on the same people from a relational perspective. Emphasize how you are connected through culture, environment and interactions. Which perspective offers a fuller account of the person and why?

2. Ask five people if you can take their individual picture. Observe what they say or do before taking their picture. What common elements exist in their reactions? What is common in the pictures you captured? Where are the relationships?

3. Reflect on how people who are no longer physically connected to you continue to influence the decisions you make. Ask a friend to share how a person who has died affects her actions today. Record her response.

4. Explain how the language of our Christian faith helps you see things differently.

5. Many of the things we accomplish throughout the day are considered individual tasks because we are alone. List the individual things that you have accomplished from the time you woke up until now. Beside each of your individual tasks, write how each has been shaped by relationships or how they prepare you for relationships. For example, brushing teeth: (a) I have been taught through my relational engagement with parents, a dentist and a health teacher that it is important to brush my teeth for the health and well-being of my teeth and body, and (b) I am preparing myself to enter into relationships with others who value good hygiene and white teeth.

6. Think about the clothes you're wearing. Why did you put those clothes on? Why not the same clothes you wore the day before? There are no directions on your clothing that tell you how to wear them. How did you know to arrange your clothing in a particular order? Why did you choose the clothing you are wearing? What relationships were impacting you as you chose your clothing?

2

The Inadequacies of Individualism

Early in my ministry career, the individuality of youth, their uniqueness as God's creation and their freedom to make their own individual choices were part and parcel of any talk I gave on Christian identity and self-esteem. I aimed to empower them with a new sense of self-worth, and I left knowing I had helped them feel better about themselves and their Christian identity. Or so I thought.

One day Lisa approached me, looking down at her black Skecher shoes. "I know I'm uniquely created by God," she said, "but I *hate* how he has uniquely created me. I hate my body, and I hate the way I can't get anything right. I feel like a failure . . . and I am beginning to hate God for screwing me up like this." Obviously she didn't listen to my Christian identity talk. Or did she?

I shrugged off her response as a result of not paying attention. Other youth seemed to get it, so why didn't she? I dismissed her criticism of my lesson and left our conversation at the church. That night I dreamed Lisa committed suicide.

All I could hear was, "I hate how God has uniquely created me," and the phrase tormented me. Lisa had come to me for help, and I had failed her. Feelings of inadequacy washed over me. Similar inadequacies that plagued Lisa also plagued me. I had crowned myself king of my self-made kingdom, assured of who I was and my position in life, yet I was trapped in a relentless process of comparison. I compared myself to everyone: other youth pastors, husbands, fathers, ministers, coaches, instructors, athletes—you name it. And I felt I had to be the best. The nightmare I had about Lisa demolished the fortress I called self-esteem. *I hated how God had uniquely created me.*

I felt sorry for Lisa, but I couldn't get past my own feelings of failure as her youth pastor to actually help her. I was inadequate too. Lisa had her own set of internal problems, and I had mine. But how could two people of different ages, genders and life stages come to express the same sentiment? We didn't harbor the same experiences of inadequacy and failure, but we fed them and nurtured them with the same story—the story of Western individualism.

BEING SELF-FOCUSED

Individualism scripts our lives at an early age. From the way we were parented to the way we were educated, we were taught to prize and prioritize the individual. We quickly learn to compete "to be the best." Teachers and coaches reinforced these attitudes with trophies, ribbons, smiley-face stamps, stickers and certificates. If we had the highest grades or the most crowd-awing athletic ability, we earned the approval of our teachers, peers and parents. External influences—magazine spreads of perfect bodies, overnight success stories, celebrities' bank accounts—aided in reinforcing our perception that we do not measure up to societal standards. Could it be that societal celebrations of individual achievements and accomplishments reduce potentials for creating meaning in life?

With thought and reason originating in the individual mind, a logical implication is that since everything resides "inside," the private world of the individual can't be known. When we can't know what is inside, even the most intimate relationships carry a sense of distrust. That's because the other person's deep interior is an unknowable region that can stand in tension and even in contradiction with my words and actions.[1]

If we understand the self as the center of our existence, and we can never fully know or trust another, self-preservation can become our central preoccupation. When a person "looks out for number one," he maintains an ongoing assessment of others and a search for their failures.[2] How can I strive to be superior to others if I do not know others' failures and flaws? Or how can I keep from feeling inferior to others by not exposing my flaws?

We spend countless hours and immense amounts of money in self-improvement, building self-esteem and finding ways to be better or equal to those around us. From our individualistic perspective, the more entangled we become in relationships, the more reminders we have of our inadequacies. When we seek to relate with others, one of the primary questions seems to be "How can this person benefit me, and what will this relationship cost me?" People become an instrument for achieving self-gratification.

When we view the uniqueness of youth as originating internally, what happens when they fail? Failure is viewed as an internal, individual problem. Any inadequate performance or public failure throws youth and us into questioning our deficiencies. Yet self-esteem, self-worth and self-value are all prominent notions incorporated in our ministry practices, which stem from our individualistic culture. The site of change is in the internal workings of the person. Can we view this differently? And can this change how we understand ourselves and our youth?

Lisa's and my feelings of inadequacy do not originate from inside us, but were formed through the relationships and stories that nourished our individualism. Let me illustrate: Lisa, who is becoming a woman, has been given the social script that provides her with an articulation and examination of what her body should do and be. By the time she becomes a teenager, she has already been instructed to think and act a certain way, according to the cultural narratives she has grasped. She knows how she is supposed to talk (that is, sweet not bitter, polite not rude, soft not loud), walk (that is, straight not crooked, delicate not forceful, smooth not rough) and look (that is, distinguished not vulgar, thin not thick, pretty not ugly). People examine her when she is in public, and she feels the pressure of that story, especially when she might not be fulfilling her role in the script society has given her. Her inability to self-manage or self-regulate is interpreted *not* as a problem stemming from the cultural narrative itself, but as her own failure.[3]

Lisa has become locked into a system of domination, and she is hoping to illustrate her ability to self-manage and self-regulate her body so that her story will be one of success and she will be admired by others. Society also provides the language that helps maintain the story of her bodily struggles. For example, if she is not pretty by society's definition, there is only one other option: ugly. If she is not categorized as good, she is bad. If she is not deemed a winner, she is a loser. She accepts these labels and stories as reality, and she never questions the negative stories and relationships that formed her reality.[4] She will continue to produce and script this story for others unless she is given an alternative script and an alternative way to understand herself in society (a focal point of chapters 9–12).

Lisa's inability to correct failures individually creates a cycle of despair, especially since she views her problems as her *individual* problems. To make matters worse, we try to throw God into the mix. Lisa not only views her perception of self as reality, but also believes it is the way God has created her to be. Ironically, our individualistic perception of God's creation seals the coffin on abundant life. When we address issues of individual failure with individual value, esteem and worth, it's like taking ibuprofen for a broken leg. It will help ease the pain, but only temporarily.[5]

AN ALTERNATIVE STORY

When youth ministers understand and emphasize students as unique individuals created by God with their individual identity, students continue to see their self-understanding as originating within them. Again, this view becomes problematic when teens identify failure solely as a personal problem.

Suicide is the worst manifestation of this view of uniqueness and the concomitant emphasis of failure. Teens who want to end it all see no way out and are trapped in a vicious cycle of despair because, if the failure is solely theirs, no one can help.[6] They see the world as being better off without them. Their individualistic worldview is so singularly focused that it blocks out the light and help—or shared responsibility—that others may offer. They do not recognize how interconnected they are and how suicide would alter not just their family but an entire community.

Therefore, to tell youth that they are uniquely created by God with their own unique identities is not enough. This statement, in itself, still has the potential to locate a youth's uniqueness within the individualistic tradition. On the contrary, a relational (and theological) perspective focuses on how any sense of an "I" or a "you" emerges from our relationships and not from any consciousness within the brain or inside the body—so much so that all notions and quests for the sacred begin and end precisely there.

Therefore, youth are created by God, not to be individuals but to be relational with God and others through using their gifts and talents that have emerged through their relationships. The uniqueness of each youth comes from his relationships, and relationships sustain his gifts and talents. God has created youth *uniquely to be in community* (the body of Christ). God has not gifted youth to go about their own doing, but to do everything in relation to God and neighbor. This perspective joins uniqueness and identity in the context of relational formation and co-agency.

Ministry is not about the individual as a separate being. When Christians affirm a unique individual identity that exists independently of others, they forfeit the very self that God intended them to be: an interdependent self (Lk 9:23-25). For Christians, the self is manifest through losing self-identity for the sake of relationship—chiefly, a relationship with Christ.[7] People may gain the whole world as an individual, but in the process, they will never find themselves without relationships.

Relationships *constitute* meaning and identity. In the West we ask, "Who am I?" and look inward for the answer. As a man who has grown up in Western culture, I viewed identity through its lens. I understood my identity

---

THE CRITIC'S VOICE

Criticism

Youth are unique individuals because they have the imago dei *(image of God). We* mean *something individually simply because God spoke each of us into existence.*

Response

That is one way of viewing the story, but the story does not require us to interpret it in the following way: God bestows the imago dei *on individuals; therefore, we are unique, individual, godlike creatures who can mean something on our own.*

Theologically, if we honor a relational (trinitarian) view of God, couldn't a plausible interpretation be that we distort the imago dei *when we attempt to live our own unique, autonomous identity—pretending we can mean something on our own—without God and others? Wasn't that the demise of Adam and Eve when they chose their own knowledge over God's wisdom and warning?*

> *If I emphasize God speaking us into being, I'm favoring one creation story over another: God speaking versus the Lord God creating from dust and rib. Even if I merit the first creation story as God speaking us into being and bestowing the* imago dei, *he doesn't speak individuals into being; he speaks them into relationships—not a person, but people. "So God created humankind in his image, in the image of God he created them; male and female he created them" (Gen 1:27).*
>
> *The second creation story emphasizes oneness and relationships too. Adam was incomplete as an individual. He could not mean anything on his own. The Lord God created animals, but meaning making did not occur with animals. It is not until God made a relationship that the man could mean anything.*
>
> *Adam and Eve were made of each other, for each other. Adam could pretend to be his own individual, but the woman was a part of him, and he a part of her. As the narrator concluded, "They become one flesh." God doesn't create meaning by creating us, nor do we discover meaning solely in the us God created. Meaning is introduced by the connection between the Creator and the created.*

according to the choices and decisions that I alone made, what I had accepted or rejected, and how I incorporated and wrestled with various understandings of myself over the years. I understood my relationships as outcomes of me joining with another person and relational influences as what I personally took from my relationships.

Who would I be if I removed all of my relationships? Would I be a Christian without my relationship with Christ? Would I be a husband without my relationship with my wife? Would I be a dad without my relationship with my son or daughter? Would I be a reader or a writer without my relationships with my teachers? Would I be a crawler, walker or talker without my relationship with my parents? Relationships and the language we coordinate with others constitute and form us.

Remove the youth from my youth group and from my community, and I can no longer function as a youth pastor. Remove my wife, and I can no longer function as a husband. Remove my kids, and I am no longer a father. As the apostle Paul stated, individually we are members of one another (Rom 12:5). It is in our relationships that we become who we are and plant the seed of who we become.

CONCLUSION

So, what does this mean for my and Lisa's struggles of inadequacy and failure? A large portion of feeling like a failure or feeling inadequate stems from feelings of relational disconnectedness. I felt helpless and disconnected from Lisa because my youth lesson did not connect with her, and I knew no other way to address her issues. However, addressing our connectedness with others is empowering. We are skilled at talking about how people are meaningful to us, but rarely do we consider how we too have an impact on them. Lisa would have never imagined that her life and relationship with her youth pastor was so significant that it would deeply affect me throughout the night—and end up in a book.

Focusing on identity, uniqueness and spirituality as internal manifestations will not strengthen the future of youth or youth ministry. It's time for youth ministry to move beyond understanding identity formation as something intrinsic and essential within the person. I believe this understanding of youth and their action is not only limiting, but also believe it devalues our relationships. We need to reframe identity formation as a life story formed within the context of relationships. Living with a relational focus on identity will change our youth ministry practices, and youth will gain what they need most: to know they are connected, to feel they belong, to see that their life matters and to love in God's relational reign.

REFLECTION QUESTIONS

1. Who is your Lisa? How can locating failure and accomplishments as something unique to the person keep youth from recognizing the importance of community and relationships? How does a relational understanding help youth have a deeper sense of responsibility and appreciation for others?

2. How have you had similar feelings of inadequacy and failure? How do you compare yourself to others? How did you learn what to look for?

What relationships and stories have helped you to see people and the world the way you do?

3. Focus on your position as a reader from a relational perspective. Although you may be reading this book alone, reflect on why you are reading it. How do those relationships affect your reading? How is your act of reading relational?

4. Paul used a body to illustrate the connectedness of the church. How could you use the metaphor of a game to illustrate your youth's connectedness? How is your church like a _____ game? Choose a game, and compare its interconnected parts with your church and youth ministry.

5. The more connected students realize they are with your community, the more importance they give to relationships. What are some ways you can help your students recognize how connected they are to each other and your ministry settings?

3

Relational Being

I want you to know that my relationship with Jesus has grown deeper than ever in the last few days, and my entire life has been transformed," Chris told me one night after a youth ministry meeting. I thanked him, feeling encouraged. In my office a few minutes later, I overheard him say to another student, "Guess who got some tonight?"

"No way! You're crazy, man," his friend shouted. Chris laughed, and as the boys passed my office, I heard him boast that he'd "gotten it" in the backseat of his car in the church parking lot with someone other than his girlfriend.

Ten minutes later, Chris's mom came to my office and asked to speak with me. She sank into a chair and dropped her head in her hands. As she began to weep, she confessed that she was worried that Chris was dropping acid with his friends and that he didn't seem to care about his family or God anymore. He had become apathetic. Then she popped the million-dollar question: "What do you think is going on with him?"

I thought about what the last ten minutes had revealed about her son: he had told me he had never felt closer to Jesus; he had bragged about having sex in the church parking lot; and his mother had said he was abusing drugs. I drew in my breath.

"I have no idea."

If you had been in my shoes, what would you have said to Chris's mother? Where would you have located the problem? Most of us would have searched for something inside the person that had gone wrong: a crisis of identity, depression, something lacking in his character. Most of us would see the issue as being Chris's dishonesty. Obviously he was lying about one of the statements that he made. How could he be growing in his relationship to Jesus and involved in such things?

But what if each of these scenarios about Chris is true, and the problem does not have to be located in his identity?

We often see incongruous elements of a person's life as impossible because of how we view people as distinct beings who operate from a core sense of self. One must be true and the other false. We presume Chris is living an inconsistent life instead of trying to examine and understand each of the selves that he comes to be from his relationships. We dismiss Chris's roles and relationships and assume there is a unified core intrinsic to his identity. In so doing, we miss a much broader understanding of Chris, his creative potential and the stories that emerge that may hinder or benefit his growth and development.

Later I asked Chris, "What's your story?" To my surprise, this junior in high school had never thought about his story. Like most youth, he was genuinely living out his life in each of his relationships, rarely giving a second thought to his story or who he was becoming in each of his roles. Chris did not see any incongruence between his growing relationship with Jesus and how he treated others. In fact, he interpreted his life in an entirely different way than I had been interpreting his life. What he considered a close relationship with Jesus was different from what I had imagined.

I would have never gained this insight if I had treated Chris as an individual with a core self. If I had done that, I would have focused on the contradictions rather than on who he was becoming in each of his relationships. I would have viewed the stories that he told me simply as stories and turned from the open window showing me how Chris was structuring his life.

Notions of Christian identity and faith formation play a vital role in how we minister to youth. In the previous chapter, we explored the limitation of viewing youth from an individualistic perspective. We will continue this discussion and illustrate how beginning with relationships leads to a fuller picture of the youth and opens space for deeper ministry practices. When youth ministry shifts its focus to patterns of communication, it moves from the individual youth to the source of meaning that forms youth.

What's your story? Or as is commonly asked, "Tell me about yourself." Chances are you have been asked this question on several occasions as an adult. But, surprisingly, most teenagers have never been asked. If they have, they may not have had opportunities to really think about their responses with anyone other than their peers. Even when most youth begin to articulate their story, they do not have much, if any, faith integration. Could it be that our popular notions of identity have become so focused on the in-

---

THE CRITIC'S VOICE

Criticism
Are you saying there is no core self? I have morals, and my morals are the same wherever I go.

Response
The morals we have emerge from our relationships. We have learned through our relationships and stories what it means to be morally good and just to others. We are like Paul, who had been morally convicted that the message of Jesus was heresy and had a change in his morality through his relationship with the risen Christ and his immersion in the Christian community. Peter was morally convicted that Christians could eat only certain foods. However, his God-given vision changed his morals (Acts 10:9–11:18). Whether it is through our relationship with the Spirit or our relationship with others, sometimes our morals shift drastically.

Our relationships liberate and constrain our morals and our religious convictions. People may be vocally opposed to Islamic religion in the United States, but they refrain from saying such things in an Islamic country where they may be executed for voicing such statements. A student may be morally opposed to her professor's views, but she may not be given the option to voice them in class. In some of our closest and most sacred relationships, we may let our moral guard down and morally be someone else.

I do believe we hold certain views that sustain our relationships. We are changing and forming in each relational encounter, and the notion of a core self limits God's transformational activity to being contained in the individual rather than in the process of our ongoing relationships.

dividual that we have neglected the stories and relationships that shape and form our identities?

SABOTAGING YOUTH MINISTRY

I sabotaged many of my own ministry efforts because I believed that the problems of youth's lives were a reflection of their identity or the identity of others. When we begin to see youth's problems as inherent in how we tell and understand our stories, we are free from the illusion that their problems have to be lodged within their biological makeup or natural identity. As narrative therapist Michael White stated, "The single isolated view of identity generates many of the problems for which people seek therapy."[1] As we understand our lives as multifaceted stories, we are able to break free of some of the dominating narratives to which we've been enslaved.

When we see youth as having a fixed and stable identity, we are more likely to attach labels to define them, their problems and their behavior.

Manufacturing labels. When we assume the youth we see in one set of relationships has one core identity—that is, is the same person in all relationships and environments—then we usually assume they have the same *problem* in all relationships. This understanding allows us to easily attach labels to our youth. In so doing, we take rich, complex and diverse creations of God and chop them up to fit our one impression.

In youth ministry, and in parenting, it is easy to label our youth. I conducted a small experiment, beginning with telling more than fifty parents, youth pastors and pastors the following story of a student in my youth ministry:

> I have a student who is passionate about most things in life. I have noticed that she has really high highs and really low lows. There is not much of an even keel to what I have observed with this student. She is either super happy or super sad. And I am trying to understand her better.

I didn't offer any more information than that, and I didn't ask for a label or diagnosis. However, almost every person offered me a diagnosis, and over half gave me an exact pharmaceutical prescription. The consensus of the group was this: she is bipolar, and she should be on lithium. Yet all they knew were four sentences about her entire life, and only a handful asked for more information. The rest of the group "knew" she was bipolar. Furthermore, everyone assumed I was giving them the "real" picture of her life. They also didn't ask how much time I actually spent observing or hanging out with her.

Quick labeling and the justification of labels are telltale signs of our reliance on a sense of an individual self and on weighing others according to our own understanding of this self. This thinking will continue to cripple our youth and youth ministry practices if we do not become aware of our tendencies toward individualism.

Although most of our culture is inundated with diagnosis and labeling, many scholarly communities react sharply against the American Psychiatric Association's *Diagnostic Statistical Manual of Mental Disorders*.[2] These psychologists and therapists argue that such labeling has perpetuated the problem of mental disorders. Yet we buy in to the popular belief that such labels in ministry are helpful because they name and thereby address students' issues. We also buy in to the idea that proper medication fixes them. Why should we explore our students' relationships and problem-saturated narratives when we "know" the problem is in their brain and such problems require medication? Or we see the problem as being a spiritual one, and our antidote is the right amount of prayer, repentance and forgiveness.

With our diagnosis and labeling, we dismiss their relationships in favor of our own conclusions. Although everyone's intentions to diagnose and label are well intended, they complicate matters for the teen and reinforce their problem narratives with additional negative stereotypes.

"Many of the problems that people encounter in life come to represent the 'truth' of their identity,"[3] said Michael White, the originator of narrative therapy. For example, most clients say to their therapists, "I have bipolar disorder," "I have ADHD," "I have depression," "I have OCD." The therapist can reinforce this kind of language and labeling.[4] Unfortunately, even though youth may use the word *have*—which normally denotes possession, not one's intrinsic identity—further conversation reveals that their identity is bound to their classified disorder and dysfunction.

Therefore, the person is really saying, "I am bipolar," "I am ADHD," "I am depression," "I am OCD." In other words, "I am disorder. I am dysfunction." These descriptions of people leave little room for other descriptions, and many times they reinforce the problem as a biological reality.[5] Listen to the conversations of youth, and observe how they use diagnostic labels to define their decisions or lack of ("I am sorry, could you repeat that, my ADHD is kicking in") and how they use the labels to classify others ("she is so bipolar"). Such language did not exist among our young twenty years ago.

I am not denying the importance of counseling; my wife is a licensed professional counselor, specializing in child and adolescent counseling. Yet we are both leery of the ways pastors, youth pastors, therapists and psychologists quickly label and diagnose as well as the limited amount of time many psychiatrists spend with their clients and monitor their clients' medication. I am not advocating that we cease all medication, but many of us blindly subscribe to medication that may have more serious side effects than benefits to youth.[6] I'm asking youth pastors to be careful not to reinforce diagnostic labels of disorder, dysfunction and deficit that are being placed on our youth; as a society we need to spend more time and energy investing in our *relationships* and *social structure* than we do in medication.

In a world of violence and pain, what is killing and wounding most people is not bullets, alcohol, drugs or the Internet, but rather the matrix of relationships that is present (or absent). The majority of people do not need prescription pills to fix them; they need a social revolution. In many circumstances, medication is seen as the fix-all to whatever problems youth encounter. But no matter how much medication is given, it doesn't change a person's belief system or provide love and support. If a youth believes she is unlovable and feels neglected by adults in her life, no pill will alter her perception. If she doesn't have healthy relationships beyond traditional therapeutic interventions, she will more than likely return to the same debilitating lifestyle.

I am in no way suggesting that we allow youth to continue destructive behaviors that put them and others at risk. The way we address these issues, however, can make them worse and reinforce the problem rather than help youth overcome them. We must help students to see that their problems are not a part of a God-given identity and that the crippling effect they feel is the direct result of their relationships and cultural narratives.

Massaging the problem. After microfracture knee surgery, my calf muscle began to hurt worse than my knee, and I knew something was wrong. After a rush to the cardiologist, the doctor found that it was two blood clots, the outcome of my blood being too thick and my lack of movement. I was trying to massage them, and my doctor quickly stopped me by saying I could break up the clot, and it could travel to the vessels in my lungs and kill me. He informed me that I should *never* touch a clot. Then he took care of the blood clot by addressing the deeper systemic issues of circulation, movement and blood thickness.

We often try to mend most of our youth ministry problems the same way I tried to take care of my blood clot. We massage the heck out of the problem, either because we're unaware of the underlying issues or because we are ignoring them. We talk with our students about sex, drugs, alcohol, lack of self-esteem and so on. But we don't attempt to comprehend sin as anything further than an individual's bad behavior; we do not see it as systemic and symptomatic of our relationships.

As we follow the stories of Jesus in the Gospels, we are confronted with a Jesus who is more interested in giving life than condemnation. Jesus does not condemn the woman who the Pharisees caught in the act of adultery (Jn 7:53–8:11). He does four shocking things: he goes against Scripture (Lev 20:10; Deut 22:24); he saves her life by reminding everyone of their brokenness; he talks to her alone (which was not culturally or religiously accepted); and he tells her he does not condemn her.

Can you imagine one of your teens being caught having sex with someone, and all you say is, "I do not condemn you. Go and sin no more." Or how about Jesus' encounter with the Samaritan woman at the well (Jn 4:1-42)? Jesus doesn't condemn her for having five husbands; he asks to share a drink with her and offers her living water. And don't forget, she's a Samaritan! Jesus shouldn't be talking to her. Yet he knows her promiscuousness and he not only talks to her but shares a drink with her while they were alone. This is scandalous!

Jesus' encounter with both women gives them a voice; he treats them like whole human beings instead of treating them as others had. The religious community couldn't see the person beyond what they considered sin, but Jesus did. Jesus is less interested in people's sin and more interested in relationally empowering them. We do not overcome sin by focusing on sin; we overcome it by accepting our new life story in Jesus.

Imagine some of the metaphors that Jesus uses: born again, drinking living water, following the light, hearing the shepherd's voice and eating the bread of life. All of these metaphors point us to our relationship with him rather than to our sin. When we taste the abundant life of being a whole and complete person in Christ, our brokenness can be overcome.

I asked a friend who ministers to prostitutes to tell me some of the hurdles the women have to overcome. I wasn't surprised to hear "Christians" at the top of her list. Her ministry team would work months with some of the women to help them overcome their feelings of inadequacy, shame and guilt. Other Christians, mainly street preachers, felt the need to tell the women that they were sinning, destroying families, hurting people and so on. Such a narrow focus on the problem drove the women further into prostitution. They desperately needed love, not condemnation.

Many Christians think they are "speaking the truth in love," but most of the time they are "speaking the truth away from love." Is it Christian truth that underage drinking, drugs, theft and prostitution are sins? Yes, this is truth. But why do we focus on sin when we speak these truths rather than on the life-giving love of Jesus that helps overcome sin?

So, how does my friend's team minister to prostitutes without becoming preoccupied with sin? They focus on Jesus. They are not concerned with condemnation or humiliation; they want to share the unconditional love of Jesus that sparks a sense of value and worthiness in these young women. They listen to the women's stories and gain a fuller picture of their relationships. And they develop strong relationships with the women. They introduce them to the stories of Jesus and his love and acceptance. They help them restory their narratives of shame, defeat and humiliation with stories of being worthy, valuable and forgiven. As my friend told me, "It is not until they recognize they are God's princesses that they begin to pull out of prostitution."

We sabotage our ministry efforts when we focus on individuals, their individual identity and their problems emanating solely from them. A tree does not come from a seed; it emerges from the relationship of the seed with the right amount of soil, water, sunlight, carbon monoxide and temperature.

THE EMERGENCE OF STORIES IN OUR RELATIONSHIPS

Let's get back to Lisa's story in chapter 2. How do we minister to students like her? Lisa shared a feeling with me that a majority of our students experience: her life doesn't matter. She felt inadequate, and after talking with her, so did I. How do we understand Lisa's identity and what was going on with her? How do I understand my identity and what was going on with me? The way we answer these questions depends on where we locate identity and the problem we see occurring. Figure 3.1 is a drawing of Lisa and me, from our conversation described in chapter two. Where are Lisa's identity and problem?

Figure 3.1.

Would you add a heart? Draw a soul? Would you place her problem and identity formation in her brain? While no drawing can capture reality, our tendency to consider identity to be internal may not be the best picture to construct in youth ministry. Our focus on individual identity and the questions we raise (who am I? do I matter? where do I belong? how do I relate to others?) are a product of our individualistic culture.

When we ask, "Who am I?" we rarely think in terms of our relationships and stories. If we begin with our relationships, we can explore *how* we co-construct our relationships with others and recognize our interconnectedness.

In every relationship, both significant and superficial, we absorb potentials for our future relationships and the stories we tell.[7] Narratives (including problem narratives) become structured in our relationships in at least three ways. First, our consciousness becomes filled with stories and images through our observation of others, and our observations serve as "*models* for what is possible."[8] Hearing stories, watching movies, reading books and heeding other cultural conventions affects our lives from the time we are born. This is traditionally how we have understood relationships to operate: relationships and stories simply affect and influence us in certain ways, and they provide specific patterns and understandings for us to live out our lives.

Second, we become a particular person and play a specific role within each relationship. These roles provide material and characters for the stories we use in our life story.

Third, we shape each other and our future in the moment we connect through language and stories.

Since the latter two are virtually nonexistent in our understanding of identity formation and youth ministry, I want to emphasize further how picturing youth in this way gives us a relational view of students that allows us to explore problem-saturated narratives that may be crippling their lives.

PICTURING RELATIONAL BEINGS

We become particular people and play specific roles within each relationship. How do we help Lisa understand that her feelings of inadequacy and failure do not originate from a locale within her called a "self"? In figure 3.1, most of us would show identity and change occurring within the person. Yet the problem is not Lisa or her God-given nature, but the stories that have given her an incomplete view of being God's precious creation.

Instead of viewing Lisa and me as self-contained individuals, let's begin with a view that recognizes the multitude of relationships that form and shape our stories.

Each of the ovals in the wings in figure 3.2 represents a single relationship. The picture below looks similar to a butterfly, and Kenneth Gergen uses this image to emphasize how any relationship is like a butterfly: its wings must coordinate to take flight.[9] One wing represents a person and the host of relationships that have shaped her. In order for meaning to occur in any relationship, she must coordinate her previous stories and relationships with the other person. Successful coordination means successful communication. We coordinate our past relationships, and the language and stories from those relationships, with another to make meaning. Failure to coordinate is failure to make meaning.

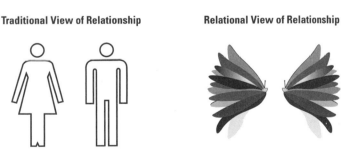

Traditional View of Relationship   Relational View of Relationship

Figure 3.2.

Youth pastors, therapists, parents and education professionals who interact with youth often assume the youth they observe in a shared context are the same in all contexts. Most of my office meetings or phone calls with concerned parents center on them discovering their teen transforming in an alien way. At other times, a mom and dad feel bewildered by their daughter's misbehavior at home when they hear that she is exceeding expectations in other relationships. Therefore, we typically approach identity and change as occurring within the person, and we do not take into consideration that transformations occur within the relationship. We are not the same person in every relationship.

Let us pull away pieces of our relational wings and use ovals from figure 3.2 to look at a few of Lisa's specific relational encounters. Each of her relationships generates particular actions and stories that she may draw from and use in future relationships. For instance, one oval may represent one of Lisa's relationships, such as that between her and her youth pastor (me).

Figure 3.3.

With each relational encounter, we become somebody. As we see in figure 3.3, Lisa becomes a particular person, and she has developed specific stories about herself from her relationships. Of course, some of her stories weigh more heavily than others in how she understands her future relationships, but for now, visually we will treat them as equal. Consider each of her roles in figure 3.3.

Do you see anything odd in Lisa's relationships? Although she has a brother and typically would emerge in the role as a sister, she assumes the role of a mother. Lisa's parents both work sixty hours a week, and Lisa's brother is six—ten years younger than her. Lisa feels pressure to be a mother rather than a sister to him. She prepares his breakfast, takes him to school, picks him up from after-school care, helps him with his homework and provides dinner for him.

Many of our problem narratives come from stories we have gathered from previous relationships. Exploring the relationships and stories that constitute Lisa helped me find her problem narratives, which gave me direction in using other narratives to help her overcome these problems. I discovered that Lisa's feelings of inadequacy stemmed from a relationship with a teacher who viewed her tardiness in her first-period class as a result of laziness and apathy.

But it wasn't apathy or laziness. It was Lisa's hard work as the primary caretaker of her brother. In fact, the pressure of taking care of herself and her brother hindered a lot of her relationships, perpetuating feelings of inadequacy and failure, simply because she could not perform the way she wanted or to the standard idea of success. Lisa was not aware of how these stories were guiding her life and hindering her from seeing how unselfish and caring she was with her brother and family.

Adolescents adopt many roles. Sometimes these roles veer from traditional cultural norms. Some youth take on the role of parent to their own parents because of drug addictions, physical disabilities or mental illness. Some parents treat their teenagers like elementary-school children, inducing these teenagers to assume that role. And teens raised by grandparents sometimes take the role of sons or daughters rather than granddaughters or grandsons.

Often we mistakenly assume that the youth we see at church are the same youth in all of their relationships. So we are shocked when we have students like Chris, who talk about their deepening relationship with Jesus after they just cheated on someone and tripped on acid. Even when I visit students on their own turf, they tend to slip into the role of youth-with-youth-pastor. They may quit cursing, or they may even end the conversations they were having with their friends.

We may view this as students putting on a mask with us. Once again, this assumes there is a core identity lurking beneath the surface and that they are hiding it from us. I am not suggesting that we do not limit information about ourselves to others. We often do. But why do we do this? Doesn't a particular relationship draw from us particular ways of being, requiring information that others don't? Indeed, all of our relationships call for different interactions and performances.

I remember being at one of the lowest points of my life before walking in to teach a college course in youth discipleship. Overcome with grief, I had five minutes to pull myself together. I looked up and saw an old college friend heading my way. Memories of our relationship flooded my consciousness, and I immediately found myself smiling and happy. Was I wearing a mask? Did my pain vanish? No, but the relationship I was now participating in called for a different interaction—one that did not require the performance of grief I was experiencing seconds before.

While it is easy for us to see how we emerge and maintain particular roles in each of our relationships, we usually ignore how the other person depends on our role to also become somebody. This is worth exploring, because it allows us, and our youth, to recognize our connectedness.

If I asked you to write about your most meaningful relationships and what makes them meaningful, what would you say? I ask my college students to do this, and I usually receive a list that looks much like this:

- Mom: My mom has always been there for me, and she has always let me share my problems and frustrations.

- Dad: My dad has been a steady rock for me. He has always encouraged me to be a better person.

- Sister: I can goof off with my sister, and she has provided me with an outlet of fun.

- Friend: My friend has always got my back. He encourages me to keep going when I'm at my lowest, and he listens to my problems.

After writing more than twenty responses on the board, I asked my students if they saw anything odd about their perspective of the relationships. It wasn't long before Lane said, "We're still looking at our relationships from an individualistic understanding. We're focusing on what our relationships do for us and not the meaning that occurs in the relationship—for everyone."

I said, "Okay, tell me more."

"Although I see my mom's caring and nurturing of me, I don't see how I also allow her to be a caretaker and nurturer. My mom depends on my role as her son just as much as I depend on her as a mom. And without our relationship together, neither of us has these roles. My mom understands herself as a certain kind of mother because of our interactions, and I see myself as a particular kind of son."

"And why is this important for youth ministry?" I asked.

"Because most of our students will never see how God has created us to be in relationships in such a way that everyone's life matters and makes a difference in all of their relationships."

"And what does this have to do with the stories we tell about ourselves?" I asked.

"In my relationship with my mom, I have the story of being a provider, a caretaker and an intellectual genius. In the relationship with my dad, our patterns of communication revolve around how he needs to teach me to do something better because I can't do it right. I'm not the same son in each of my relationships with my parents, and they certainly are not the same parents. The story that emerges from my relationship with my father (I can't do anything right) sucks, and I need to be reminded of other narratives that I neglect, like the narrative of being God's beloved and the narrative of my mom that acknowledges I do lots of things right."

We develop dominant narratives that aid in the structuring of our life stories. Sometimes these dominant narratives can be debilitating, and sometimes they can be liberating. Many of our youth neglect how they enable people to exist in particular roles, and without them, they can't fulfill those roles. As we help youth explore their multifaceted life stories and relationships, we also point to their relationship with Jesus. (This will be discussed in more detail in chapters 11 and 12.) The life story of Jesus becomes a dominant structuring story for youth ministry that reminds youth that their relationships do matter and their lives do have significance.

DANCING THE DANCE: COORDINATING OUR RELATIONSHIPS AND STORIES

A small dance school called Cripple Creek in Burgaw, North Carolina, opened its dance floor on Saturday nights to allow teens a safe place to dance. I will never forget my first slow dance. I was a sixth-grader, and I was awkwardly breakdancing to MC Hammer's "Can't Touch This" until the DJ faded the song to Brian Mcknight's "Every Beat of My Heart." I approached

Adelia, stretched out my hand and led her to the dance floor. For the first time, we were face to face and fully interlocked.

I had danced this song before—alone in preparation for this moment. When I locked my arms around Adelia's waist and she wrapped her arms around my neck, everything changed. I tried to dance the way I had practiced—the same rhythm, movement, speed—but Adelia had a different rhythm, a different speed. I kept stepping on her feet and she on mine. The first minute was filled with apologies and uncomfortable laughs. Step by step we worked to synchronize our movements to the song and to each other's rhythm. Contrary to many cognitive and theological models, coordinated action changed my thoughts and behavior, not the other way around. This is something we tend to neglect when we focus on the individual.

By the end of the song, we were dancing without stepping on each other's toes and experiencing a small slice of heaven. This picture of a dance illustrates an idea that I believe is missing in youth ministry and in our understanding of human development. We begin with the individuals who come together, rather than the relational dance that shapes and forms us.

The movements we make in our relationships and the language we use really do make the difference between stepping on toes and fluid rhythm. We literally form our stories in the moment of coordination, and we shape our future actions.

Practically speaking. Let's consider Lisa's initial comment (action) to me: "Do you have time to talk?" What kind of meaning is made if I do not hear Lisa speaking? Until I acknowledge her greeting, her words mean nothing. Like a billboard or a sign that's never seen, the message fails to communicate. Neither her question nor my response means anything without a larger body of understanding how to communicate.

What if I respond with, "Absolutely, I have time right now"? My response becomes an affirmation of our relationship. Meaning is not made until I respond (supplement her action). We depend on each other to create meaning. I can't walk around saying, "Absolutely, I have time right now." I need Lisa's question for my response to be meaningful, or I will raise the suspicion of everyone within earshot.

Lisa is not just listening for my response; she also knows our pattern of communication before she speaks. Even when we ask a question, we know the relationship between questions and responses and how they function in our culture. Lisa can't simply listen for my response without recalling her question. And I can't simply respond without recalling her question. We are interlocked. Both question (action) and response (supplement) alone are sterile; only in coordinated action is meaning born.

Gergen illustrates how this happens with our coordination of body language too:

"I thrust out my hand and
          . . . you grasp it in yours,
I have offered a greeting.
          . . . you push it aside to embrace me,
I have underestimated our friendship.
          . . . you kneel and kiss it,
I have demonstrated my authority.
          . . . you turn your back,
I have been insulting.
          . . . you give me a manicure,
I am your customer."[10]

Notice how the same gesture can be coordinated with completely different meanings and ways of relating. The person is positioned a certain way with each response (supplement): greeter, friend, authority, insulter and customer.

Consider the numerous responses that I could give to Lisa, and imagine how Lisa might interpret our interaction.

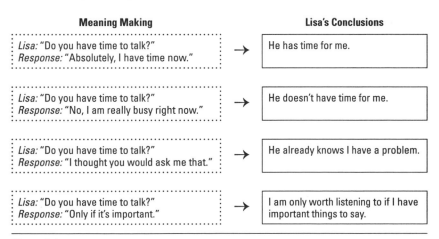

Meaning Making		Lisa's Conclusions
Lisa: "Do you have time to talk?" *Response:* "Absolutely, I have time now."	→	He has time for me.
Lisa: "Do you have time to talk?" *Response:* "No, I am really busy right now."	→	He doesn't have time for me.
Lisa: "Do you have time to talk?" *Response:* "I thought you would ask me that."	→	He already knows I have a problem.
Lisa: "Do you have time to talk?" *Response:* "Only if it's important."	→	I am only worth listening to if I have important things to say.

Figure 3.4.

Each response/supplement coordinates meaning with Lisa in specific ways. Lisa and I are creating new potentials for our future in the moment of our conversation (co-action).

Responses (supplements) both constrain and create meaning within relationships. As soon as we begin to coordinate our language, we create potential for meaning.[11] I use the word *potential* because, depending on the response, it may grant, restrict or obliterate meaning.

Notice how these supplements coordinate meaning with Lisa, but they also constrain meaning. If I responded with, "Did you not understand the lesson?" Lisa is constricted to respond to my question within our cultural understanding of communication. If she ignores my question, meaning breaks down.

By focusing on the internal and trying to guess what's inside, we miss how our conversations form us in the very moment of our interaction. What we think changes from our interactions with others. How many times have you prepared for a conversation only for it to end completely different from what you imagined? As soon as we speak, we are at the mercy of the person we are trying to coordinate our language with. For example, the statement "You look nice today" can be interpreted by another person as a compliment, joke, harassment, insult or flirt.

If we don't ignore the power of constructing our lives in the moment of our interactions, and we help our youth understand this too, incredible differences may occur. What can happen when we have youth who value co-constructing their lives when they communicate?

"Why are you always late?" Carrie asked her boyfriend, Greg, as he walked into our youth room.

"Why do you have to be so critical?" Greg responded.

"I just asked you a question, Greg! You don't have to bite my head off," Carrie shouted.

Both sat in silence with their arms crossed until Hillary said with a smile, "You guys don't have to end your performance that way."

"Shut up, Hillary! This is serious," Carrie roared.

"I am serious. Remember what we talked about last week? You are creating your relationship right now in this moment, and you can change it in this moment too. I know you don't want to be mad at each other. You can redo your interaction."

"The damage has already been done," Greg said.

"Yes, but you can do things differently and create something better than you have right now," Hillary insisted.

"I am not going to sweep this under the rug and let him get by with being rude to me," Carrie said.

Hillary leaned closer to persuade her. "You will not be ignoring your little tiff; you will be trying to overcome it and practice better communication. Greg, why don't you go outside and walk in just like you did before, and you guys can focus on saying something positive. Just give it one shot."

"This is stupid, but I will do it one time, and that is it." Greg walked outside and walked back in.

Carrie drew in a deep breath and said, "I've missed you being here, and I wished we could have experienced youth group together tonight."

Greg's entire demeanor changed. "I missed you too, and I hate being late. I'm going to be more considerate of our time together."

"Well, that's all I need to hear." Carrie reached over and hugged Greg.

"Dang, it actually works," Hillary said with amusement.

Imagine what type of environment we can co-create with our youth when everyone believes "it actually works." What if our moments of interaction become central?

The way we coordinate our language with our youth matters. We can co-create positive, life-changing meaning in one interaction, and it can be destroyed in the next. If our in-the-moment communication is that powerful, why not invite our youth into the meaning-making process to create a loving and accepting environment in Christ?

If language shapes us and meaning is not within the private mind *but in the process of relating through language,* understanding adolescents' identities through the stories they gather and tell can be beneficial to youth ministry practices.[12]

CONCLUSION

Lisa felt inadequate, and so did I. We were both paralyzed and under the impression that our past was shaping our future. However, if I had viewed our conversation as an interpretive dance in which our interaction was shaping and changing our feelings of inadequacy, how would I have responded? Furthermore, how would my reaction change if, in this interpretive dance, Lisa and I could both restory our negative views in a way that shaped our future stories with others?

When talking with teenagers, it doesn't take long to realize most of them really do not believe they can make a difference in anyone's life. Yet they literally make a difference with every word uttered in every conversation they engage.

For youth like Chris, who rarely think about the life they are living or all of the different roles they are playing, this process helps them articulate their own life story, and it provides them with the ability to begin recognizing some of their own destructive narratives, which brings to light alternative narratives that have the potential to liberate them.

REFLECTION QUESTIONS

1. List labels that professionals use to describe and diagnose youth. Beside each of the words you list, write an explanation of how the label can have negative consequences for the youth.

2. List five names of people who have been meaningful to you. Beside each of the names, write their relational role (for example, mother, teacher, sister, coach, son) and beside their role write your name or calling (for example, mother—son; teacher—student; sister—brother; coach—player; son—parent). Beside the relationships you have listed, write a short summary concerning how this relationship has formed you. After the summary, write about how your relationship has also affected the other person you listed and allowed him or her to exist in that role.

3. How can focusing on the outcomes of problems, such as drugs, alcohol and sex, lead us to miss the problem?

4. Think about the relationships you have engaged throughout the day. How did you change in each of those relationships? Explore how you also allowed the other people to exist in their particular roles.

5. Our relationships depend on specific cultural coordinations. Anything out of the norm may lead to confusion and frustration or to not communicating "properly." Observe the patterns of communication you use with your friends. The next time they ask a question, respond with "What do you mean?" Keep asking this question in response to their responses, and record what happens. For example, a friend asks, "Are you going to Mc-

Donald's to eat?" Respond, "What do you mean, am I going to McDonald's to eat?" "For the group Bible study that is being held at McDonalds!" "What do you mean for the group Bible study that is being held at McDonalds?" Record how their cultural anticipation of an answer to their question is subverted and called into question with another question.

4

The Reality and Not-So-Reality
of Our Life Stories

Stories are a vital part of human interaction. Can you imagine humanity without stories? Stories constitute us, and they are the vehicles through which life is made meaningful. What if I gave you a one-word response to every question you asked me?

"What have you done today?"

"Fun."

"What did you do that was fun?"

"Scream."

"What were you screaming at?"

"People."

"Why?"

"Fun."

A continuation of my one-word responses would not enhance our relationship, and you may become frustrated. The context is not given; stories do not unfold; meaning is not made. Now imagine me telling you a story of a road trip with several of my crazy college friends to the world's largest haunted amusement park.

Although I did not type out a specific story above, this scenario is more meaningful because of the overlapping stories we find ourselves in. In other words, "road trip," "crazy college friends" and "world's largest haunted amusement park" aren't just words taking up space in a sentence. These words mean something based on our shared relationship, culture and language.

Our lives depend on stories.

LIFE STORIES ARE NOT "REALITY"

Our life stories are not "reality," but they are "*our* reality." None of us can tell our whole life story, because we can't remember everything that has happened in our lives. If we could, no one would listen, because it would take us almost the same amount of time as we are old. Obviously our ten-minute life stories are condensed and fabricated. There is always more to the story than what we recall or choose to share. Therefore we can never tell our true and full life story. Every telling is interpretive and selective, and there are other alternatives to how we tell and structure our story.

"Just because it is a condensed version of my story doesn't mean that it's not what really happened," a student said one day in class.

"Do our parents tell the same story of our lives?" I asked. "How about our brother? Sister? Friends? Who has the true version?"

"Okay, I see what you're saying: our stories will all be different because they come from different perspectives. But certain descriptions that I have of this world and of myself are real for everyone. I can describe my experience of this room and give a vivid description that is real. And it's not just real for me, but my description is real for everyone." He thumped his hand on the table and said, "This is obviously a hard desk."[1]

I asked the class to describe the room and its reality. After a few minutes, this is what they told me:

- gray block walls

- a computer for our instructor to use with the projector and for searching for information

- the carpet adds a cozy feel to the room and serves the purpose of eliminating an echo that would make it more difficult to hear

- we exist as students who are here to learn and gain a college education

- you exist as an instructor who is paid to guide us in our education

- book bags and laptop cases are present to carry our laptops, books, pens, pencils, paper and other important items essential to learning

- a ceiling exists with an adequate amount of light so we can see our work and each other

- laptops for taking notes

- sound system to amplify sound for presentations or videos which enhance learning

- a door to enter, exit and keep outside noise from interfering; an honor code hanging on the wall to remind us of our academic integrity

- a white board and markers for the instructor and students to use for writing or drawing.

After they exhausted their description of the classroom, I reminded them that what often seems obvious might be what blinds us. "From whose perspective did you describe the reality of the room?" I asked.

Rachael chuckled and said, "From the perspective of students in a classroom. And neither this room nor the objects in it have to be seen as a classroom, nor do we have to be students." The tabletop would not be considered a desk if my students were not constructing the reality of the room as a classroom. But since they were in this role every time they walked into the room, it was difficult to imagine the room being anything other than a classroom.

As in the telling of our life stories, my students had excluded many other realities or functions of the room. How could this happen? How can we see and understand other realities? Philosopher Ludwig Wittgenstein sheds light on this issue by looking at how relationships and language shape what he calls "forms of life" and "language games." First, forms of life are broad patterns of social activities that give language and stories significance, and the language and stories aid in holding the forms of life together.[2] Our forms of life configure our life story. Youth use language situated within their particular forms of life.[3] They can't talk about being Christian and deny the existence of God. A person can't claim to be a baseball pitcher and throw a football to a batter.

My students had difficulty seeing the room as anything other than a classroom and themselves as anything other than students because of the university form of life within which they are participating. Certain roles and identities require a specific form of life in which to couch them. A youth's point of view depends on his view from a particular point in his form of life. Every point of view should be understood as a view embedded within particular relationships. Without particular forms of life, there would not be corresponding points of view.[4] In other words, there is no such thing as a football player without the game of football, just as there is no such thing as a Christian outside the form of life of Christianity. Identity is formed within the multifaceted forms of life that youth engage.

Within each form of life are language games. The concept of language games points to the rule-governed character of language within a form of life. Each form of life has a specific language game that is unique to the relationships established. My students' description of the classroom is an example of language game. They form a particular way of talking and using their language that generates a form of life in a classroom setting.

When I discuss this topic, I ask my students to participate in a role-playing game.[5] Each group is to discuss a form of life and describe the room from its language game. As they describe the room, the other groups attempt to guess the form of life that the group's language represents. For example:

Form of life: Firefighter
Description: The bags and laptop cases on the floor are clutter. They should be hanging on racks or placed on top of the tables so the students can leave the room quickly. The wiring around the computer station needs to be secured with electrical tape. The sprinkler system in the room is a plus, but I don't understand the logic behind the evacuation plan on the wall.

Form of life: Interior decorator
Description: The gray paint on the walls must go. The windows are too plain. We can keep the carpet, because it will match a variation of color schemes. This room is starving for vibrant colors, curtains, artwork and crown molding.

Form of life: Brick mason
Description: Head joints and bed joints need filling in some places. The jointer was obviously rushed, as some joints are struck with a concave jointer and others are flush. The walls are plumb and level, and the overall structure looks good. The interior is comprised of eight-by-sixteen-inch blocks. A rowlock is missing on the exterior of the window, which may encourage water damage to the window frame. The drop ceilings were attached with concrete nails in the bed joints.

The list goes on, from an electrician's and a sound engineer's view of the room to a middle school youth's and a senior adult's view of the room. After describing several forms of life, I ask my students which is the "real" description of the room.

THE SUBJECT OF THE MATTER: SOME HELP FROM NOOTKA INDIANS

Of course, all descriptions are all "real" and "true" within their form of life. But if my students continued to operate from the role of interior designer, their grades would suffer. Although we can construct multiple realities, we will favor some over others according to their utility and according to what our form of life requires.

On a broader scale, all of these perspectives see the room and our world according to its parts. Through our English language, we have established a large language game and form of life that divides our world into objects as if they are separate. When we tell our stories, we talk about subjects acting on objects, because the English language places primary importance on subjects and objects rather than on processes of relationship.

The language of the Nootka, a North American tribe in Western Canada and Washington State, is one of many that create a different world. The Nootka do not speak of objects and subjects but streams of transient events. Their worldview is more fluid, integrated and action-oriented than ours. Where we would see a house as a physical object, the Nootka see it as a long-lived temporal event with a literal English translation of "it houses" or "housing occurs."[6] It is difficult for us to imagine such a world, and without the language we can't. As Wittgenstein states, "The limits of my language mean the limits of my world."[7]

In one sense, we are not going to transcend our English language of subject and object agreements. But if we acknowledge that we chop up our world through our language and that this is not the "real," we can conceptualize more fruitful approaches to human action, youth ministry and adolescent development. No matter what stories our youth tell or we tell our youth, we must keep in mind that there are always other perspectives and different ways of interpreting our stories.

OUR LIFE STORIES ARE OUR REALITY

The biggest misconception many have is that stories mirror the life we live.[8] In other words, we live our lives, reflect on what we live and then tell the story the best we can from our lived experiences. This perception comes from a longstanding tradition that treats language as a form of picture. Our stories do not mirror our lives or represent reality; they are our reality. With every telling and retelling of our story, we are shaping our lives.

Psychologist Jerome Bruner observes,

> I believe that the ways of telling and the ways of conceptualizing that go with [stories] become so habitual that they finally become recipes for structuring experience itself, for laying down routes into memory, for not only guiding the life narrative up to the present but directing it into the future. . . . A life as led is inseparable from a life as told—or more bluntly, a life is not "how it was" but how it is interpreted and reinterpreted, told and retold.[9]

As psychologists, sociologists and anthropologists began observing how we create ourselves and our world through stories, many began using terms like *narrative* and *story* as metaphors for experience. No longer were they pointing to experience as if experience exists outside culture. Rather they began drawing attention to relationships and stories as the shaping, cultivating and altering force. Instead of seeing language and stories as simply tools with which to communicate, I began to understand language and stories as our world itself. Stories do not represent our reality; they are our reality.

INTERPRETATION PRECEDES EXPERIENCE

From the time of our birth, we enter into our culture's interpretive language, and our experiences of the world are framed, separated and segmented through the language and stories we learn. We interpret reality first, and if we have the ability to frame the perception, we may recall it as an experience.

I point to trees, and I say, "Trees." My eighteen-month-old repeats, "Teeees." I point again, "Trees." She comes closer and says, "Twees." Currently, those tall things that sway in the wind and get naked in the fall are not just trees; they are twees. Before I name anything, what exists? Of course things exist, but before they are named and labeled, they do not exist in our language of classification and usage. Even pointing to something and calling it a "thing" becomes a classification.

My daughter sees twees as a whole; she doesn't distinguish the bark, roots and leaves. She also doesn't notice the differences between one tree and another, because she hasn't learned how to classify those differences. They are all twees. Eventually, I will teach her *leaves*, *limbs*, *roots* and *bark*. As she continues to learn our language games, she will learn classifications of trees: maples, spruce pines, gums, dogwoods, redwoods, cedars. She will also discover that types of furniture, houses, paper, cups, plates, necklaces and much more gain their existence from trees. She will learn that trees not only provide the material for many of the things we build and use, but they also provide us with a central ingredient for life through photosynthesis. When she learns our language games of trees, her preschool twees will disappear.

David Yamane, drawing on the work of anthropologist Edward Bruner, distinguishes between the everyday flow of reality that he calls "experiencing" and what we frame and recall with our language as an "experience."[10] No one can capture "experiencing" (reality). As soon as we try, it becomes just another "experience" (something recalled and framed with our language). Therefore _____ (insert your word here) may exist, but until we have the language to name, classify and organize it, _____ does not exist for us in this particular way.

Our world is organized according to our forms of language. Instead of beginning with some kind of inner or general experience, we encounter the world in a particular way that is limited to our cultural conventions.[11]

The reality we perceive is interpreted first, and if we have the ability to frame the perception, it may be recalled as an experience. If we do not have the language to frame our perception of reality, we have no way to express the reality through language.[12] Without language, our "experiencing" would be shapeless, ungovernable and chaotic.[13] Like a newborn infant, we would be reduced to our senses, without the ability to understand and interpret our perceived reality.[14] Imagine having a sensation or experience without having a language to describe it. What would it be? Even as we imagine such an occurrence, we are guided by our language of imagination, sensation and experience. We may feel something, but how do we know it is the Spirit or a biological urge without the language to name and classify such an event?

As early as 1929, anthropologists were identifying how language formed communities and their social realities:

> Human beings . . . are very much at the mercy of the particular language which has become the medium of expression for their society. . . . The fact of the matter is that the "real world" is to a large extent unconsciously built on the language habits of the group. No two languages are ever sufficiently similar to be considered as representing the same social reality. The worlds in which different societies live are distinct worlds, not merely the same world

THE CRITIC'S VOICE

Criticism

"Change your language; change your world"? You are obviously a white, American, middle-class male. Tell a starving child to change his language and that will change his world. Tell a man dying of cancer to change his language and that will change his world. Say it. I dare you to say it!

Response

I appreciate your compassion for people who are living on the fringes and your defense against what seems to be another person who overlooks pain and suffering in favor of clichés. It is starving children, losing a best friend to cancer and living through intense emotional pain and trauma myself that compels me to say such a statement. I have also stared into the eyes of those who have been labeled with deficits, disorders and abnormalities and who have become disabled by professional language.

I am interested in finding better ways to describe and fashion our world that lead to wholeness and healing. Of course, I would never look a starving person in the face and say, "Change your language; change your world." The use of my language in this way goes against the very rationale for making such a statement. The idea is to create a better world through using better words in how we interact with people. Even the language I use to describe the "poor" and "starving" is important.

Consider the teenager whose dad sends him on a mission trip to a Third World country so he can appreciate all the wealth that his family has by encountering the poor. The dad expects to hear gratitude and thanksgiving when his son returns. But the son speaks of remorse for how their wealth and belongings bind them. The joy of the poor in the midst of unhealthy and nearly starving conditions altered this adolescent's view and therefore his language of the poor. The poor were looked down on as the unfortunate who needed his God and Western riches. For this adolescent, the poor became his teacher, and he met God through them.

with different labels attached. . . . We see and hear and otherwise experience very largely as we do because the language habits of our community predispose certain choices of interpretation.[15]

Those who minister to youth have far too long neglected the world-changing power of language. We have been lured to brain-based studies, personality inventories and other individualistic conceptions of human action. Yet the language coordinated among our youth creates our youth ministry environment. A different language means a different world. Change our language; change our world.

MAKING IT PRACTICAL

Todd, a junior in high school, came to me for help. He told the following story:

> I'm a lazy, manipulative cheater. Basically, I don't like doing my homework so I talk some of my classmates into doing it for me. My teacher calls me a lazy, manipulative cheater. I have been caught twice now, and my teacher says she will fail me if I don't stop. I'm not sure if I manipulate my friends—they're always willing to help me—but I know I'm cheating. I just hate doing homework by myself.

Now let's apply this statement: our life stories are not reality, but they are *our* reality. How can we understand Todd's story?

Todd's life story is not **the** *reality.* A few years ago I would have interpreted Todd's story as the real story. I would have agreed with his teacher that he was cheating and being manipulative and lazy. I would have tried to figure out ways to help Todd stop his destructive cheating. In the process, my emphasis on him being a manipulative cheater would have reinforced his problem narrative, and he would have continued to see the world through that lens. Now I know that his story is not reality and that I can help him rewrite his story in different ways.

Todd's life story is **his** *reality.* Todd is "storying" his life with the language of being a lazy, manipulative cheater. This has become his reality. How can we help Todd reconstruct or rewrite a life story (reality) that could empower him to learn without cheating?

As I listened to Todd's story, I detected a glaring strength that I wanted to confirm. So I said to him, "Let me get this straight: you had your friends do your homework for you?"

"Yes."

"Did you bribe them?"

"No."

"Threaten them?"

"No, they just wanted to help me because they know I would do anything for them."

"Wow, Todd! You have an incredible gift. You are so compassionate to your friends that they are willing to risk their own grades and do your homework for you." This was the side I knew of Todd: a compassionate and caring student who would give the shirt off his back for another person. Unfortunately, the language of being a lazy, manipulative cheater hindered him and his story. So I asked, "Do you think you could use your gift of compassion to get your friends together for a study group so that you could do your homework together?"

"Yes, I never thought about doing that. I just hate doing my homework by myself, but if I could do it with my friends, they would be able to help me have a better understanding of the material."

A month later Todd was scoring A's on his homework and tests. His mother told me at the end of the semester that Todd's teacher remained suspicious of his new grades. On his final exam he scored a ninety-five, missing the exact same question as his close friends. The teacher thought she had snagged him again, so she gave him a different test, and he made a 100. The only reason Todd missed the same question was because they were in the same study group, and they had all memorized the wrong answer.

In Todd's eyes, he was a manipulator and cheater because of his friends doing his homework. Someone in authority reinforced those labels, which further impaired him. By pointing out his compassion and influence, Todd and I were able to rewrite his life story. We did not deny that his actions had been wrong, but we moved beyond this destructive use of talent by focusing on relational gifts.

Life stories are our youth's reality of themselves. The way we coordinate our youth's life stories with them can make all the difference in *our* world.

REFLECTION QUESTIONS

1. List forms of life in which you participate weekly. Beside each form of

life, write your role and describe the language game used. Table 4.1 is an example from my life.

Form of Life	Role	Language-Game
Construction	Brick Mason	Estimates, architectural drawings, city codes, types of brick, mortar
Youth Ministry	Youth Pastor	Upcoming trips and events, God's love, discipleship, prayer, church body, Bible, Gospel of Luke
Publishing	Author	Editing, revisions, deadlines, proposals
University	Adjunct Faculty	Attendance, contracts, grades, deadlines, syllabus
Coffee Shop	Customer	Venti white mocha nonfat milk, stirred, with whip and caramel drizzle

2. Reflecting on your answers to question 1, how do your language games shape your relationships in each form of life? How does the form of life shape your language game? How could you change the language in your youth ministry to alter your form of life known as youth ministry?

3. Think about something that has happened in your life. How do you tell the story? How could you tell the story differently? If you have difficulty telling your story differently, choose a character in your story and attempt to tell it through his or her eyes.

4. How would beginning with relationships and language alter theological models that begin with experience? How would it add a reflexive element that is usually overlooked in theological models?[16]

5. Think about what you see around you. How might we view our environment if we saw everything as a set of connected actions? Look around and describe the room by changing your objects (nouns) to action verbs. As I look around, I see chairing, tableing, coffeeing, peopleing and dooring. Describe how changing your nouns to actions helps you to view the room differently. Instead of seeing a door that is attached to a wall, I see the door as a continuous gateway that enables me to enter and exit; it participates in allowing me to reach my destination. Although changing our language in such a way may seem silly and trite, our change of language changes how we view our environment. Imagine restructuring our language in youth ministry. What would you change?

6. Think about your understanding of spirit and spiritual experience. How

might your language shape those experiences? If we value the language of God being "close," "personal," "present," "spirit" and "revelatory" instead of "distant," "separate" and "impersonal," how will we experience God by privileging one language over another?

7. Todd's relationship with his youth pastor and teacher are quite different. Who does Todd become through his relationship with his teacher? Who does Todd become through his relationship with his youth pastor? What makes those differences?

8. Ask people to tell you about their day using one word. Next, ask them to tell you about their day using a story. Note the differences in connectedness between you and the person in each scenario.

Part Two

COORDINATING
A LIFE STORY

Relational Narrative Development

5

Life Stories

If I were conducting a baseball clinic with tee-ballers, teaching them the proper techniques of hitting a curve ball would prove ineffective. Developmentally, a tee-baller can't even begin to throw a curve ball, and pitching is not allowed. I would begin by teaching them the basics of the game, like keeping their weight back when they swing, so that one day they could progress to hitting a curveball.

Sharing the biblical story with children, youth and adults is no different. In this chapter, we will explore the basics of story in the lives of youth: story as it is constructed in relationship and story as it serves to build a sense of identity. We will establish relational lenses through which we can see the role of narrative in the identity construction for both children and adolescents. This framework will help us understand how we communicate, share the biblical story, provide counseling and connect youth with Jesus' life story.

COORDINATING OUR LIFE STORY

If we met for the first time and I asked, "What's your story?" what would you say? Where would you begin? What would you include? How and where would you end your story? We all tell stories about ourselves. Have you ever thought about *how* you organize your life story? Have you thought about *what* details you include or exclude? Have you contemplated how your listener may alter the way you tell your story?

We begin telling stories about as early as we begin walking. Meaning, identity, understanding and intelligibility are all encapsulated in our ability to narrate a story with others. We learn to tell different types of stories, one of which is a life story. A life story "en-tales" various lived and anticipated stories, all arranged and told through specific narrative conventions and coordinated with others. Ask a high school youth to tell you his story, and you will get a convergence of stories, in one shortened unified story, that functions as his defining narrative.

Although we tell stories every day, a life story requires advanced narrative abilities to integrate, connect and organize all the disparate and episodic narratives of our lived experience. These skills do not fully emerge until midadolescence (high school age).[1]

Four kinds of coordinations are essential to our life story.[2] First, we construct life stories according to *cultural coordination,* which includes our *cultural concept of biography* (for example, how we begin and end our story, family life, growing up, geographic locations, school transitions) and *cultural life scripts* (important transitional events expected to take place in a specific order and time within a typical life, such as driving, college, marriage, family).

Second, *temporal coordination* is the arrangement of our life story with markers of time that allow others to locate events in our story. The most basic temporal ordering is chronological, but stories may deviate from this pattern and use other markers, such as flashbacks and foreshadowing, that move the story along. By middle school, children have used cultural and temporal coordination to form a basic, skeletal life story. Although middle school youth can tell a life story, they have not yet developed the ability to causally and thematically order their story with an interpretive posture. In other words, they can tell life stories but are unable to make sense of their diverse stories or to restory the incongruences.

Third, *causal coordination* provides a sense of direction and purpose to our life story. In late high school, students begin to pull together their separate life narratives. This coordination provides the linkages between stories in explaining how and why they moved from one episode (like their dedication to soccer in middle school) to another (their hatred of sports and their passion for writing music in high school).

Fourth, *thematic coordination* is the most advanced form of life story, because the youth is able to look at her entire life and extract certain continuities across change. Thematic and causal coordination work together. Youth have themes that emerge from their causal connections, and they causally connect their stories according to these themes.

All of these coordinations have distinct qualities and characteristics, but they are interconnected and interdependent when it comes to the formation of a story, especially a life story. I will touch on each coordination in this chapter, and in subsequent chapters I will expound on each from childhood to adolescence.

CULTURAL COORDINATION

Cultural coordination begins as soon as we learn to communicate. Since life stories are shared in the language of others, we must learn the basic language (verbal and nonverbal) of our culture and the language games involved in each form of life.[3]

The biographical elements and cultural concepts included in our life story depend on the form of life (discussed in chapter 4) in which we participate. If I were to share my life story with one of my college baseball teammates, my language and story would be different than if I were to share it with a church member. We see this in the New Testament when comparing the Gospels. Luke's awareness of his Gentile audience meant he generated a different slant on the story of Jesus than Matthew with his Jewish audience. And these are not just different perspectives; the Gospel writers intentionally arranged certain stories to fit their audience's understanding and to convey particular messages.

If we do not make allowances for our cultural form of life, we will not be able to coordinate our story with others. The 1960s sitcom *The Beverly Hillbillies* gained its humor from a lack of cultural coordination between the hillbilly way and the Beverly Hills way of life. The Clampetts—hillbilly mountaineers—arrive in swanky Beverly Hills, but only see from their hillbilly form of life. For example, when Jed Clampett discovers the billiard table in his new mansion, he thinks it's a fancy dinner table with the pool cues serving as pot passers and meat stickers. The feisty and short-statured Granny believes the Beverly Hills people are always out to get her. When she visits the supermarket for the first time, she fails to coordinate her language with that of the cashier. Granny returns home, telling her story to Jed:

> Then she tells you how much money to give her. She says to me, she says, "That will be twenty-eight twenty-five." And I says, "Now you make up your mind. Is it twenty-eight? Or is it twenty-five?" She says to me, she says, "It's twenty-eight twenty-five." Now I see I ain't gettin' no place with her, so I give

her the benefit of the doubt, and I plop down twenty-eight—a quarter and three pennies. . . . You'd have thought that pleased her. But not her. As I started through the gate she says, "Hold on! Madam, you're short!" And I says, "Maybe so, but I'm big enough to take you on."

All of the stories and cultural concepts of the Clampett family are coordinated with others through their mountaineer form of life.

Unless the Clampett family learns the language games of the Beverly Hills form of life, they will continue to fail at coordinating meaning with them. Elly May Clampett's double-barrel slingshot may have a purpose and usefulness in her hillbilly way, but as she participates in the Beverly Hills culture, she would be better suited wearing it as a bra.[4]

While *The Beverly Hillbillies* is light-hearted entertainment, failing to coordinate our story with others is no laughing matter. It can mean the difference between conflict and communion. When we fail to coordinate our stories, we fail to establish meaning and hinder relational growth. Our students, who are just learning to share their life stories, can benefit from us serving as healthy and loving mentors who model how to coordinate a life story by sharing ours and inviting them to tell and retell theirs.

When we ask people to tell us their story, we expect a certain kind of response. What elements do you anticipate hearing? Or if you are telling your story, what would you include? Generally we expect to hear the person's name, occupation, family members, current residence, place of birth and where she grew up. All of these elements conform to our culture's concept of biography.

Cultural concept of biography. As early as two years of age, toddlers begin learning basic concepts of biography: the location of their home, their name, their family members' names and their position in the family, such as a daughter, sister or granddaughter. As we get older, we learn other important biographical elements, such as school transitions, geographic moves, family dynamics and changes, economic conditions, grade, educational status, degrees, employment, family dynamics, pivotal experiences (tragic events such as death, illness, suffering, injury), significant relationships beyond family (teachers, coaches, girlfriends/boyfriends) and faith experiences (conversion, baptism, youth camp).

The difficulty for youth emerges at the point of deciding where to begin and end their life story. A narrated life, unlike most literary narratives, is open at both the beginning and the ending.[5] Everyone's birth has an obscure element that causes reflection on family history and family values. As Alasdair MacIntyre says, "We enter upon a stage which we did not design and we find ourselves part of an action that was not of our making. Each of us being the main character in his own drama plays subordinate parts in the dramas of others, and each drama constrains the others."[6]

Supporting cast. Although most midadolescents view their life story from an individual perspective, a supporting cast is always present. How adolescents tell their life stories and how they include or hide their supporting cast shows whether or not they are aware of the importance of understanding their life story in community. Most youth tell their life story as if they did everything all by themselves. I like to ask questions that bring out their supporting cast and help them recognize how interdependent they are with others.

Furthermore the very act of youth performing their personal narratives sets the stage for further interdependence and secures a relational future.[7] Adolescents and adults not only need a supporting cast to talk about their own selves, but they also need their supporting cast to be in agreement with their roles.[8] Narrative validity depends on the affirmation of others. Youth identities suffer when people who have been cast in their supporting roles disappear from the stage. As Gergen says,

> A fundamental aspect of social life is the network of reciprocating identities. . . . This reliance on others places the actor in a position of precarious interdependence, for in the same way that self-intelligibility depends on whether others agree about their own place in the story, so their own identity depends on the actor's affirmation of them.[9]

An adolescent can scarcely boast of being at the top of her class academically if her teachers or classmates are not willing to comply as supporting roles. A youth's identity can be thrown into question or suffer loss when supporting cast members drop out or choose to recount the narrative in a different light.

After high school, many of the actors and actresses (the supporting cast) in midadolescents' life stories disappear, and they engage in new relationships (a new supporting cast from their new forms of life). For most Christian youth, the supporting role of youth pastor, pastor, Sunday school teachers and mentors become void when they move from high school to college or the workforce. When youth have formed their Christian identity

THE CRITIC'S VOICE

Criticism

Aren't you just trying to make a case for the nurture side of the nature-versus-nurture argument? A plant needs the right amount of water, soil and care from us to grow. And adolescents are like plants that receive the right amount of nurturing when we listen to their stories.

Response

Psychologists (including social psychologists) have utilized the metaphors of a machine and organism. They focus on human development from the perspective of the self-contained individual in either a mechanistic (child behavior is the output of environmental inputs) or an organic (child behavior genetically develops like a growing plant with certain stages of growth and development) perspective.[10]

For Lev Vygotsky (one of Jean Piaget's early critics), these metaphors of machine and organism that separate the individual from their surroundings can only be achieved analytically—as an exercise in theory—for they are inseparable.[11] *In other words, "independent thought" is never independent. It always relies on and reflects social life and social processes, as there is nothing in the mind that was not first in society.*[12]

Nature-versus-nurture arguments focus on the individual and how she is influenced by nature or biology. The perspective that I am proposing here operates from a completely different paradigm. I begin with the relationship first and how we coordinate our stories with youth.

I'm attempting to emphasize that we co-construct our life story with our youth. We do not simply give them a voice and nurture them; they also give us a voice and nurture us when their stories are shared. In the moment of their sharing, we are not innocent listeners; they are constructing their story according to our questions and responses. In focusing solely on biological or social, nature versus nurture, we miss how our moments of coordination define and shape "us."

only within the form of life of their Christian relationships, their Christian identity is threatened with the loss of these relationships. How can youth continue their form of life as Christians when their form of life and the roles that supported their Christian identity no longer exist? Unless youth have a deep relational integration of their Christian faith and deep storied experiences of it, it will be no more than simply another supporting role that no longer exists when the supporting cast ceases to exist.

Cultural life scripts aid in developing a life story within cultural coordination.[13] Our life narrative conforms to what the culture expects us to convey and illustrate.[14] Cultural life scripts define those expectations within a particular culture.[15] They include experiences that may not have actually occurred during adolescence but have become part of a life story—for example, getting a job, going to college, getting married, being a mom or dad, owning a house and any other expectations friends, family, church and the culture at large have of a prototypical life.

A person's life story also includes other cultural concepts and ideas. These concepts vary among youth: understandings regarding sex and dating; their view of self as independent or interrelated; the language they use to label others; how they locate characters in their life story; and on and on it goes. It is important to note the cultural concepts our youth attempt to coordinate with us and to inquire about them to acknowledge how they are interpreting such concepts with others. Each life story has a particular order, and this order provides a sense of how the person's life has evolved thus far. This linear ordering, which provides a sense of time, is known as temporal coordination.

TEMPORAL COORDINATION

Stories must be temporally located, and this ability begins before children are five years old.[16] Narratives provide a sense of time. Imagine telling your life story without temporal coordination. If we jump from past experiences to future anticipations without indicating a shift in time, our stories make no sense.[17] Time provides markers in our stories, giving them intelligibility. Below are common temporal markers used in life stories:

Age specification: twelve, fifteen, nineteen

Seasons: winter, spring, summer, fall

Months: January–December

Tense: past, present, future

Transitional words: then, next, after, and then, previously, from now on

Temporal indicators: "I remember," "Back in the day," "Once upon a time," "A long time ago," "When I was little"

Segments of the day: morning, noon, afternoon, day, evening, night

Activities that denote time: breakfast, lunch, brunch, dinner

Dates: January 12, 2010

School or school grade: Elementary school, eighth grade

Cultural events: "After 9/11"

Distance from present: five days ago, two years ago, two minutes ago, right before I came here

Temporal coordination includes not only temporal indicators and linking many stories into a cohesive timeframe, but also the very act of coordinating with the other person in a timely manner.[18] Functioning outside the agreed-on temporal coordinates risks a loss of meaning. Movies that go over two hours, novels over three hundred pages and Sunday morning services that extend beyond noon all might lose their audience. Life stories are no different. After being asked by a student in the college youth discipleship course I teach, I only shared five minutes of my life story. Instead of giving me their full attention in this brief timespan, my audience packed up their laptops and clenched their book bags as though they were on the starting block of an Olympic four-hundred-meter race. The time was 11:45; my class ended at 11:40.

We organize our lives around time.[19] Chronological time is a human construct that has to be adjusted to capture the earth's slow revolutions and orbits around the sun. We consider Western chronological time to be *the* time, but death, birth and nature illustrate otherwise. We find different ways of coordinating time that do not fit our chronological clock.[20] Temporal coordination establishes consistency and allows us to locate events within our common understandings of time. We eat, sleep, meet, work, study and play according to time. We would not dream of telling someone to meet us at a specific location in the near future without using temporal coordination. It can't be done.[21]

Not until age ten do students learn how to think about the calendar, associating particular months with particular seasons and life events with certain days contained in certain months within certain years.[22] Flashbacks are also difficult for young children to understand, but a person who has developed a thick and rich understanding of temporal coordination (usually around the onset of adolescence) understands the sequencing of time with flashbacks and foretelling in spoken and written narratives.[23]

With temporal coordination, children can arrange their language, experiences and sequences of action. This basic cultural and temporal ordering develops as early as preschool when children learn to tell single-episode stories. With maturity, children deepen and connect with stories that have many episodes. They understand causal and thematic connections when they reach midadolescence.

CAUSAL COORDINATION

Causal coordination is the ability to connect episodic links into causal chains in which certain life events caused, ended, resulted in or related to other life events.[24] Causal coordination is supported by temporal and cultural coordination. Without temporal and cultural coordination, causal coordination can't emerge. With the advent of causal coordination, youth gain the ability to link their multifaceted and developing life story and to provide explanations of their actions and changes over time.[25] They are able to determine and explain physical causality and human motivation.[26] Causal coordination increases the most between ages twelve and sixteen.[27] Reason and meaning are added to the life story through causal coordination.[28]

Causal coordination provides the central structure to a life story.[29] Consider the metamorphosis in your own life story. How do you explain changes in your life, and what kind of meaning and motivation do you attribute to them? To explain those changes, you use causal coordination. I played football and baseball in high school, and although I performed well at both sports, I played only baseball in college. A causal connection in my life story is the fact that I dislocated my throwing arm during my junior year while playing football. At that point, I decided my love for baseball and rehabilitating my throwing arm was more important than playing football my senior year. So I connect two important dimensions in my life story with an explanation of an injury that led me to make a final decision between my two favorite sports.

The discontinuities of the past—the experiences we may never have inspected—are causally linked for the first time in midadolescence. Only in midadolescence do students relate motives and the presentation of others' understanding of their motives to their life history and life choices.[30] Early adolescents may repeat information gleaned from a parent or older sibling, but they have not yet developed the skill to integrate a person's spoken life history and to causally link their past choices with the development of their present motives.

If we do not have causal coordination, we present our lives to others without any motivational or relational understanding, which makes our lives appear meaningless.[31] Causal coordination not only connects various stories in our life, but also helps us make sense of our experiences, attribute value and meaning to those experiences and adjust our lives for future stories.

In middle and early high school, it is normal for students to live and tell their life story with contradictions they are not unaware of. A middle-schooler may tell her life story by focusing on her tightknit family unit, how she loves her parents and how she would never do anything to hurt them. In her very next story, she may talk about the joint she smoked at Saturday night's party and how crushed her parents would be if they found out. While we recognize the contradiction in her two stories, she may not.

Students at this age do not have causal coordination, but I believe a loving adult who questions these differences provides lenses for middle-schoolers to comprehend them. This is one of many reasons I argue for more relational adult involvement in the lives of middle school and high school youth rather than buying into the destructive narrative that adolescence is a time for separation and independence from adults—especially parents.

A central task in youth ministry is helping our youth tell their life stories as well as comprehend how a life story in Christ might revise their current story, giving them a different interpretive stance concerning previous causal connections and future integrated actions. I grew up with the culture narrative that if people hurt me, I hurt them. And many of our middle-schoolers live by this modern rule: "Do unto others before they do unto you." After encountering the life story of Christ and realizing that a central task of Christianity is to restory my life based on the way of Jesus, I realized that my eye-for-an-eye method only added more evil and destruction to the world, solving nothing. Now I try to approach all people as made in

God's image, and I accept that God's love is manifest and shared in our relationships. I ask my youth, "What do we do with mean people?" They say, "We try to love them." Restorying my life in Christ compels me to see people's hurt and love them in spite of the circumstances.

We hear this in many of our teens' stories when we ask why some of their friendships ended. The causal connection that most teens live by includes some kind of hurt that resulted in retaliation and more hurt that eventually severed the relationship. Cultural themes like "If someone hurts me, I hurt them back" causally connect parts of our life in negative ways that hinder our motivation to action and sabotage our future actions.

THEMATIC COORDINATION

The final and most advanced form of coordination is thematic coordination.[32] Although thematic coordination requires cultural, temporal and causal coordination, it also shapes them. In particular, thematic coordination constructs causal coordination, and causal coordination builds thematic coordination. It requires the highest level of interpretation. With thematic coordination, we gain the capacity to integrate the cultural, temporal and causal coordination through which we extract a certain theme or meaning.[33] Thematic coordination influences how we tell a story and find meaning through our story.[34] It emerges between the ages of sixteen and twenty.[35]

To understand a theme in an episodic narrative is one thing, but to take a narrative with multiple episodes—or, as in a life story, multiple narratives with multiple episodes—and extract a theme or summary takes a high level of relational thinking. Life narratives are very complex and do not always have the clear structure and goals that written narratives do.

Children and most early adolescents who take events in life as facts and nothing more do not need to interpret their life situations. However, by the time they reach midadolescence, they have a relational need to interpret various situations (instead of simply accepting them as fact).[36] Researchers have found that a clear and compelling belief system correlates with strong thematic coordination.[37] If we evaluate our lives, we generally understand our values and beliefs.

We interpret stories with certain slants and meanings according to our thematic coordination. Thematic coordination is typically evident at the beginning or ending of a life story through evaluative statements, such as

"Let me tell you about how awful my life has become," or "Looking back, I can see how God has blessed me."[38] You may remember the oft-repeated line from the movie *Forrest Gump*, "Mama always said, 'Life is like a box of chocolates. You never know what you're going to get.'" What if Forrest's mother had told him that life is like a den of lions? If he would have believed this hypothetical proverb, he would have told his story with pessimism and fear. *Forrest Gump* abounds with stories and causal connections that delight watchers with its own brand of "chocolates": themes of surprise, curiosity and the great adventure of a life truly lived.

Thematic coordination generally reflects what a person believes to be right and true, whereas causal coordination organizes those beliefs. Popular themes that help organize our narratives as an end point or goal are progressive narratives (end point is positive), regressive narratives (end point is negative), happily-ever-after narratives, heroic saga narratives, tragedies and romantic comedies.[39] Problem-saturated themes structure a problem-saturated outlook. Causal links adapt to the negative, problem-saturated theme. The causal structure helps form the theme, and the thematic form helps structure the causal links. If I believe that my life is full of problems, I will select and connect parts of my life story to reflect that belief and to show others how bad I have it.

Thematic integration. When it comes to integrating our life story and our youth's life story with that of Jesus, thematic coordination is most important. We use the same understanding with Scripture as we do with our own life story. There is no such thing as applying Scripture directly to our lives. We would be limiting a dynamic text that speaks new life into our current situations, because we live in a different time.

In the Gospel of Luke, Jesus encounters a leper who asks to be made clean. Jesus touches him, heals him and asks him to present himself as clean to the priest. This is a powerful story, but I am no Jesus and there are no lepers around me. We do not emulate the story and pretend to be Jesus, find lepers to heal and send them off to a priest. In a strict reading of the story, Jesus' healing of a leper has nothing to do with us. Instead *we interpret a theme* from the story that we can use in our own relationships. In narrative homiletics we call this the GTT, or governing theological theme. With what kind of central theme can we restory our lives? What themes that govern our life story do we need to rework?

One theme we may want to convey to our youth from the story of Jesus healing the leper is Jesus' compassion for and acceptance of the man. People pocked with leprosy congregated in colonies because they were deemed unclean; they were social outcasts. People considered the skin lesions and sores as a sign of God's punishment for their—or their parents'—sins. Jesus illustrated otherwise and restored the untouchable to touchable, the unclean to clean, as the leper became a functioning and whole human being within his society. While many focus on Jesus' miraculous healing, I think the real healing occurs when Jesus touches the man who had not been touched most of his life by another human—especially not by someone else who held power and value in society.

Who are the rejected and outcast in our society? Sometimes our own youth may feel that way. How much of our story are we willing to rewrite according to the compassion and love we see in Jesus? Do we feel untouchable, unclean, unworthy, shameful, cast out? What do we do with those around us who are socially shunned? How far are we willing to extend God's love with others? Will our acceptance and love only include people who are like us (look like us, think like us, sin like us)? Or will we be so bold as to reach out and touch the untouched? All of these questions raise issues regarding our thematic interpretation of the story of the leper and of our own life story (see Mt 8:1-3; Mk 1:40-45; Lk 5:12-13).

Drama genius Curt Cloniger said, "You tell me your view of God, and I will tell you how you will live your life." Curt illustrates six different themes of God: God as sheriff (out to get you when you mess up), God as a grandfather (old man who sits back and watches children play), God as a mechanic (fixes everything), God as a partier (everything is a celebration), God as the one in a box (neatly packaged and fitting within our categories) and God as a waiter (here to give us anything we need). Curt said this twenty years ago; if he performed these scenes today, he might add God as a therapist (here to make us feel better and happy).

When we carry these views of God, our reading of Scripture is also affected. If we imagine God as a sheriff, we interpret and focus on the passages that we believe convey that kind of God. If we believe Curt's final dramatization of God—who lavishes us with love and invites us to create that love with him—we see God through a completely different lens. Thanks to Curt, we see how these themes can bind or liberate us.

CONCLUSION

Instead of trying to guess what is inside a youth's mind and question his identity, we would be better served to move our focus to coordinating our life stories. The brain is understood as an instrument that achieves culturally and spiritually constructed ends.[40] The crossroads of causal and thematic coordination is where Jesus' life story intersects most meaningfully. If youth construct problem themes in their lives and causally connect their life stories according to those themes, how can we introduce them to the themes of Jesus that liberate, restore and make us whole?

COORDINATING LIFE STORIES WITH OUR YOUTH IS IMPORTANT FOR THE FOLLOWING REASONS:

- It forms "our" identity.
- It is how they make sense of their life.
- It presents a fuller picture of the youth, their life and their families.
- Most introductions between people require us to tell our life story (for example, job interviews, scholarship applications, college interviews, court testimonies).
- They provide access to how youth structure their problems and make sense of them.
- They help us understand how youth organize information, interpret past events and anticipate their future experiences.
- They give us access to their values, beliefs, hopes, intentions and plans for their future.
- They help develop and maintain social bonds.
- We learn about characters important to their story and their relation to them.
- We learn about their understanding of Jesus and how his life story fits or does not fit with their own.

REFLECTION QUESTIONS

1. Share your life story with a friend, a stranger, a minister. What changes do you make in your story with each coordination? Why do those changes occur?

2. If thematic and causal coordination are not fully present until late adolescence, how can we prepare children and middle school youth to develop these skills at an earlier age?

3. Ask a sixth-grader to tell you his or her story. Ask a twelfth-grader. Record the differences.

4. What is different about how middle school youth and high school youth tell their life stories? Provide an example of this difference. Why do you think it is important for youth workers and parents to know these differences?

5. List the four coordinations of a life story. Ask a friend to tell you about his or her life and write out pieces of his or her life story, highlighting each of the coordinations. To grasp the thematic coordination, you may need to ask what his or her overall impression of life has been and ask for an elaboration.

6

Childhood Foundational Elements for Adolescents

"Has Devin talked with you about him using marijuana?"

Not the question I wanted to hear from a high school principal. I took a deep breath, "Yes, he informed me a few days ago."

"Okay, that is all I wanted to know. Devin and Travis [both youth in my ministry] were caught texting about their usage of pot. They both told me they had talked with you about their marijuana problem, and they were seeking help. I wanted to make sure Devin was telling me the truth."

I assured her he was, and she thanked me for my time and hung up the phone.

That was the most awkward phone conversation I have had with a principal. It was even more uncomfortable because Travis had never told me he smoked pot, only Devin. Yet their principal was only concerned with knowing if Devin was telling the truth.

Why not Travis? I didn't have to ask. I knew exactly why the principal trusted him and not Devin. It wasn't too long before this incident that the boys were caught peeing in a bottle on the back of our church bus. After talking to them, I also wanted to excuse Travis for his behavior.

Travis and Devin are caring and compassionate youth. They both love people and enjoy making others laugh. One distinct difference distinguishes the boys the minute they speak: Travis has a deep Southern accent, and Devin does not.

Travis was born and raised in Gastonia, North Carolina. Devin grew up in New York City, and he has lived in Gastonia for a couple of years. Travis knows how to talk the language valued by older teachers and principals in our region. He knows how to be polite, how to apologize and when to talk and not to talk to adults.

Devin grew up being taught that "Southern manners" are backward and ignorant, and he refused to use such language. When I talked with the boys about urinating on the back of a bus full of youth, Travis looked me in the eyes with compassion and concern, and he politely responded with "Yes, sir" after a few of my comments. Meanwhile, Devin stared at the ground. When I finished, Devin had nothing to say to me, and he walked away. Travis didn't. "Brandon," he told me, "I am sorry for disrespecting you, the youth and our church. I know you and the other adults have taken your time and energy away from your friends and family to be with us. What I did on the back of the bus was inconsiderate of those around me, and it will never happen again."

"Travis, I appreciate your apology."

"I will also talk with my parents about my unacceptable behavior."

"I appreciate your sincerity, Travis. I will call your parents in a few minutes, and you can fill them in on anything I missed."

"But I apologized to you!" Travis suddenly protested. And I had anticipated his protest. I had heard him tell too many stories of politely and respectfully talking his and Devin's way out of getting into trouble. Most adults respected Travis, and they were always quick to talk about how polite and well mannered he was. No one ever said anything about Devin.

When word reached a few high school parents that Travis and Devin were caught texting about their use and purchase of marijuana, everyone assumed Devin was the supplier. Even after Travis admitted to supplying marijuana to Devin, several adults excused Travis by saying he was probably taking the fall for Devin.

If Travis and Devin were transported to New York City, Travis's Southern accent and polite manners would not hold the same value and may even provoke sharp criticism and distrust. The differences between Devin and Travis are not issues of respect but of their exposure to particular ways of talking and interacting during their childhood. When youth enter our ministries, we gain the relationships and stories that have shaped them from childhood. If youth have not strengthened certain foundational elements through childhood, they will struggle with their identity and life story through adolescence.

As a brick mason, I relate to foundation metaphors and questions such as "What type of foundation are you building your life on?" I appreciate the foundation metaphor because it is not as concrete as many assume. The footing (the hole where a foundation must be poured) dimensions (width, length and depth) need to correlate with the size and weight of the structure built on it. The concrete for the footing must be mixed to certain specifications, including chemical admixtures, certain kinds of crushed rock (limestone, granite, sand) and binder aggregates (fly ash, slag cement), with a certain amount of water to achieve an appropriate compressive and tensile strength. All of these mixtures are adjusted according to the type of concrete needed. The natural environment (climate, frost conditions, type of soil/clay/rock) and type of structure the foundation will hold determine what type of concrete is needed. Therefore no two foundations are exactly the same, and the makeup is interrelated to the environment and type of structure it will hold.

Similar to the complexity of the right mixture for a foundation (type of structure and environment), youth should be exposed to certain elements in childhood so that they have a suitable foundation for constructing their relationships and stories in adolescence and into adulthood.

Just as structures need strong foundations with an adequate mixture to support their weight, youth need strong foundations that prepare them for adulthood. We can't go back in time and add the missing foundational element, but we can help youth strengthen those areas.

We do not have enough space here to exhaust all the elements needed for a good foundation. Therefore, I have highlighted a few that affect the youth's life story development.

FOUNDATIONAL ELEMENT 1: RELATIONSHIPS AND NARRATIVE TONE

Gerald scolded Jonathan for dunking on a basketball goal in our gym. He told me the teen owed him an apology for disrespecting him by walking away when he was speaking. I held out my hand, and said, "Give me a hundred dollars."

Gerald looked at me like I had lost my mind and said, "I can't give you a hundred dollars!"

"Gerald, I really need a hundred dollars right now."

"I don't have a hundred dollars on me."

"Gerald, you are asking something of Jonathan that he can't give you either. Demanding respect from him will not get you respect any faster than I can get a hundred dollars by demanding it from you."

Jonathan didn't need one more adult he had never met scolding him. His life was littered with adults telling him what he was doing wrong and then leaving him. Abandoned by parents, in and out of foster homes, Jonathan hadn't had a single adult involved in his life for more than two years.

Jonathan could not show respect or compassion for others because no one had shown it to him. He had never experienced unconditional love. Every person he encountered placed conditions on how they would love and accept him: as long as he followed their rules, helped around the house, showed them respect and so on.

I wonder if Jesus pointed to young children as being the greatest in the kingdom of God because early childhood is one of the few times that our sense of value and dignity stems from unconditional love rather than what we do or don't do. It is not long into our "growing up" that we aspire to be better than others, take life too seriously, assume we are right, strive for independence and place conditions on God's love toward others and ourselves. The Christian story proclaims that God's unconditional love seen in Jesus is our source of dignity and value. Our worth is rooted in our relationship to God, not in our individualism. And because God loves and pursues us all, we affirm that everyone has value and worth, and should be treated as such.

My friend Fred Burnham (a retired Episcopal priest and director of Trinity Institute at Trinity Church Wall Street from 1984 to 2004) says we would be better off replacing the word *commandment* with *relationship*, especially when it comes to the Great Commandment.

What is the greatest relationship? Jesus said, "'You shall love the Lord your God with all your heart, and with all your soul, and with all your mind.' This is the greatest and first [relationship]. And a second is like it: 'You shall love your neighbor as yourself.' On these two [relationships] hang all the law and the prophets" (Mt 22:37-40).

We have placed many limits on God's love and our love for others. We do not love God because it is a command or some rule to follow. We love because God loved us first (1 Jn 4:19). And we love others from the abundant, life-giving love that we experience and see in Jesus. Imagine how Jonathan might view people and the world if he had experienced this kind of love as a child.

Childhood relationships. The first few years of life provide some of the most important resources for constructing a life story.[1] We learn the language of love in infancy through hugs and kisses before we can ever speak it to another person.[2] What happens if infants are not exposed to such love?

In 1945 Rene Spitz compared American babies raised in orphanages with those raised in an institutional prison nursery. The main difference between the two environments was the child-to-adult ratio. The orphanages had one nurse to eight infants, and the prison babies had direct contact with their mothers. Spitz found that 37 percent of the children in the orphanages died before they reached the age of two, whereas none of the prison babies died. The prison babies thrived with fewer infections, healthy weight and height gain, and emotional and intellectual stability. Spitz concluded that the lack of individualized care and attention wasn't just unhealthy; it was fatal. As neuroscientist Bruce Perry notes, "A lack of love was what was killing the orphanage children, not unsterile group living."[3]

Infant-parental attachment is one of the greatest achievements during the first years of life. Infants are not immediately "attached" to their caregivers at birth, nor are their caregivers immediately attached to them.[4] Bonding is a mutual process.[5] Healthy attachments need to occur between infants and their parents or guardians for infants to develop relationally and positively. If healthy attachments are not formed, the child may suffer severe trauma and a lack of cultural and physical development that will affect him for the rest of his life.[6] Infants need relationships. Without them, they become impaired.[7]

Infants and children need a secure base to which they can return when they feel threatened and need comfort. This attachment does not dissipate in adolescence, but the frequency, duration and function of the attachment evolves from infancy, through childhood and into adolescence.[8] At every stage, children need to know that their environment is safe. This safety has more to do with their relational environment than with their physical environment.

Children come to see the world either as a dangerous place or as a place where people are available when needed to meet their needs. The stories our caregivers use from their relational narratives in caring for and nurturing us as infants scripts how we will respond to and tell stories in the future. While storytelling does not begin in infancy, the tone of our future stories does. Narrative tone can be either optimistic or pessimistic, based on whether or not we experience a secure attachment with our caregivers.[9]

Valuing the relationship. It took me a year of showing Jonathan that I was not going to abandon him before he began trusting me and telling me his story. There was a pessimistic tone in every story he told. He believed the world was out to get him, and he told his stories with this theme. During one conversation, Jonathan told me I was the only person he trusted. I was honored and saddened by this revelation. I couldn't imagine being a teenager and only having one person in the world that I felt I could trust.

How do we minister to youth who are similar to Jonathan?

Jonathan didn't stop dunking on the basketball goal after Gerald scolded him—that is, until Von approached him. What was different? Von's knowledge of working with teens and his focus on valuing Jonathan and their relationship made most of the difference.

Von was another adult Jonathan began to trust. He spent time with Jonathan and knew his story. When Jonathan slam-dunked the basketball, Von ran over to him, gave him a high-five and said, "That was incredible!" After the high-five, Von pulled him aside and said, "I want you and your friends playing on these goals for a long time. Right now we don't have the money to replace these goals if they get bent. Could you work on your basketball game without dunking? Or can I help you improve your jumping where you can dunk without touching the rim? We don't have rules posted, because we want to focus on building relationships, and I need your help to spread the word that we can't hang on these rims."

Jonathan never dunked on our goals again. Why? Von knew Jonathan's life story, he complimented him, he illustrated his concern for Jonathan and not the goal, he offered to help, and he showed trust in Jonathan to partner with him. Underneath all of this language was the unspoken and unconditional language of God's love with which Von approaches all of our youth.

FOUNDATIONAL ELEMENT 2: CULTURAL COORDINATION— LANGUAGE GAMES

> Give ear, O my people, to my teaching; incline your ears to the words of my mouth. I will open my mouth in a [story]; I will utter dark sayings from of old, things that we have heard and known, that our ancestors have told us.

We will not hide them from their children; we will tell to the coming gener-
ation the glorious deeds of the Lord, and his might, and the wonders that he
has done. (Ps 78:1-4)

"Preach the gospel at all times; if necessary, use words." This is one of my
favorite quotes, attributed to Saint Francis of Assisi. I have seen too many
people abused by religious words and never shown the gospel in action. Yet
Psalm 78 reminds us of another perspective. If we don't tell the stories of
God and use words, we will be like the Ephramites, who lost their identity by
forgetting what God had done (Ps 78:11). The psalmist is adamant about
sharing the stories inherited from his ancestors with the children (Ps 78:5-6).

Actions may speak louder than words, but what kind of identity can our
children and youth develop if they do not have the stories to provide context
for the actions? Using our faith language with our children is vital in maintaining our faith. Let's take a look at how we learn through our use of language.

Beyond words as pictures to our use of words. I remember the first time
my son interacted with what we call a globe. He put his finger on the round
object and said, "Ball." I was stumped. How would I teach him that it was
like a ball, but was not a ball? Furthermore, he placed his finger on an area
that we would call blue or water. How would he ever distinguish that the
object he was pointing to was not a ball? It rolled like a ball and looked like
a ball, but it was a representation of our earth. I had numerous corrections
I could offer. I could have said, "Kaden, that is not a ball; it is _____ " (fill in
the blank with blue, plastic, salt water, an ocean, the Atlantic Ocean, round,
the Earth, a planet, a globe, a model, a sphere, thirty degrees north latitude
and forty-five degrees west longitude, the Northern Hemisphere).

Determined to teach my three-year-old son that what he had pointed to
represented our planet Earth, I moved the globe to its base and found our
current location. I pointed to the left of Charlotte, North Carolina, and said,
"Kaden, this is where we live."

Kaden looked at me and laughed. His laugh helped me realize how ridiculous I sounded pointing to his ball and saying we lived on it. The only
way my son will eventually recognize that his ball is also a representation of
Earth is through learning the language games of models, representations,
balls, shapes, planets, solar systems and geography. As he grows older, he
will learn to coordinate his understanding of what he points to and the
language his context requires him to use.

If children had no one with whom to coordinate their language, they would not advance in their vocabulary proficiency, and they would not know how to play our language games. In extreme cases when children were not exposed to language before adolescence, they eventually learned through exposure how to speak full sentences, but they were never able to tell their own life story.[10]

Our coordination becomes more intricate than simply attaching pictures or names to objects. Think about all the words we use every day in our coordination with others that do not have a direct picture or meaning attached to the word, but gain significance through their utility. Look at the previous sentence and try to separate the words from the context and imagine a picture that the words generate: *think, about, the, all, words, we, use, in, our, coordination, do, not, a, have, picture, direct, or, meaning, but, they, gain, significance, its, utility, through.* Not one word correlates to a single direct picture.

Children not only learn how to attach words to signs or objects (this is one language game), but they also learn the utility of words in our language and how to coordinate them with others. As Ludwig Wittgenstein pointed out, our words are coordinated with others like a game.[11] Most of our talk makes sense only within certain language games. A person throwing a baseball off a small hill to a person squatting would not make sense without the game of baseball. Since most of us are familiar with the game, we might call this scene "practice."

The same is true in our youth ministry practices. Children do not learn the language of faith solely through word pictures or by memorizing verses. They learn from their active use of their faith language with others.

Preschool. The preschool world bursts with images and stories that provide essential elements for the life story. Preschoolers may eventually be able to tell and listen to entire stories, but images and characters are more important than the stories themselves.[12] While toddlers learn to differentiate between four-legged creatures, colors, grandparents and so on, older preschoolers and early elementary school children learn to differentiate and classify images. With the help of their caregivers, they can classify, for example, a *Chihuahua, Schnauzer* or *German Shepherd* as a dog. *Siamese, Persians* or *Bengals* they call cats, and they recognize that *Grandma, Granddaddy, Maw-maw* and *Paw-paw* are all grandparents.[13] Just as the games of baseball, football and chess have different languages and ways players interact, children learn the same with language.

Even though preschoolers are able to classify objects, they can't distinguish words *and* objects.[14] For preschool children, words and objects themselves are inseparable.[15] For a child, an exchange of names would mean an exchange of fundamental attributes.[16] I told my preschool daughter that we were going to start calling our cat, Molly, a dog. I explained that Molly was still going to be a cat and do all of her cat sounds and behaviors, but we were going to call her a dog for one day. She laughed and was excited to play my silly game. I pointed to Molly and I asked her, "Molly is now called what?"

"A dog."

"And what sound does she make?"

"Ruff, ruff."

My daughter had not yet learned our more complex language games.[17] This is a comical exercise when we switch cats and dogs, cows and lions, monkeys and elephants, but I hope we all stop laughing when people switch the child's name with a negative attribute. It may be funny to watch a preschooler protest someone calling her "stinky," but it is not so funny when we realize the child is associating stinky with "poop," and all the preschooler hears is that she has the same attributes as poop. Our words shape their world and describe their reality. In a few years, the child will learn the various word games that people play, and she will know that such name calling can be understood as joking.[18]

Stories are too complicated for preschoolers to comprehend fully. Their focus is on images and characters,[19] and the world revolves around them. They will pretend to be certain characters from a story or from their cultural setting "to suit their immediate wishes and desires."[20] The world of another is understood from within the context of the preschooler's own experience. He has not yet learned the world in a systematic and logical manner within the context of culturally agreed-on systems and standards.[21] Therefore, he dictates the character's actions, conforming behavior to fit his desires. If we want to keep the attention of preschool children during a lesson, we highlight the characters and images as we tell the story. We dress up like the main character or have the preschoolers dress up and participate.

Elementary school. In elementary school, around the age of six or seven, children better understand human behavior in stories and in life.[22] Children can now understand the rules and regulations that govern characters.[23] Children move from a subjective understanding of the world to a more objective viewpoint. They learn how life operates according to "rules."[24] Everything is thoroughly objective.[25] Differences appear when we observe preschool and elementary school children playing together. If an elementary school child throws a Wiffle ball past a swinging four-year-old, he hollers, "You're out!"

"I am not!" the four-year-old says, stomping.

The frustrated six-year-old screams, "Three strikes and you're out! That was your third strike!"

The four-year-old may respond, "I am not out until I hit the ball!" He has not yet developed the understanding of the language game and rules of "being out," "three strikes" and the relationship between them. Much of elementary school is a socialization process of learning societal rules such as grammar, math and science.

Elementary children begin to recognize that characters in stories are guided by certain motivations and thoughts, and that the characters strive to attain particular goals within a limited time.[26] Children understand and read *The Wizard of Oz, Alice in Wonderland* and the parables of Jesus as straightforward stories. What is told is what happened. Early adolescents begin to understand that something deeper lurks beneath the text. They may feel the shame of the woman accused of adultery or experience the emotional loss of Jesus when his disciples abandon him. Young children can't attain this depth of understanding without a lot of explaining.

Cultural construction of emotions. Much has been written about how emotions are culturally constructed. We may be born crying and screaming and may appear mad, angry or scared, but our emotions are shaped and formed early in life from the culture in which we participate. What we consider anger and what makes us angry are all products of our culture and what we have learned to value.

One way I have come to a better understanding of this is to view emotions as a social performance. In our culture, I can't display my anger to someone by smiling. And I can't be angry without reason. If I am trying to show love to someone, I do not scream and curse in his face. And even though Paul may have encouraged the Romans to greet one another with a holy kiss (a common Middle Eastern practice—see Romans 16:16), such a greeting in our American cultural context is grounds for sexual harassment. Just as we teach our children how to perform emotions, we also have the opportunity to show them different ways to regulate them.

My wife and I gave our kids jars filled with water and glitter. We told them when they became angry, they could grab one of the jars and shake it up. After they shook up the jar, they could watch the glitter settle in the bottle and that would help them cool down. The first few times our kids became angry, the bottles became missiles launched at the other sibling. Eventually our kids took to the anger bottles, and they used them to calm down before they said or did anything hurtful. One time my wife and I were in a heated argument and our daughter brought us each a bottle to use.

The way we culturally construct emotions with our children makes a difference in how they act out such emotions with others. How do we perform anger? Love? Hurt? Pain? Compassion? Think of the people who may have shown you compassion and concern. The way they cared for you became a model you can imitate to care for others too.

THE CRITIC'S VOICE

Criticism

You seem to be privileging relationship over personality. A person is born with a personality before they are in a relationship. Shouldn't you focus on the individual personality first?

Response

Consider some of the personality characteristics: outgoing, shy, caring, organized, messy, nurturing, honest, patient, open and so on. Most words used to describe our personality would lose their meaning if the person was alone on a deserted island. Without the presence of others, can a person be nurturing? Shy? Caring? Our personality traits are not so much inside us as in the relation between ourselves and others.

If personalities were innate within all of us, we would find them in all cultures, but we do not. Even in our own culture, the idea of personalities and the ways we define them have changed over time. Vivian Burr illustrates how we have taken words that illustrated actions between people and made them about private feelings inside us:

> *When I was a child, my grandmother sometimes used to say, "Come here and give me a love," or "Let me love you for a minute." To "love" someone here means to physically embrace them, and perhaps to comfort them. . . . In the vast majority of cases when we talk about loving someone, we are talking about private events, our feelings, things which are taken to exist inside us and which influence how we treat people. Love has therefore become something which is seen as motivating our behavior rather than as a word which describes our behaviour.*[27]
>
> *With words such as* loving, caring and happy *moved to the internal domain, it is easier to separate such "feelings" or "personality traits" from action and conduct. We can then use this separation to justify the most appalling behavior: "I hit her when I am angry, but I really love her."*[28] *More and more of our language is being relegated to describe the internal rather than our actions toward people.*
>
> *What would happen in our relationships if we did not focus on individual personality traits, such as internal love, but on how love is acted out and sustained in each of our relationships?*

My former pastor, sixty-five-year-old Ned Buckner, knows the importance of this kind of role modeling. I will never forget the first time I saw him coach a soccer team of five- and six-year-olds. When the team huddled for coaching instructions, Ned disappeared, vanishing into the circle of elbows and shin guards. He crouched to their level to put them at ease, looked them in the eyes and conveyed a genuine love for them. When I started coaching the same-aged soccer team a few years later, I huddled my team and I disappeared too.

FOUNDATIONAL ELEMENT 3: TEMPORAL COORDINATION

Jenny, one of my ninth-grade students, was telling me about her friend Sarah. "She is such a sweet friend, and so considerate of others," she said. "Yesterday, she bought me ice cream and purchased some to take to our friend, Jill, who is sick. She invited me skiing with her family, and they paid for everything. I love Sarah's family. . . . Oh, she bought me a nice flat iron too!"

"All of this happened yesterday?" I asked.

"Oh, no. Just her buying me ice cream and taking some to Jill. Everything else was at different times."

If Jenny had been testifying in court she would have confused a lot of people, and without a coherent order in her story, her testimony might have been in jeopardy of being considered false.[29] It is not so much the truth that we are after, but a proper story.[30] If what a person shares is not embedded in a proper story, we begin to question its validity. All of Jenny's statements may be true, but chronologically they do not make sense. Whether or not we are on a witness stand or talking to a friend, we are listening for stories to be arranged and ordered according to chronological time. Without temporal indicators (see chapter 5), Jenny's story fails to communicate.

I asked Jenny a few questions about when the events occurred in her narrative, and she retold it with an emphasis on ordering the events: "Sarah is such a sweet friend and considerate of others. The first time I met her she invited me skiing with her family, and they paid for everything. Just a few months ago, Sarah bought me a nice flat iron for my birthday. Yesterday, she paid for my ice cream at Ben and Jerry's and bought extra to take to our friend, Jill, who is sick."

Questioning Jenny about the story helped her see how incoherent it was, and she was able to practice telling the story in a more coherent and orderly manner. Such simple retellings may not seem like much, but they allow our youth to reflect on how they tell their stories.

Temporal coordination in childhood. One of the most fundamental changes that occurs during the preschool years is the emergence of temporal coordination.[31] Temporal coordination begins to develop as preschoolers learn their culture's construction of time; they begin to distinguish between what has happened, what is happening and what may happen. Parents or guardians guide children to voice their understanding of events through language, as children's shared representation of time becomes critical for children to gain a sense of self.[32]

Children before the age of three have not yet figured out that their memories are representations of past events and that their memories may differ from others' memories of the same event.[33] Thus they have not yet established a sense of self. A sense of self hinges on a child's ability to discuss the past with others and to know that she recalls an event differently from others.[34]

The preschooler begins to understand that the cultural sign "yesterday" can be collaborated temporally with others as something that has already taken place (even though the preschooler may equate it with any day in the past), and "tomorrow" is collaborated with others as something that will take place but has not yet happened. At age three, my daughter would say, "Remember yesterday when we went to the beach?" The last time we had gone to the beach had been three months prior. I responded with, "Yesterday we went to Kaden's Christmas play, and you went to preschool. Do you remember that? We went to the beach several months ago." Although my daughter had no idea what "several months ago" meant, she learned to associate it with something in the distant past.

"Do you remember when we went to the beach 'seferal mons' ago?" she had asked, trying again.

"Yes, that was fun wasn't it?"

"Yeah. I want to go back!" she said as she jumped up and down.

Telling stories with an ordered time sequence to our children helps provide them with a pattern for how they can arrange their stories. One of the most beneficial things we can do with our children and youth ministries is to provide an account of the biblical story that helps them understand how it temporally unfolded. The importance of this hit me a few years ago when one of my youth asked, "Was David, the guy who killed Goliath, before or after Jesus?"

How adults guide children to create more collaborative and integrated narratives influences how children construct life narratives in adolescence.[35] Elementary school children can provide sequences of episodes and a generalized extension of events that are ordered temporally but otherwise not related.[36] By late elementary school, children can write narratives of single events that are almost an adult-level performance.[37] Between the ages of five and ten, temporal coordination applies heavily to single autobiographical events rather than causal connections between different events.[38] Not until midadolescence can youth connect different biographical events into their life story to make meaning with others through thematic and causal coordination. If children and adolescents have not spent an ample amount of time talking with others about what they have experienced in the past, they do not represent themselves in the past nor do they project themselves into possible futures.[39]

Endpoint. With any coherent story that we tell, there is an endpoint. Everything is temporally ordered and structured toward the endpoint. Early adolescents and children can only arrange their stories toward an endpoint with temporal and cultural coordination. In midadolesence we begin to see youth building on temporal and cultural coordination to arrange their stories thematically and causally according to the endpoint. Jenny's endpoint was to focus on Sarah's kindness and friendship. The ordering of events is important because Jenny is also trying to establish that Sarah has remained a faithful friend over time.

Most of the time, the endpoint of our stories must also relate to the stories that others are sharing. You may have been around a middle school youth who tells a story and someone asks, "What was the point in that story?" The student missed the context of what the group was discussing. Rarely do older high school students make this error, because their friends will certainly let them know: "Get to the point!"

Adults help children reach the endpoint of their stories by asking questions or giving commands: What did you do today? Tell me about your favorite vacation. Why did you do that? What was your worst experience? Children need this coaching and practice to learn how to organize their stories.

Goals. Imagining future possibilities that change our present circumstances is an important skill for children to learn and practice. Without this skill being developed in childhood, adolescents will have a difficult time setting goals to achieve a task, and they will struggle to understand the gospel and its eschatological component.

Joy announced that she was going to be a mental health therapist. This was the second time I heard Joy make that statement. I asked her why she was interested in counseling. She shrugged and said, "I don't know. I guess I just like to help people."

"What school do you plan on attending?" I asked.

"I don't know. I just don't want to be in college for more than four years."

I asked, "Did you know to obtain a degree as a counselor in mental health in the state of North Carolina you must attend six to eight years of higher education as well as complete about three thousand hours of clinical work before you can take the licensure exam?"

Joy stared at me. "No, I didn't know any of that. You are the first person who has asked me these questions. I should probably know these things since I am graduating in a few months," she said, slumping down in her chair.

In the past I had heard Joy describe her counseling in detail. She already had a named picked out for her counseling practice: "Joy's Hope." I know many teenagers whose dreams, hopes and future plans were crushed because they didn't take the appropriate steps to achieve their goals. Now she was faced with additional information about her future that led her to rethink her present decisions, and I was able to help her through the process.

A deeper sense of the Christian gospel also requires youth to imagine God's future reality and begin implementing it in the present through what has taken place in the past through the life, death and resurrection of Jesus.

The first time I tried to introduce youth to eschatology (the study of last things), it didn't go so well. I was excited about helping them imagine their future story grounded in the full culmination of God's kingdom. I wanted them to grasp how our future hope in God's reality shapes who we are becoming right now. I thought I overused the word *eschatology*, but seventeen-year-old Aaron proved me wrong.

Aaron went home after our youth lesson and couldn't wait to tell his mom about what he had learned. His mom, Ruth, told me what he had said: "Mom, I am blown away by this concept that Brandon talked about tonight. You can look it up; it's called scatology." Ruth wanted to participate in her son's enthusiasm, so she went to the dictionary and found the following definition for *scatology*: "an interest in or preoccupation with excrement and excretion." This was the only time in youth ministry when I wished I had used the term *eschatology* a few more times, with more explanation.

Don't we youth ministers tend to avoid eschatology as if it were scatology? Yet it is vital that youth wrestle with the way God's future story changes our goals for our lives. Youth tend to be more interested in their present circumstances than their future, and they tend to interpret Scripture that way too.

One of my youth expressed this well with the story of Simeon and Anna in Luke 2:21-38. He said, "They are old and about to die, so why does it matter if they see Jesus? He's just a baby." Great question. If Anna and Simeon made God's redemption about their own personal redemption and their own life story, it really didn't make much of a difference. But they viewed their story as part of a much larger narrative in which they were participants in and witnesses of God's work for the whole cosmos. God's future, in the Christian story, is vital in shaping Christian identity in the present.

Ask youth and adults what they do when they feel down or stuck, and they may give one of the following responses: listen to music, play a game, talk to a friend, contact a family member, pray, draw or paint and so on. All of these activities can spark our imagination. They help us to see beyond our current circumstances and imagine something different.

John, the author of Revelation, encountered early Christians who felt abandoned by God, taken advantage of by others, powerless and—like many youth—despairing because they were having a difficult time seeing beyond their present circumstances. He painted a portrait of God's reign and rule that ignited his readers' imagination of reality and future. Although it looked like Caesar was on the throne, John reminded them that God was on the throne. Although it looked like Caesar was victorious through violence, Jesus conquered through nonviolence, giving his love and life away. Although it looked like the early Christians were losing an impossible battle, they would experience victory through Christ, even though they faced losing their lives. John gave them a dose of imagination that helped them overcome complacency, apathy and indifference so that they could see God's future reality.

For children and early adolescents, our sharing of eschatology does not have to be complicated. It can be as simple as holding on to a hope that things will be okay, because God promises us this.

I watched my best friend and eleven-year-old cousin slowly die of cancer when I was thirteen. His future did not include high school, driving, marriage or children. His future included a death sentence from the medical field. This was the way many saw it. Yet Rodney Jones did not see his future that way, and he convinced me to see his end differently too. For Rodney, his future was the beginning of life—one without chemo and radiation, without pain and suffering. He had hope. Like the psalmist in Psalm 42, Rodney had hope that included questions, fear and some doubt. But he clung to God's hope and believed that God would make "all things new."

We need to teach our youth that God's future kingdom is not separate from God's present kingdom work. We are rescued and delivered from our broken relationships to become agents of God's love and reconciliation in this world (2 Cor 5). We can begin practicing God's new kingdom now because Christ inaugurated it on the cross.

FOUNDATIONAL ELEMENT 4: EVALUATIVE NARRATIVES

Angela, a white high school student who was relatively new to our youth ministry, was turning the corner when Michael, one of our black students, came rushing out the door and bumped into her. He turned and said, "I am so sorry. I didn't see you."

Angela walked away with her friend, Shirley. "Typical," Angela said, rolling her eyes.

I heard her and asked, "What do you mean, 'typical'?"

"Well, you know, that's how they are," she said. "Always inconsiderate of people around them."

"No, I don't know. Michael is one of the most considerate teens I know, which is why he apologized to you," I said.

Part of Angela's narrative included a negative evaluation of black people. In fact, a little further into my conversation with her, she revealed that she thinks all Democrats are stupid and all black people take advantage of white people. I have also heard the opposite stories from some of my black students about Republicans and whites. It is no coincidence that their parents use the same type of language and share the same views. How we evaluate others with our children present provides a template for how they evaluate others in adolescence.

I was surprised to walk into our playroom that also functioned as a workout room and see my son with dumbbells in his hands and my four-year-old daughter lying on the floor.

"What are you doing?" I asked.

My daughter, with her hands clasped behind her head, attempted a sit-up. "We are exercising like you, Daddy."

I didn't know my daughter knew the word *exercise*, much less associated a sit-up with it. I chuckled at the scene until a wave of anxiety washed over me. What else had they heard me say or watched me do?

Children are *not* like sponges. They may absorb everything, but we can't squeeze out what they have absorbed. Trust me, I've tried.

I was livid when Randy, a faithful church member, told me we should be helping only the youth who attend our church on Sunday morning. We argued back and forth, both of us refusing to budge from our theological rationale. I finally told him, "This is stupid, Randy. God's love is so much bigger than that!" No one had ever put him in his place, and I felt good about my choice of words—until I walked away with my son, who parroted, "Stupid Randy!"

How we interact with others in the presence of children models patterns for how they can—and will—talk about others or themselves. It is not only the verbal content that children learn, but also how we position ourselves in relation to others. Psychologist Lisa M. Tillmann-Healy recounts this story:

> The brush whooshes softly as it rolls off the ends. She stands in front of the mirror attached to the pine dresser her father made. I look up at Mom's re-flection, and she smiles at me. When her gaze returns to her own image, a different expression washes over my mother's face. She sets the brush down. Turning to the side, she squeezes the skin beneath her rib cage. Back to center, Mom's hand sweeps over her slightly rounded middle. Her eyebrows curl and her lips purse as she watches herself intently. Mom turns away and dresses hurriedly. While she dons baggy sweatpants and a long shirt, I reach under-neath my sweater and feel for excess flesh. I am 4 years old.[40]

Lisa's mom did not tell her she was fat, and hopefully she would never do such a thing to her four-year-old. But she did teach her how to survey her body and what to focus on during her examination.

In a similar way, church wars between traditional or contemporary music do not teach our children which music is more sacred or relevant; they teach them intolerance. They learn how to place their stake in the ground and claim their narrow turf in the whole body of Christ. Children mostly learn from their parents and caregivers the form and function of memory and the manner in which they will tell stories to others in the future.[41]

If parents view their child as an individual and autonomous agent (pre-dominately a Western cultural view of self and world), parent-child remi-niscing will focus more on the child's individual emotions, thoughts, de-sires and actions.[42] Alternatively, if parents value community and highlight the importance of how the self relates to others (predominately an Eastern cultural view of self and world), parent-child reminiscing will focus on moral emotions and lessons that draw attention to communal responsibil-ities and belongings.[43]

The parental view of self and world, as conveyed through reminiscing with preschool children, influences how elementary children and adolescents understand and tell stories of their selves in the world. Mothers who use evaluative narratives in their mother-child reminiscing (for example, "Didn't we have a great time sliding together?" or "Wasn't that fun?") have children who later use evaluation in their own narratives.[44] Evaluations in narratives are important because they enhance reflexivity and provide scaffolding for the later construction of thematic coordination.

When caregivers encourage children to talk about their past, the children can move beyond past actions and objects, and tell orienting information, such as the class took a field trip (what happened) to a strawberry farm on Friday (where and when the event occurred), and they can report evaluative information, such as, "It was hot, but I loved it" (thought and feeling concerning the event).[45] Essentially, they begin to form and tell a rough narrative.

Only around age four do children begin to have an enduring sense of self.[46] At that age, they begin to link past emotions with present feelings and situations.[47] If the family dog was hit by a car, the child may exhibit concern that a new dog might face the same fate. Even when the child's speech becomes internalized, the child's emotions and ideas are always linked to his cultural influences. The child's experience is external before it becomes internal.[48] Ideas and emotions (internal states) are a product of their outward cultural experiences: a child learns to count on her fingers before she does in her mind, and she feels love through hugs and kisses before she feels it in her heart.[49] The same is true with narratives. Children learn the raw evaluative narratives for coping with stress and future problems long before they know how to use them as coping mechanisms.[50]

Elementary school child can imagine the intentions and actions of others because of certain motivational patterns and schemes they have developed. After coding the narrative content of children nine to thirteen years old, Fivush and colleagues discovered that the more children talked about their problems and provided negative evaluations of others, the less they were able to cope with their problems.[51] In other words, talking about problems doesn't help. Older children need someone to help them structure their problems in more causal and coherent ways that leads to a better understanding of the problem and stress management.[52] Once again, critical to a child's well-being is the provision of a coherent, causal and emotional framework for coping with and enduring difficult events.[53]

Throughout childhood, parental involvement and reminiscing with children, including sharing family history, is "significantly correlated with . . . better family functioning, greater family cohesiveness, lower levels of anxiety, and lower incidence of behavior problems."[54] This assessment correlates with other studies that linked eating disorders with a lack of coherence in narratives and family sharing, which allowed the person to contemplate possible alternative narratives and alternative views of self and cultural narratives of beauty.[55]

In order for youth to develop any kind of healthy sense of being, they need to be able to offer an evaluative narrative of themselves.[56] A parent that tells a child she is dumb in order to motivate the child to work harder in school is likely to provide an evaluative template through which the child underscores her mistakes and failures and to tell stories that are saturated with her "dumbness."

Nine- to eleven-year-old children whose parents are expressive and causal in talking about negative events have higher self-esteem after a two-year period than those whose parents are less expressive and causal.[57] Although parent-child communication regarding positive events does not seem to make a difference, talk about negative events appears to be particularly important because children need help in making sense of and coordinating these events.[58] Parental and caregiver assistance to children as they develop their stories is essential as "storytelling is at the heart of both stability and change in the self."[59]

The way we approach children and youth, and the posture we take toward them, plays an important role in their evaluative narratives of others and themselves. I wonder what kind of view the children would have had of Jesus and his disciples if they had not been permitted to see Jesus? How would they have viewed God? How would they have viewed their relationship to Jesus?

Jesus tells us, "Whoever welcomes one such child in my name welcomes me" (Mt 18:5). Like praying in Jesus' name, our welcoming and praying is done in the likeness and humility of Jesus. And such praying and welcoming within the likeness and humility of Jesus makes a world of difference in our children and youth ministries.

CONCLUSION

Relationships result in the formation of stories, and stories are part of the formation of relationships. They constitute our identity, and if one is lacking, then so is the other.[60] In contrast to our ancestors, where the adult-to-child ratio was 4:1, we live in a relationally impoverished world where the ratio is 1:4.[61] Humans are fundamentally relational creatures, and healthy development extends from the person's relational connectivity with others so the child can develop to be socially appropriate, empathic, self-regulating and humane.[62]

In cases of neglect and trauma in children, psychiatrist Bruce Perry has recommended not pharmacology or psychiatric labels, but a "therapeutic web."[63] The central prescription to this web is healthy and invested people in the child's life, such as youth ministers who can provide quantitative and qualitative relational support. The church can play a major role in shaping children's lives in a positive and loving way. The church can be a family of families to our children and their families.

In the 2007 animated film *Meet the Robinsons*, twelve-year-old Lewis is an orphan who longs for a family. His creative knack for inventions sabotage him throughout his childhood as experiments go wrong at the worst possible time—when he first meets prospective, adoptive families. After many failed inventions, which result in families refusing to adopt him, he finally meets his dream family, the Robinsons. At a meal, the family robot tosses out bread and attempts to spread peanut butter and jelly with one pull of the trigger. But the gun freezes, and their robot can't fix it.

Lewis's friend, Wilbur, pushes him to fix the gun in hopes that Lewis will regain confidence in his inventive abilities. Lewis refuses, but the family's pleading finally encourages him to try. He fixes the gun, and when the robot attempts to shoot, the machine explodes, and peanut butter and jelly cover the room and everyone in it. Lewis's fear of failure had come true. But contrary to the other families' responses, the Robinson family reacts differently and rewrites Lewis's future story.

"Oh, no. No. I didn't know. I am sorry. I am so sorry," Lewis says, burying his face in his hands.

Grandpa Bud lifts his hand in celebration and says, "You failed!"

Lewis looks up, confused. The rest of the family chimes in with congratulations, and Uncle Gaston says, "If I gave up every time I failed, I never would have made the meatball canon."

Then, to prove his point, Grandpa Bud lights his pants on fire and says, "I never would have made my fireproof pants." The flames consume his pants leaving him standing in his underwear. "Ah, still working out the kinks."

Grandpa Bud laughs at his own failure. Mrs. Robinson comments, "Like my husband always says"—there is a slight pause and the room erupts with signs, banners, and a chorus breaks out with the message—"KEEP MOVING FORWARD!"

Then Mrs. Robinson continues. "I propose a toast to Lewis and his brilliant failure. May it lead to success in the future." Everyone toasts and cheers.

Lewis's entire outlook on life, family, failure and success changes at that moment because of the Robinson family's acceptance.

Will we help our children restructure their fragile stories with affirming language so that they can see their importance through their connectedness with others? Youth ministers can provide evaluative narratives that guide children through solving problems and making sense of their lives. We and the larger church body can be a loving Robinson family that actively pursues and encourages our young to keep moving forward (see Phil 3:12-14).

REFLECTION QUESTIONS

1. If children learn our language by how they *use* the language with others, how can we use this understanding to help us minister to children in our ministries?

2. Reflect on a recent interaction with a child. What did you coordinate with the child? How did the interaction mold you? How did the interaction shape the child?

3. If preschoolers gravitate to characters and images, how could you share the story of Jesus' servant-leadership when he washes the disciples' feet?

4. How can we incorporate evaluative narratives in our children or our youth ministries so that it helps them with their future stories? Give an example of helping a child or youth reinterpret a failure into a success.

5. How can ministers to children or youth provide a relationally safe environment? What would that look like? What would need to change in your own ministry environment?

7

Relationships and Stories in Middle School

Middle-schoolers in my youth ministry wrote down hurtful words their peers had called them. The list included everything from *stupid, fat, bipolar* and *ugly* to *moron, emo, jerk* and *loser*. We discussed each word and how deeply those words had wounded each student.

The following week I taped a blank piece of paper to the wall and handed out pieces of paper. "Ball your paper up," I said. "Now imagine the blank piece of paper on the wall represents the person you dislike the most. This is your chance to say anything you want to that person."

It didn't take two seconds before one student hurled her balled up piece of paper at the wall and said, "I hate you, you ugly excuse for a human being." The rest followed suit, flinging their papers—and insults—one after the other. As I had anticipated, they all threw their wadded-up paper without a prompt and spewed venomous words to the person they had imagined.

After the chaos settled, I removed the blank paper from the wall to reveal another paper I had taped under it. On that paper were all the hurtful words they had given me the previous week. In the barrage of paper throwing, each student had shouted at least one of the words that they had listed. In the center of the paper was Jesus' statement in John 8:7: "Let anyone among you who is without sin be the first to throw a stone at her."

I reminded them that I had never asked them to throw their paper (or stone), and they could have said anything—positive or negative—to the person. Yet as a group, they resurrected the same hurtful words that had hurt them. We talked about how Jesus' statement neutralized the violence and reminded people of their equality. We analyzed the negative word *adul-*

terer and how, according to the religious leaders of Jesus' day, the woman who had been caught in adultery not only deserved the label, but she also deserved death. Jesus refused to participate in the language or condemnation of the religious. Instead, by defending the woman and treating her with respect and dignity, he tangibly showed her grace. The class read the story three times, imagining ourselves to be the woman who had been captured, the religious who wanted to stone her, and Jesus, who refused to condemn her.

We explored what a similar scene might look like today and how we could stop joining the crowd of condemners. As one seventh-grader suggested, we ended in prayer and tossed our paper in the trash as we left.

YOUTH ARE EASY TARGETS

I was the last to walk out of our youth room, and I heard an eighth-grade girl say, "Please stop! Why are you always picking on me?" My heart sank. In that moment I felt like John, the author of Revelation, who hears and anticipates one thing and sees another that changes his entire perspective. When I turned to look down the hallway, I saw my assistant leader respond, "Because you are such an easy target."

One label we use as the scope to enhance our sight on youth is the word *adolescents*. We don't hear youth identifying themselves in this manner. It's a scientific and psychological label used to classify the person who is more than a child but not yet an adult. Adolescence is typically known as the period through which the adolescent "grows up" into adulthood.[1] A historical study of adolescence will illustrate that such a period did not exist over a century ago, and the timing and duration has lengthened. In the 1950s, adolescence lasted no more than three to six years. Today, some argue that it lasts twelve to fifteen years. In fact, a new phase has been argued for called "emerging adulthood," which represents the transition between post-high school and adulthood.[2]

Several adolescent psychology textbooks separate adolescence into three distinct stages: early, middle and late.[3] But there is much disagreement as to where these fit. Most agree on early adolescence representing middle-school-age youth (ten to fourteen). The major disagreements are about when adulthood begins and whether or not emerging adulthood is recognized as a separate and distinct period.[4]

Take a stroll through the last decade on adolescent research. The differences of opinion according to how we should understand adolescents are as broad and diverse as there are fields: psychoanalytic, cognitive, behavioral, social psychology, cultural psychology, family therapy and so on. As child psychologist William Kessen states, "No other animal species has been cataloged by responsible scholars in so many wildly discrepant forms, forms that a perceptive extraterrestrial could never see as reflecting the same beast."[5]

When we venture beyond psychology into biology, neuroscience, sociology, anthropology and theology, the differences of opinion multiply. Which one is correct? If you feel overwhelmed and don't know, relax, because your position of "not knowing" may be the best view to have.

Adolescence is a social construction; no one can claim the "truth" of how to view it. Accepting that we do not know keeps us from adopting the latest theory to label youth. We should study every view of adolescence, including the one proposed in this book, as simply one perspective among many. And we should ask what these views do to our youth and their roles in society? How do they help or hurt us in ministering to our youth? Do they allow our youth to have a voice? Do they promote youth becoming whole and complete human beings in the way of Jesus?

Target practice. Middler-schoolers should star in Nike ads because they "just do it." They react. They are "all in." Most people who have children in middle school or who work with them find these comments entertaining because we have experienced at least one middle-schooler acting that way. I recently decided to stop making these statements, because they frame *all* youth in middle school as incompetent and lacking sound judgment. While we may see some students matching these descriptions, we unfairly label—and immobilize—students with such causal statements.

In what other ways have we unfairly targeted our youth?

One way is through our discourse of naturalization. A discourse is a specific way we talk about our world. In the social sciences, *discourse* usually refers to the assumptions we voice through statements that we deem "real" or natural. Reflect on the statements below made by parents, teachers and youth pastors. Think about how we unfairly target youth through such discourse and abandon our relational involvement with them:

- They act that way because their brain's prefrontal lobe has not fully developed.

- Teenagers go through "storm and stress"; that's what it means to be a teenager.

- The peer pressure is just too much for them.

- They are supposed to be separating from us.

- They are just trying to become their own independent adult.

- Youth are at risk because biologically they are wired that way.

- They are having an identity crisis.

- Teenagers are all hormonal.

Whether or not these statements are "true," each focuses on direct causality and the belief that youth behavior is the result of their nature. This bypasses the importance of relationships and stories in shaping adolescent identity.

FROM CAUSE AND EFFECT TO CONFLUENCE

How and when does a child become an adolescent? When is the label no longer required? In answering these questions, most of us look for the *causes* of adolescence and for the *causes* that affect the developmental changes that signal the transition from adolescence to adulthood. Understanding adolescents and their transition into adulthood from the categories of cause and effect limits our understanding of the relational complexities that occur throughout life.

If we look around our environments, we can easily see cause and effect at work. We have been acculturated with this perception of the world from as early as preschool. I can see in my current environment that door chimes, a cool room, children laughing, coffee brewing and typing are the direct causations of people opening the door, air-conditioning, tickling, people ordering coffee and fingers tapping keys. We view adolescents, study adolescents and interpret data about adolescents through similar cause-and-effect relations. We look at the biological, psychological and neurological causes of adolescence, and we miss a more holistic view of our youth.

Kenneth Gergen suggests replacing metaphors of cause and effect (for example, a bat hitting a ball and setting it in motion) with metaphors of baking or chemistry.[6] We look at the relationships of ingredients or elements as being essential instead of an individual cause that propels an individual effect. Consider a traditional cause-and-effect metaphor: "The bat hit the ball, and the ball flew through the air." What caused the effect of the ball flying? A typical cause-and-effect response would be "the bat that hit the ball."

However, this outlook hamstrings the complexity of the relationship between the bat and the ball. First, bats do not hit balls without a batter, and the ball does not reach the bat without a pitcher. Second, the relationship between the bat and ball and their coming together creates the achievement of the ball flying through the air. The bat does not cause objects to fly in the air. If a bat collided with a tomato, the outcome would be quite different. Third, the bat-and-ball scenario wouldn't make sense unless we understood the "form of life" of baseball. When we see the action of the ball flying through the air, we should look for the co-action (relationship) that exists between the bat and ball and the larger relational dynamic.

Biology. How can we apply this understanding of confluence to adolescence? John Conger's comment is often quoted: "Adolescence begins in biology and ends in culture."[7] However, this statement suggests that the onset of adolescence is due to biological changes. Biological changes may be a marker of adolescence, but they do not "cause" adolescence. Of course, biological changes occur, but some of the changes and how we perceive those changes are influenced by relationships and by our cultural understanding of adolescents.

As Jeffery Jensen Arnett states,

> Biological events interact with cultural influences. Culture influences the timing of biological events, and cultures respond in a variety of ways to the biological changes that signify adolescents' attainment of physical—and sexual—maturity. Adolescents, in turn, rely on information provided by their cultures for interpreting the changes taking place within their bodies and in their physical appearance.[8]

Consider the pubertal changes that are emphasized as a marker of adolescence. The early adolescent may grow ten inches in one year; male voices may drop from a high pitch to a lower register; girls experience menstruation; pubic hair begins to grow; erotic pleasures and sexual fantasies create new feelings and longings; pimples form; deodorant and other self-care products begin to be used. While all of these changes are important, they do not explore the relationships that shape the early adolescent. A more holistic understanding of our teens does not begin with biological changes but with how our youth and their relationships interpret such changes. For some youth, such biological changes change everything. For others, we may make a bigger deal out of it than it is for the teen.

Why do pubertal changes become a marker of adolescence? If it is because they are "major" changes, by what criterion are they defined as major? They become major changes only in the context of the relationships that the adolescent deems major. For example, by the time children reach early adolescence, they have been introduced to the Western concept of beauty, and pimples are not one of its attributes.[9] Plus, a huge industry targets adolescents and depends on them buying into the need to remove or cover up pimples. If pimples came to be considered a mark of beauty and maturation, companies would lose millions of dollars. Of course pimples trouble adolescents, but this attitude toward blemishes has nothing to do with pimples themselves. Rather, it has everything to do with how the pimple is viewed in the context of the adolescent's relationships. To cover up or remove a pimple is to cover up or remove a flaw that diminishes beauty in the eyes of others.

When I was talking about this in a college class one day, a student protested, "You are not denying biological realities, are you? My sister and I grew up in the same environment, with the same coach, and I throw a softball much harder than she does and with more accuracy. That biological reality means something, and it meant something when I was recruited over her to play college softball."

No doubt such interpretations of biology mean something within the form of life of softball. The relationships and games played in softball have value and meaning. Throwing harder than another person is interpreted as valuable because the game and the relationships value it. Throwing hard in a theology class will not grant success in the classroom.

We have biological differences. Some people can run faster than others, throw harder than others and swing a bat better than others, and their biological makeup has a lot to do with the velocity, speed and skill of such movements. But even movements themselves are learned and only important because of our cultural processes. Swimming may be a valuable asset to people living in coastal cities, but such a skill loses its value in the desert.

The teenage brain. Youth ministry practice is in danger of becoming enslaved to brain-based teachings and understandings of youth. We have become culture-washed with our emphasis on the brain. Many books and articles in psychology and youth ministry concentrate primarily on causal relations beween the teenage brain and developmental changes and behavior.[10]

Furthermore, when the teenage brain is emphasized, our relational interactions and stories with teens are largely ignored. When adolescents are socially constructed as faulty thinkers and risk takers as the result of under-developed brains, we may use this understanding as an excuse to withdraw from them until their brains fully develop.[11] As a local middle school teacher said, "What is the use in teaching them certain concepts if their brains are not ready to learn? I'm wasting my time."

Let's think about brain scans (for example, MRI, PET, EEG, MEG and TMS). Are we using our brains? Of course, but isn't our thinking about brain scans the direct result of our relationship? What comes to mind? Isn't it my questioning of such thoughts that lead you to thinking in such ways? Can we think however we want? Can we think in German? Japanese? Indonesian? We are bound by our relationships and language, and so are our brains.

Studying brain function can be helpful if we are looking into the neural mechanisms involved in Down syndrome, Parkinson's disease, aphasia or brain tumors. But in terms of neural activity, human action will remain unintelligible. To understand forgiveness and reconciliation as expressions of cortical architecture is to void them of value and meaning.[12] Gergen suggests that we view the brain as an instrument that is in the service of cultural processes. Neural research can tell us a lot about the blink of an eye, but it tells us nothing about a wink.[13] In youth ministry, we are interested in cultural and interpretive matters concerning our spiritual connection with God and others—nothing that brain scans can reveal.

Independence and separation. Transitioning into early adolescence is a social process involving the transformation of child-parent relationships. As mentioned earlier, the way in which parents and others narrate their experiences (through words, concepts, ideas, evaluations and understandings) and the adolescent's relationship to those narrations play an important role in how teenagers come to understand their identity. Identity stories in Eastern cultures are "organized around holistic, interdependent,

THE CRITIC'S VOICE

Criticism

What about abstract thinking? Middle school youth are concrete think-ers because they have not developed the prefrontal lobe of their brain; therefore, they can't think abstractly.

Response

Most literature on midadolescence (high school age in psychology) points out that a major difference that occurs is the development of ab-stract thinking. The brain is credited to the formation of an adolescent's ability to think abstractly as the midadolescent moves from concrete op-erational thinking to preoperational thinking (terms that have become popular thanks to psychologist Jean Piaget).[14] *However, in this process of "brain talk," abstract thought is understood as being the primary cause of adolescents' less concrete reasoning. While abstract thinking does seem to emerge in midadolescence, it should not be seen as pri-mary or originating solely from brain development. Abstract thought is secondary to relationships.*

In some cases, adolescents are understood as having a deficit un-til they develop abstract thinking; in other words, teenagers' lack of judgment becomes equated to a lack of abstract thinking. This view of adolescent development provides another opportunity for adults to withdraw from teenagers (they believe there is nothing they can do un-til adolescents' brains develop abstract thinking). When the problem is limited to the realm of cognition, many perceive lack of judgment and critical thinking as being an individual's problem. This line of thinking ig-nores the organizational power and influence of language and symbols through relationships.

Abstract concepts such as love, justice, honesty, equality and spiri-tuality are important to most traditions. However, teenagers who are learning to think in such abstract terms do not do so independent of oth-

> *ers. The definition of the terms and the rules that indicate when, where and how such words apply requires participation in a form of cultural narration.[15] Abstractions within themselves are empty of significant content; they contain no stories of enactment. Therefore to think abstractly means to be familiar with the culture's abstract terminology and the diverse stories in which such abstractions are given meaning and definition. After all, one's abstract understanding of justice may be another's abstract understanding of injustice.*

interconnected, interactive, and contextual lines, not around personal autonomy" that is characteristic of Western cultures.[16]

Central organizing units in understanding identity stories in many non-Western cultures (family, social group, culture, nature or religion) would be termed "non-self" from many Western perspectives.[17] The Western understanding of being a "unique individual," where there is a constant evaluation of individual thoughts, feelings, wishes and desires is quite different from non-Western understandings of self.[18] For many non-Western people, the person is not the most basic part of the whole from which the whole originates; the person is constituted by the whole.

Child psychologist William Kessen asserts that we ought to regard development as a social construction and the child as "a modulated and modulating component in a shifting network of influences." Furthermore, he believes that

> the seminal thinkers about children over the past century have, in fact, been almost undeviating in their postulation of the child as container of self and of psychology. Impulses are in the child; traits are in the child; thoughts are in the child; attachments are in the child. In short, almost every major theory of development accepts the premises of individualism and takes the child as the basic unit of study, with all consequences the choice has for decisions that range from selecting a method of research to selecting a therapeutic maneuver.[19]

Youth ministry is also a social construction, and the transformations that have occurred over the past one hundred years are a startling reminder of our eternal call to be scrupulous observers and imaginative ministers. We must understand that we are both creators and performers in our cultural inventions of youth ministry.

A view of adulthood that values autonomy and individualism over interdependence and community tends to view adolescence as a period of separation and independence.[20] Cigdem Kagitcibasi highlights how individual autonomy has been influenced by the psychoanalytic tradition (Blos, Erickson, Freud and Mahler):

> Psychological theory and practice have traditionally stressed the importance of individual independence, achievement, self-efficacy, self-reliance, self-actualization, privacy, and freedom of choice. Individual independence is a cherished value and is reflected in much popular psychology from parent education courses to self-help books particularly in the United States.[21]

If counselors and psychologists understand separation and independence from parents as necessary for healthy adolescent development, the relational needs of adolescents may go unmet.[22] Adolescents need adults as much as adults need adolescents. To ignore either will continue to perpetuate separation and independence.

From this perspective, achieving adult status in culture means the adolescent journey becomes one of separation and increasing autonomy as she "matures" to become a free and independent adult. As a unique individual, she makes her own choices and decisions. Although she may belong to a particular community, the community is a matter of her individual choice. She is not accountable to anyone other than herself. Her problems are "her problems." She has her own thoughts, and she chooses whether or not to act on them. She is free. Or is she? Consider the constraints:

- She can't even begin to think without the language she has gained through relationships.
- She can't communicate without another person.
- She can't make meaning with her actions or words unless someone else acknowledges them.
- She can't make intelligent decisions apart from the constraints of her past.
- She can't make sense of others' actions until she understands the context and "rules" of her environment.

The freedom to be a person operates within the constraints of relationships. To ignore this is to ignore God as a relational being who has created us in God's image to also be relational beings. As Gergen says, "All that we find to be real, true, valuable, or good finds its origins in coordinated action."[23] In the process of searching for the causations that lead to the effects of adolescence, we can get stuck on the individual biological, cultural and cognitive changes, rather than ascertain the confluence of these and their interpretations in the adolescent's relationships. Let's instead reconceptualize a child's psychological, biological and neurological motivating factors in favor of their interpretive function within relationships and society.

THE RELATIONAL MIDDLE SCHOOL YOUTH

Observe a few middle school youth if you can. Watch them navigate a multitude of roles that didn't exist in elementary school. Watch them morph into different characters in each relationship. Listen to their language. Hear the stories they tell and how they construct meaning with others.

Let's take Tori, a seventh-grader, and look at her roles: She is a student of social studies, science, math, English and PE. She's also a softball player, soccer player, Bible club participant and cheerleader. She has friends—and a host of relationships with her peers that she attempts to juggle in classes, on breaks, at lunch, during special school events and so on.

Now consider her roles outside of school: She is a youth group participant (Wednesday and Sunday night), a daughter (two sets of parents), a granddaughter (four sets of grandparents), a sister (two biological brothers), a stepsister (two stepsisters), a stepdaughter (to a stepmom and stepdad), a girlfriend (at least one boyfriend a month), a friend and a "virtual" friend via Twitter and Facebook (and the many ways she attempts to maintain these relationships through email, text messaging and cell phone conversations).

Not all of these relationships would have been formed in the present year. Tori has cultivated relationships with former teachers, coaches, neighbors, other family members and childhood friends. In each of these relationships, a unique pattern of understanding is developed and new relationships are co-constructed.[24] Tori has numerous relationships, and they influence her relationships and interactions with her parents.[25]

As discussed in chapter 3, we can better understand youth as relational beings, as navigators of intersections of multiple relationships in which they are capable of presenting a variety of external personas for the many roles and relationships in which they participate.[26] When relational beings come together, they negotiate a common reality concerning what they value together; however, extending the duration of this relationship requires more complex negotiation.[27] With the slew of roles that a middle school youth has, the roles become extremely difficult to manage and negotiate for a long period. Boyfriends, girlfriends and friends in general may shift quickly and drastically. Long-term childhood friendships are the last to dwindle in middle school if they have survived sixth grade. Usually, this is due to the familiarity between the teens.

In the life of a middle school youth, there is not a lot of stability. The two constants that I see as most prominent in society are the family and church. Schools change; sports teams wax and wane; and teachers rotate. Few organizations offer free services and a stable environment. This is why youth ministry has an opportunity to make a huge difference in the lives of our young and provide stability to a rapidly changing teen.

Perceived audience. We were in a restaurant on a youth trip, forty-five minutes away from our lodge. One of my seventh-graders, Traci, asked, "Can you take me back to the lodge?"

"Why?"

"I need to change my shirt."

"What's wrong with your shirt?"

"I spilled tea on it."

"Where?"

"Right here," she said, pointing.

"Oh, that? It will dry up in ten minutes," I said.

"*Everyone* is looking at it," she said, scowling.

I looked around the restaurant. *Everyone* seemed preoccupied with their food, not Traci's T-shirt. "I can barely see it from this close," I said with a squint.

"Well," she said, clearly put out now, "everyone *else* can see it."

Perhaps you could tell similar stories about teens who are worried about others seeing their hair, face, clothes, makeup or what-have-you. If so, you witnessed what psychologist David Elkind calls their "imaginary audience."[28] Personally, I don't like the term *imaginary* because it undercuts the real pressures that early adolescents face. I prefer to say "perceived audience."[29] The perceived audience is constructed as the early adolescent believes that she is "on stage" as the primary actor, and everyone else is focused on her behavior and appearance.[30]

And why not? Have we taught our children to be responsible or concerned for anyone other than themselves? From schooling, home life and church life, don't we teach our young to be individually responsible, to take care of themselves, to do their own work, to mind their own business and to focus on self-care, self-improvement, self-esteem, self-surveillance. And they project this way of seeing the world on everyone else. They perform on a small stage—much like actors in a community theater—in front of family and close friends as children, but when they progress to middle school, their stage morphs into Broadway—with lights, smoke, grips, soundtrack and packed house. Since the early adolescent is bombarded by so many changes, he is primarily concerned with himself, and he assumes that others are as obsessed with his behavior and appearance as he is himself.[31]

Before we become critical, dismissive or judgmental of the middle-schooler's perceived audience, let's consider our own for a moment. When was the last time you sang in front of thousands of people? Spoke to thousands of people? Had a conversation with the president or someone famous? I would be willing to bet you did these things from your home or car. I am not talking about real encounters but imaginary ones. How many times have you imagined an audience (maybe your youth or church) and prepared a speech, sermon or lesson according to how you imagined their responses? These imagined performances become real participatory actions that help us articulate in preparation for our relationships.[32]

We all carry traces of the perceived audience with us. A mother may leave a restaurant with her crying baby because she thinks everyone wants her baby to hush, so if she remains she is not being a "good" mother. A father may feel the perceived pressure of other adults in not being a good coach to his son because his son is not performing well in a sport. A youth pastor may feel that the church is out to get her because of a few comments. What about our hair? Dress? Weight? Don't adults still care and obsess over these things too?

Now imagine being transported into middle school without as many lived experiences or the realization that people are not as concerned with ourselves as we are. While the audience may not be physically present in every situation, some pressures from society (for example, magazines, peers, television) are constant reminders of societal standards for adolescent behavior. In addition, the middle school youth may not be scrutinized while she is in public by others, but she certainly is in her middle school environment. Take time to visit a middle school cafeteria and observe their conversations. Rarely will you hear a fifteen-minute conversation that doesn't include a critique of another middle school student.

Could it be that early adolescents' perceived audience has more to do with belonging and their longing for community and acceptance through relationships than an internal misconception?

I wasn't going to take thirty students back to our lodge for a small tea spill on a shirt. I thought Traci left something behind at the lodge, because I believed she just couldn't be that concerned about her shirt. At our next stop, Traci took the last bit of spending money she had and bought a new shirt to wear. Her audience was real enough to her that she spent the remainder of her money rather than face her perceived audience's ridicule and shame.

Perceived audience in action. When adolescents perceive that everyone is looking at them and interested in them, they are more keenly aware of their attributes. Parents may notice that their carefree children enter adolescence and become acutely aware of their clothing, bathing, hair style, physical build and so on. Clothing options become reduced to particular brands, cell phones become more important than food, and iPods and mp3 players are seemingly social deal breakers.

My church had a local weekend event, and my youth were staying in host homes, where the hosts had made them homemade ice cream. I was making rounds and visiting my groups before they inhaled the ice cream and went to sleep. I visited the host home of my sixth-grade girls, and they had bowls filled with ice cream and topped with everything from marshmallows to gummy bears to caramel. I left my sixth-graders in a sugar haze to visit with my ninth-graders in another house. The host had prepared the same amount of ice cream and toppings, but the girls were eating a spoonful of ice cream with no toppings. I asked why they didn't want more. All of the girls were thin, and they were all on a diet. Three years of middle school had changed their understanding of body image. Although they were concerned with their physical weight, they could not see how their perceived audience was what really weighed them down.

Parents find it difficult to understand the new demands and wants of their middle-school youth. They normally conclude that the changes are due to peer pressure. Early adolescents may want certain things that their friends have because they feel the pressure of their perceived audience, but not because their friends pressured them. Herein lies the confusion that most parents have with their early adolescent's behavior. If parents attempt to understand their children's behaviors according to individual influences, they may fail to see their motivation. They may not observe that their youth are acting out certain roles according to their perceived audience through the new relationships they have established, not necessarily because of any direct pressure.[33] Who pressured you to get your hair cut or styled the way you did? Who pressured you to dress the way you did today? No one in particular, but we feel the weight of relational expectations on our backs. Similar to adults, most of the things early adolescents want have more to do with belonging and being able to relate to their peers than with the actual product or individual pressure.

LIFE STORY: PERSONAL FABLE

Keep in mind all of the roles middle school youth pilot every day. When do they have time to reflect on who they are becoming through all of their diverse roles? Have you asked a middle-schooler to tell you his or her life story? You may get questions: "Huh?" "What do you mean?" "What's that?" "Where do you want me to start?" Even if you ask them to tell you about themselves, you will see the difficulty many of them have. Most will focus on their attributes, and their narratives will be choppy.

Here is the life story of a rising eighth-grader: "I have a mom and a dad. I have a sister. I like to play softball. I am nice. I was born here. I have a cat. I have four close friends: Bo, Cory, Timmy and Teddy. I want to be a doctor. What more do you want me to say?"

If you want to enhance the life of youth, engage them in telling their life story. If all youth are doing is telling their fragmented stories to each other, why would we expect them to have a whole and complete understanding of their life for making informed decisions about their future? We dish out rules and regulations that will never help them make sense of their lives. Rules are needed for order, but without helping them negotiate their life story, we put them in a game without teaching them how to play. It's like giving a rulebook to someone who has never played basketball and expecting him to walk into a gym making shots and running plays. Most of the time, what we give our youth will never help them with their life story. What they need is for us to co-construct their life story by asking them questions and providing opportunities for them to articulate their life.

The idea that a person is a self with a personal story to share concerning her past, in her present context, while anticipating the future, emerges in early adolescence.[34] Bohn and Berntsen observed that the interest in writing a life story increased considerably from ages eleven and twelve onward.[35] Once prompted and guided, an early adolescent should be able to tell about her past, her family heritage and certain transitions along the way, such as the birth of siblings and geographical relocations.[36] Ten- to eleven-year-olds, not eight- to nine-year-olds, were found to refer spontaneously to their past when trying to understand a given situation.[37]

Since causal and thematic coordination have not yet developed, youth will not be able to unify their life stories in such a way that it helps them understand their future choices. Without causal and thematic coordination, middle school youth do not take an interpretive stance on their life story without the help of an adult.

The cultural concept of biography coupled with temporal coordination gives the early adolescent the ability "to select and arrange life events into coherent life narratives" that "create skeletal coherence in life narratives in terms of sequential order and normative content."[38] These two elements enable adolescents to create life stories that are realistically constructed and culturally accepted. With cultural and temporal coordination, an attempt at making a life story begins, but without causal and thematic coordination, what results is a fantasized personal fable.[39]

The personal fable of an adolescent can be seen in her journals and heard in private conversations with other early adolescents, as she conveys how no one else understands her and how her situation is unique. We can stop telling our students they are unique. They believe it! Problem is, they don't believe anyone is like them, and therefore they think no one understands their problems. In a paradoxical way, many believe they know the thoughts and feelings of others and their perceived audience, but they simultaneously believe that no one knows (or understands) their own thoughts and feelings. This sense of uniqueness, coupled with the development of biographical and temporal coordination, creates the right environment for the construction of the early adolescent's personal fable.

One of the benefits of remaining in the same ministry location for several years is that I have witnessed the changes that have taken place with my own youth ministry students from middle school to college. Every year I would hand out a sheet of paper to my middle school youth and ask them to describe their lives in twenty years with as much detail as they could muster. Out of a group of fifteen to twenty, I had doctors, lawyers, dentists, presidents, hair salon owners, psychologists, major league baseball players, NFL football players and WNBA and NBA athletes. Most lived in mansions, had a family with kids, owned their own businesses and made six figures. Some got detailed in naming their wife, kids and pets.

I held on to most of these descriptions, and when the students became high school juniors and seniors, I gave them back. One of two responses took place: outbursts of laughter or gasps of embarrassment. For most, the grandiose dreams of early adolescence were tamed by the advent of causal and thematic coordination in midadolescence, and they rewrote their personal fables.

CONCLUSION

Over the course of my youth ministry experience, I have spoken several times on harmful names. I have used the exercise of the blank sheet of paper (representing someone we dislike) and balled-up pieces of paper with most of my new middle school youth. One year a student did something completely unexpected. In the middle of everyone throwing their "stones" at the blank paper on the wall and hurling the insulting words, Laura walked up with her piece of balled-up paper and placed it on the floor beneath the blank sheet.

"Forgiven," she said, and turned and walked back to her seat.

In the chaos and uproar, her gentle action and one-word response silenced the room. Her small act of forgiveness stopped everyone's stoning. Her act of love and compassion unveiled our hurt and pain.

She also exposed my limited expectations of my youth. I expected them to fail at this exercise. In fact, the exercise doesn't work unless they fail. If no one throws stones or says insulting words, I really don't have a reason to lift the blank piece of paper and reveal the hurtful words they voiced the previous week. A sense of irony washed over me as I thought about the religious who anticipated stoning the woman they had caught in adultery, and how Jesus' love and compassion changed their course of action, stunning them to silence.

Laura taught me a lesson about expectations, love and forgiveness. What expectations do we place on youth? How do we unfairly target and label them? Do some of our expectations set them up for failure? How can we view them in a way that empowers and connects them with God's kind of love?

REFLECTION QUESTIONS

1. How have you seen youth become easy targets? How can you help remove the bull's-eye from their chest?

2. How have you understood youth from a cause-and-effect perspective? How does your view change when you focus on confluence or use metaphors of baking or chemistry?

3. How can youth ministry help early adolescents with their roles without becoming just one more role?

4. Give an example of how you have observed youth reacting to their perceived audience. When do you feel the pressures of your own perceived audience?

5. Share your middle school personal fable, or share one you have been told recently by a middle school youth.

8

The Life Story in Midadolescence

"Do you know your youth?" If I had been asked this question five years ago, I would have responded with a definitive yes. What youth pastor would say no? I take pride in my relationships with my students. I know them. I could give you their family history, latest struggles, relationship status, favorite activities and sports, and recent accomplishments and failures. I know more about them than some of their parents know.

But now I realize that what I thought I knew of my youth was superficial because it was from how I had interpreted their lives. When I began asking my students to tell me their life stories, I gained a new perspective. It's one thing to know a lot about youth's lives; it's something entirely different to know their life stories and how *they* interpret their lives. Could most of our youth ministry efforts prioritize meeting youth where *we* think they are, when they are interpreting their lives otherwise?

One after another I listened to youth articulate their life stories, and I was blown away at what I heard. A few things became apparent to me: (1) The vast majority of youth interpret their lives unlike me or their parents; (2) adults do not often ask youth to share their life stories; and (3) knowing the elements of the life story helped me coordinate a broader and deeper life story with youth.

A DIFFERENT PERSPECTIVE: YOUTH'S LIFE STORIES

Hearing my youth's life stories gave me a new perspective on them.

Luke, a freshman, played varsity baseball. Anyone who talked with Luke would have said that he loved the sport—especially his father. I thought he did too. Later I discovered he was not living out his dream but a nightmare as he shared his life story, which included how his controlling father pushed him to play.

I assumed Tyreek lived with his mother and father, since they dropped him off at youth group every Wednesday night. But from his life story I found out he lived with his grandmother, and the only time he saw his parents was on Wednesdays.

Leah is a devout Christian youth. Church members speak of her Christian example among her peers. Her parents beam with pride at their daughter's dedication to following Jesus. Ask her questions about her faith, and she will illustrate a deep knowledge of Scripture and love for God. Leah's life story revealed something else: she hated the pressure of being the "good kid," and her Christian lifestyle had more to do with her parents than a sustainable faith in God.

After hearing a multitude of youth's life stories, I wonder how much re-search data is skewed because researchers ask preconceived questions geared to their research project rather than asking youth to tell their life stories and attempt to understand how they are interpreting certain situa-tions. It is also not uncommon for youth to tell contradictory stories within their own life story when they have not yet discovered or thought about the contradiction. There is a big difference between hearing generic stories from the life of a teenager and hearing how they articulate their identity through their life story.

THE IMPORTANT ROLE ADULTS AND YOUTH MINISTERS PLAY

If we are not asking youth to share their life stories, who is? From middle school to high school, most youth do not have an adult who asks them to share their life stories. How will our youth make sense of and find meaning in their lives if we do not offer them opportunities to coordinate their stories?

I remember in high school thinking about my life story and how I would articulate it to others. I thought everyone knew his or her story. The adults in my faith community asked me frequently about my life and future plans, and I was led to reflect on my life and learn how to articulate it because of their questions. None of them rushed my story nor did they jump into their own when I finished. They were genuinely interested, and they were always asking me more questions about my life that conjured up memories that I had either forgotten or not considered. Our conversations changed my life.

And that was eighteen years ago. Today, youth are rarely surrounded by adults who genuinely want to hear them articulate their life story. Yet most youth long to tell their life stories. Have you observed how youth share their stories with their peers? It mimics their daily patterns of communication. One youth tells his story while the other youth fights the urge to interrupt and tell her story. Generally they do not question each other or help their friends to process their stories. The conversation appears more like a tennis match: one youth swats a piece of her life story to the other youth, and he returns his as fast as hers was served to him, with little reflection or questioning on what has been shared. When do youth have the opportunity to consider how they are structuring their life stories?

One of the main ingredients necessary for youth to act in violence, rage and anger is the inability to communicate through language.[1] If youth are angry and they have learned how to voice (or perform) their anger in constructive ways, their use of destructive expression lessens. Imagine students who are never heard by adults or friends or who do not trust anyone to process their anger and frustrations. How will they learn to cope? Who will teach them?

Psychologists have observed that reminiscing within families and in therapeutic settings adds to the development of a teen's emotional stability.[2] Recall from chapter 5 that midadolescents begin to coordinate causations and themes in their life stories for the first time. The only way they become skilled at this meaning-making process is through practicing coordination of their life stories with others.

Beyond listening and telling stories. Have you ever thought about your role when a student shares his or her story? I never gave it much thought. I would repeat the popular mantra, "Youth ministers are listeners and tellers of stories." Therefore, I saw my role as either a listener or a teller. I understood the role of listener as being acted on by the teller. The traditional picture of listener and teller separates sharing stories into two distinct, individual modes that aren't helpful.

If I "tell a story" to my sixth-graders, it seems like I am simply the teller, and they are the listeners. As discussed in chapter three, a closer look reveals we are listening (and using all of our senses) while we are telling, and we are dependent on their telling (their posture, body language and verbal responses).

I was speaking to sixty high school students, and they were glued to my story. Right at the climax, twenty students in the middle of the group began squirming and laughing, which created a distraction for the rest of the group. I was flustered, and I couldn't see where I'd lost the group. Then I smelled it—someone had passed gas, and I squirmed and chuckled too.

Knowing that teller and listener can't exist independently, youth ministers can place the emphasis on the construction and coordination of the story. Instead of simply listening to youth's stories, youth ministers can accept that their actions and reactions shape and change the story experience too.

A young person may set out to tell one story, but through the interaction with his youth minister, he may halt the story, extend it, exaggerate it and so on. Youth and youth ministers are dependent on each other for the storytelling experience, and the stories they share are only fragments of a much larger story web.

Relational narrative youth ministry values the storytelling process, focuses intently on the verbal and nonverbal (and attempts not to separate

THE CRITIC'S VOICE

Criticism

What about empathetic listening? I learned to do this in my counseling practices, and it works.

Response

Empathetic and sympathetic listening are two popular methods in counseling. We teach people to empathize with the other person and try to see the world through his or her eyes. These forms of listening, however, are generally understood from an individualistic perspective of communication. When the focus is centered on the relationship and the dialogue, the focus turns from guessing the internal states of the other and the meaning behind his words toward the meaning that is made in the relationship. Stewart and Blake explain this:

> *Empathetic listening can be helpful, but dialogic listening requires a move beyond empathy to a focus on "ours." It can make*

a big difference whether you are trying to identify what's going on inside the other person or are focusing on building meaning between. When your focus is on the other's thoughts and feelings behind their words, you spend your time and mental energy searching for possible links between what you're seeing and hearing and what the other "must be" meaning. "Look at those crossed arms. She must be feeling angry and defensive." Or, "He said he'd 'never' pay all the money back." That means it's hopeless to try to get him to change his mind: When you think in this way, you're moving back and forth between what's outside, in the verbal and nonverbal talk, and what's inside the person's head.[3]

If communication is genuinely focused in the space between two people, the pressure of having to know what is inside the mind of another ceases to exist. There is more concentration and attentiveness to the relationship.

I believe empathetic listening works, but does it deepen and extend the relationship? I can try to see through the eyes of my spouse and understand where she is coming from, but by doing so I remain focused on her individuality. Instead, focusing on our relationship and who we are becoming through the language and stories we share paints a fuller picture of who we are.

Most problems in a relationship are not because we can't see through the eyes of the other, but because it's not clear how our relationship might move forward and function after we understand where the person is coming from. Paraphrasing—a function of empathetic listening—can become a mere parroting of words. By beginning with the relational coordination we may still paraphrase what the other has said, but we use the paraphrase to explore the context of our claims and how such an understanding helps or hinders the relationship. What are we creating here together? As we describe and explain, so do we create our future.

them) and does not assume anything beyond these. This is not a prepa-
ratory style of communication. When a person is preparing a response
while someone else is talking, there is a good chance of the speaker's words
failing to connect.[4] Preparation tends to subside, however, as people learn
to trust the relationship.

COORDINATING A YOUTH'S LIFE STORY

I thought I knew Blake's story. The day he *told* me his life story changed my
perspective of him forever. The way I had interpreted his life from the information I gained from our conversations was quite different from how he
articulated his life. From my point of view, Blake seemed to have it all together. He had a close family. His father was a heavyweight kickboxing
world champion. He made good grades and was accepted into his A-list
college. And the list goes on. When I interacted with Blake, I often asked
him how his day or week had been, what his favorite hobbies were, what
was his summer like, what he planned to do after high school, if he had any
prayer requests, how I could help him and how he felt about the youth ministry. I never gave him a chance to articulate his life story.

Instead of exhausting pages writing about the emergence of a life story in
midadolescence, I hope to show the importance of using the elements we
have discussed as a framework to better understand our youth's life stories
and help them structure and organize their stories in loving and holistic ways.

Listen to how Blake told me his life story. Notice how he coordinated his
story with me. Also, think about your own life story, and practice coordinating life stories with your youth or any youth you encounter. Using chapter
five as a guide, what were the cultural concepts of biography that Blake used?
What were his cultural life scripts? What cultural concepts provided the
content for his narrative? What temporal coordinations did he use? How did
he causally connect his stories? Around what themes did he structure his life?

> I have a mom and dad, sister and two half-brothers from my mom and dad's
> previous marriage. They are fifteen and twelve years older than me. My
> birthday is in four days; I will be eighteen. I was born in Rock Hill, South
> Carolina, but we moved to Gastonia, North Carolina, when I was little. I do
> not remember living in Rock Hill. When I was three I almost died. I fell into
> my pool, and all I remember is seeing the sky from under the water. Appar-
> ently, a couple of minutes later my dad rescued me.

When I was in second grade, I had a big thing happen at my daycare. My daycare worker lost her temper with me and choked me. I had bruises all over me. We went to court and everything over it. Ever since then, I can't stand for people to grab me around my neck. Sometimes I can freak out about it, but I will not hit anyone over it. It doesn't bother me beyond that. If I saw her today I would probably go up to her and tell her I forgive her for doing it. People lose their temper. Just different people express it in different ways.

I got picked on a lot in elementary and middle school. I don't know why. I guess I was just different. I remember Dustyn used to pick on me when I was little, and now I am bigger than him [laughs]. We are cool now. He still picks on me, but he doesn't mean anything by it now. He probably didn't mean anything by it then either, but that is how it goes. I've done it; other people have done it. Everyone just picks on each other, and you have to learn to deal with it. If you put "I am sorry" at the end of it, then it goes away.

In seventh grade, I started cutting myself, and I continued until ninth grade. I stopped in November of ninth grade. I stopped because I didn't want to be like that. I didn't want my kids to look at me when I was forty and ask me, "Dad, what is that?" "Oh, that is where I cut myself because I was young and stupid and I didn't know what to do with my emotions." Ever since then I have been trying to control my emotions, because I had a lot of anger problems. I used to get mad a lot—I guess because people picked on me so much. I have controlled that a lot. I don't really ever get mad. Whenever confrontation approaches me, I try to push it away and cut into something else and try to get my mind off whatever it was.

I dated a girl in seventh and eighth grade, and she broke up with me. I didn't sleep for two days because I was in *looove* with her. Me and her are actually best friends today. But when that happened, I felt really alone and that no one cared for me. And it was on New Year's Eve, so what a way to celebrate the New Year. I felt really alone. From then on I don't think there was a day that went by that I didn't think about killing myself [long pause].

Actually [laughs] I remember standing on top of a swing set in my backyard and there were two ropes that hung down. And I thought, *If I tied that rope around my neck and jumped off, would anyone care?* But I remember telling myself that that doesn't make me a better person by doing that. And even though I may not feel like people care, people do care, even if I don't see it or people approach me; I know that people do care. Like my mom and dad. That would probably destroy them if I killed myself. Not to put a lot of emphasis on me being a good person, but I am their kid. If my kid killed himself, I would cry. That would be horrible.

Freshman year, my sister-in-law actually passed away in January, and I didn't talk to anyone for like a month, and I lost a lot of friends. Then I started dating Ashley a couple of months later, from my freshman year until sophomore year, around February-ish. And then she broke up with me. Didn't result in cutting myself, even though I was really sad about it. Actually, the day after Ashley broke up with me, my grandmother was diagnosed with stage-four cancer: single-cell carcinoma, in her throat. I was really close with my grandmother. I started doing martial arts and that helped me get through it. Actually it was this week two years ago.

Junior year, November 7, my grandmother died. I went to school that day because I didn't want to stay home, because that would have torn me up. But I still cried the whole day at school. I have never experienced someone that close to me dying. I was closer to her than I was anyone. It still hits me hard. I remember one day last week, I couldn't go to sleep because I couldn't stop thinking about her. It is just really hard thinking about that still [long pause]. We never really had a funeral for my grandmother. She was cremated, and we were supposed to scatter ashes, but we didn't. So I never really got the closure that I needed.

I have good days and bad days ever since junior year, actually since seventh grade. Actually, I have weeks that go by where I don't want to do anything. I have days where I just want to drive off the road and run into the tree. But I don't want that to be who I am remembered as. I want to be stronger than that. When I see people who are sad, I try to be their friend. I look at people's arms when I befriend people to see if they have marks. And if they do, I eventually ask about it. It would have helped me out a lot if someone would have talked to me about it.

I have to say that believing in God has helped me a lot. I have to remind myself that if no one cares about me, he does. I have times where I will walk through the backyard and sit at the swing set with my iPod or lay down flat on the floor with my head to the floor and just pray and cry for hours at a time. So with all of that, I am at a much better place than I was before.

Exploring Blake's life story. What happens if we explore Blake's life story and we take the role not of an expert youth pastor or empathetic listener but (with Blake) of a curious detective? Our role in our relationship with Blake becomes one of investigating his life with him. A detective attempts to remain neutral and tries to uncover as much information as possible without jumping to conclusions. The detective is not concerned with sharing his own story at this point. In the exploration of Blake's story, we help create his picture of himself. In the story above, I did not ask questions until the end. When I began asking questions about his life, Blake extended and thickened his life story, adding elements and further explanations.

Many times we want to tell our youth what to believe and how to live. I suggest we do this as often as Jesus practiced that method with his followers: rarely. Most youth pastor-to-student advising contradicts the spirit of Jesus. When we view students as containers to be emptied of harmful contents and filled with good, we assume action and agency and instill an unintentional pattern of passivity and disengagement in the student. As a result, youth will not be experienced at making their own faith decisions when they reach college age, because their parents or minister did it for them. We do not want to narrate our students' lives for them, but we want them to learn how to narrate their lives with anyone they encounter.

Most would have no idea that Blake struggled with such things. His parents may even have been unaware of how he was interpreting his life. I thought I knew Blake, because we'd been on trips together, and we'd had lengthy conversations. In that ten-minute encounter, he unveiled more about himself than I had ever known. I was able to hear how he structured his life story and the important themes he used to narrate his life. Knowing this allowed me to understand previous stories he had shared with me, and I was able to see how he interpreted future stories through his life story lenses.

Cultural coordination of Blake's life story. Let's take a look at the cultural elements in Blake's life story:

Cultural concept of biography:

Location of birth: Rock Hill, South Carolina

Current residence: Gastonia, North Carolina

Age/date of birth: "turning eighteen in four days"

School transitions: daycare, Lingerfelt Elementary, Central Piedmont Charter

Supporting cast:

Familial relationships: mom, dad, sister, two half-brothers, grandmother, sister-in-law

Other significant relationships: daycare worker, two girlfriends, friends, martial arts instructor

Familial positioning: youngest child, son, grandson, brother, half-brother

Loss of supporting cast: sister-in-law, grandmother, girlfriends

I already knew that Blake's parents were divorced and that he had two half-brothers. What I didn't know was that Blake's mom and dad were not divorced from each other, but from their previous spouses. Until I heard Blake's life story, I pictured him living between homes. Knowing the supporting cast also helps us to become more aware of those who have the most influence on our students, with whom we need to be communicating.

The supporting cast is also important to inquire about when searching for alternative storylines or positive encouragement for the student. With Blake's story, we may want to highlight his parents' love and concern for him. The supporting cast of a youth's life story provides important voices around which he structures his life. Pay attention to the people students bring up in conversation; you may need to turn the volume up or down on some of the voices of supporting cast members.

Life scripts in Blake's story:

Dating: two girlfriends, two breakups

Becoming a parent: wants a family

Life scripts can both help and hinder a person. In Blake's story, the life script of growing up and having a family enabled him to stop cutting. Later in life, if Blake never has a family or children, this same life script may be a reminder that he has not lived up to his (and society's) expectation of being a father or husband. For now, his life script is beneficial, but I want to add more support in his narrative so that this life script does not one day cripple him. To do this, I can ask a simple question: "What are some other reasons that you no longer cut?"

Cultural Concepts in Blake's Story

People caring

Martial arts and self-defense

Death, grief and mourning

Happiness

Anger, temper

God

Music

Nightmares

Handling confrontation

Concept of "picking" and "making fun"

Value of physical size and strength

Belief that everyone picks on each other

Belief that apologies dismiss hurtful words

Concept of cutting

Dating

Concept of best friends

Suicide

Concept of self: individualistic—struggles with seeing connectivity with others

Relationship with God

Mom and dad relationship

Cultural concepts in youth's stories are telling of how they interpret and use certain cultural elements. Each of these cultural concepts varies from culture to culture in how we practice them. They may also have variations in our own culture. At any point in a youth's telling of her life story, I may ask her to elaborate on particular cultural concepts. I do not correct or challenge any of her interpretations, but ask so that I can fully understand her perspective and what shaped it.

Blake's belief that apologies dismiss hurtful words and his ongoing participation in making fun of others are actions that I strongly oppose in youth ministry. Yet I withheld challenging these. I continued to ask questions about how he came to such choices. It is common for youth to use certain cultural concepts without any thought concerning what they mean. They are usually unaware that they may interpret and use most of the cultural concepts differently in their life stories. In his story, Blake triumphs over his anger. In our conversation after his initial telling of his life story, I highlighted his strength to overcome his anger and cutting. In so doing, I began to help Blake see his strength to overcome acting out of anger.

Anger is a social construction. The way anger is expressed and what we become angry over depends on how we have come to see and live in the world. Blake believed that his anger may result from being mocked. Although we have a multitude of images of what picking on may be in our culture, this is another concept that I further investigated with Blake. What did he mean by "always getting picked on"?

Hearing the cultural concepts from our youth and providing them the opportunity to explain them helps our youth develop thicker and "meaning-full" stories. We develop totalizing language in our life stories when we include cultural elements that we frame as *always* or *never* occurring. Again, we don't have to challenge these descriptions, but further questioning helps loosen their grip and determines how we include them in our future stories.

Temporal coordination of Blake's life story. Temporal indicators help locate events and lend cohesiveness to the story. A lot of our students do not think about how our stories change over time or how we can rewrite our past. Yet our aspirations also mold our present. As we see in Blake's story, his focus on the future life script of becoming a father led him to stop cutting.

Temporal Indicators in Blake's Story

Age: two; eighteen in four days

"Little": denotes childhood and time in the past

Transitional temporal indicators: ever since then; from then on . . .

"I remember": denotes time in the past

Tense: past, present, future

Death: end of time for grandmother and sister-in-law

School year/grade: freshman, sophomore, junior

Shift in time and change: then I started; the day after

Getting youth to imagine alternatives to their future life stories stretches their imagination and thickens their story. Richer storytelling is the outcome.

The Christian narrative plays an important role in how youth structure and understand their lives in regards to time. We do not teach our youth to imagine or cling to hope, but we enact it with them. We know the end of the story: God is victorious. This victory is not one of force and brutality but of love. The cross was Rome's *no* to Jesus' love and way, and the resurrection was God's *yes*. It is God's victory and *yes* that we cling to, knowing that when we live and love in the way of Jesus—even when faced with death—we will be okay too.

Living in this narrative relieves anxiety and tensions that suffocate us from living life as it unfolds one play at a time. It's like TiVoing our favorite football team and accidentally finding out that our team wins.[5] Our anxiety lessens when we know how the game ends. We don't sweat the fumbles or interceptions, and we don't worry if our team is down and facing insurmountable odds. Instead of worry and anxiety, we are excited and curious as to how they win. Interestingly, the crazier the odds, the more excitement. If only we could remind ourselves and our youth that we can live and story our lives with this kind of excitement and joy because we know the final outcome.

Causal coordination of Blake's life story. Causal coordination is the developmental ability to connect episodes into causal chains where certain life events caused, stopped, resulted in and/or related to other life events.[6] It is supported by temporal and cultural coordination. Without temporal and cultural coordination, causal coordination can't emerge.

With the advent of causal coordination, midadolescents now have the ability to link their multifaceted and developing life stories and to provide explanations of their actions and changes that occur over time.[7] Because of causal coordination in the life story, midadolescents are able to determine and explain physical causality and human motivation.[8] Causal coordination increases the most between ages twelve and sixteen.[9] Reason and meaning are added to the life story through causal coordination.[10] Causal coordination contributes to the "inter-story connectivity" of youth as they link past events with their highlighted and enduring aspects.[11]

We are so inundated with cause-and-effect relations that most of our life stories are built on them. If we keep in mind the confluence that occurs in a person's life story, we may help our youth see more broadly and relationally connected stories. Below I provide significant events that Blake used to link his life story. Can you locate the missing links that he used to connect his causal explanations? The missing links correspond numerically with the causal explanations. After looking at each of these causal connections, look for the confluence that leads to the outcome.

Explanations.

1. Almost drowned to present state of being alive

2. Choked by daycare worker to present state of being alive

3. Dustyn picked on him in elementary school, and it really bothered him, to Dustyn being his friend, and it doesn't bother him

4. Anger and emotional problems from early childhood and high school to no longer having much anger or emotional problems

5. Dating a girl in the seventh and eighth grades ended in no longer dating her and being sad.

6. Wanting to commit suicide to not committing suicide

7. Beginning a second serious relationship with Ashley to no longer dating her

8. Grandmother diagnosed with throat cancer and his closeness to her, to how he got through it

9. Grandmother died to it still hits him hard and it is hard thinking about it

10. Cut himself for a couple of years to stopping

11. Self-injurious behavior to how he is better off now

12. Big thing happened in daycare to parents going to court

13. Daycare worker choking him to Blake forgiving her

Links.

1. Dad saved him.

2. Mom and dad intervened and took daycare worker to court.

3. Blake recognizes Dustyn is not a threat in size and excuses Dustyn's behavior because everyone does it.

4. Blake learned how to push confrontation away.

5. She broke up with him.

6. Blake thought about how devastated his parents would be.

7. Ashley broke up with him.

8. He began martial arts, and it helped.

9. He was closer to her than anyone else, and they did not have a funeral or scatter her ashes, so he had no closure.

10. Blake thought about having kids and did not want that kind of image with his kids.

11. He tries to help people like himself who cut, and he believes in God, prays and cries.

12. Daycare worker choked him.

13. People lose their temper and express it in different ways.

As mentioned in chapter five, causal explanations form themes and themes shape causal explanations in our life stories. This is how our high school students begin to make meaning of their lives when they use causal coordination. Notice how Blake has several interpretations of his life. I would want to explore some of these areas with Blake. Most of the time youth see themselves as being passive recipients of their supporting cast. Notice in Blake's story how most of his causal connections involved his supporting cast acting on him. We can help him see how he is also an active agent who has affected and formed those relationships.

While some of these interpretations are helpful, I want to draw support from other voices in Blake's life. We can do this from any of the mentioned supporting cast—mom, dad, grandmother, half-brothers or sister—and we may inquire about other meaningful relationships that we may include. Who in Blake's list of relationships might you get more information about to help him handle some of these issues?

Sometimes I begin with the relationship that means the most to the student. I would ask Blake to describe his relationship with his grandmother and what she would say about how he stopped cutting if she were still alive. I would also ask him how his relationship with God has helped. Bringing healthy, positive voices to the forefront of our conversations strengthens and thickens our youth's stories so that they have more to draw from when conquering future problems.

Thematic coordination in Blake's life story. Most of our youth will not give a specific overview or theme to their life stories. Certain themes may be obvious to us, but not so obvious to them. We may ask them, "What do you think about your life as a whole?" Most of the themes that older high school students give are the very thing that they have used to structure the majority of their life stories.

Children and early adolescents establish narrative evaluations through relationships with their guardians. These become crucial in midadolescence, as youth move from evaluating and establishing themes in particular roles and social life to evaluating all of their roles and forms of life for their life story. Thematic coordination is the ability to interpret life's many narratives and to recognize similarities and differences that can be combined to create a central theme.[12]

Thematic and causal coordination are rarely observed in early adolescence, but they increase throughout midadolescence into young adulthood.[13] By linking their past stories, midadolescents determine their evaluative trajectories.[14] They may have a lot of positive events happen in their life story, but they may choose to highlight and extract negative interpretations that result in negative thematic coordination.

When our youth tell their stories, we can give an unlimited amount of responses. Imagine the unique outcomes of the responses that we could give Blake:

- Wow, that's an interesting story, Blake. I have a similar story. When I was twelve I also cut.

- It sounds like you still have suicidal thoughts, and I want to help you get rid of those before they destroy any more of your life.

- Your life has so much more value than what you are giving it. I am shocked that you ignore all of the positive things in your life.

- God seems to be tagged on at the end of your story as an afterthought. If your relationship with God were stronger, your story would be filled with more hope and joy.

- I had no idea you went through so much pain in your life. You have lived a difficult life, and I'm sorry you are going through so many problems. Please let me know if there is anything I can do to help.

In the past I have dismissed many students' life stories by responding with statements similar to those above. Today, when youth share their stories with me, I want to help them thicken and deepen their stories in such a way that helps them conquer future problems and that sustains them beyond high school.

The first few times we attempt to do this, we may not have much to say or we may not be able to think of questions. That's okay. I have reflected on some of my youth's life stories and months later asked them questions from their initial telling that helped them navigate their life. An ongoing dialogue with our youth adds value to their stories because an adult desires to hear, and keep hearing, their stories. As one of my students said to me, "You are the only adult who actually cares to listen to my story."

What theme does Blake give us concerning his life story? We may be able to see several, but one that he mentioned at the end colors his entire life. Blake's life story has a progressive theme. Although it is similar to a rollercoaster, he ends stating, "I am at a much better place than before." He has encountered a lot of grief and heartache, but he has overcome. He also attempts to help others who are in similar situations as his own. The theme I attempt to emphasize and thicken as Blake shares his story is his theme of overcoming and survival.

Using the words of our youth also helps them see that we were listening to their stories. The following comments and questions have the potential to thicken Blake's theme:

- That's crazy how your daycare worker choked you. I am even more amazed that you reached a place where you could forgive her. How were you able to get to that point? How does that help you forgive others when they wrong you now?

- Your grandmother and your parents are important figures in your life. You shared how close you were to your grandmother, how your father saved you from drowning and how thinking about your parents when you were about to commit suicide kept you from doing it. What are some other ways that your grandmother and parents have helped you? (After Blake's response, I also asked him how he has helped them.)

- You talked about how everyone picks on each other. Is some picking worse than others? How do you think we can stop it? How did Jesus react to people who were hurtful toward him?

- I bet your grandmother would be proud of how you have overcome such difficulty in your life. What do you think she would say to you if she were alive today?

- I'm sorry that no one was there for you to talk with when you were cutting. Your story encourages me. Instead of being bitter and complaining about no one helping, you have decided to follow the way of Jesus and help others. Can you describe an experience where you helped someone? What did it feel like? How do you think God's love was shared in that experience?

- What do you listen to on your iPod when you lie down and pray and cry for hours at a time? How does that help you to feel better?

- You said weeks can go by in which you don't want to do anything, and sometimes you want to drive off the road and run into a tree. But you said you don't want to be remembered that way. How do you want to be remembered? What kind of memories do you want to leave behind for people? How would those things help others?

- What is it about believing in God and knowing God cares that helps you?

We could go in many more directions with Blake's story. Yet the goal is to extend and thicken the depth and awareness of the life story of every student in our ministries. When we help them thicken their narratives they will have a deeper and richer identity.

CONCLUSION

Youth experience a plethora of new emotions and feelings, and it is a struggle for them to find the right words to express their emotions. Since most adults do not make time to listen to the beginning formations of the life story of teens, all that most adults hear are phrases of a much larger story—a larger story that is fluctuating and changing. Youth may think pot is cool for a week, and the next week they may lead a resistance against such drugs. Midadolescents are learning to make meaning with others and with their life stories, and they sometimes struggle in this meaning-making process. How many youth's lives will God use us to impact by the simple practice of coordinating their life stories with them?

REFLECTION QUESTIONS

1. Have a friend tell you stories about his or her day or week, and then ask your friend to tell you his or her life story. What difference does this make? Does hearing your friend's life story help you frame his or her everyday stories?

2. How can you move beyond traditional listening and telling stories in your youth ministry practices?

3. Record how you thought you knew one of your youth or a friend, and how hearing his or her life story altered your perception of that person.

4. After reading Blake's story, what supporting cast's voice would you use to emphasize positive qualities about him? How would you use his or her voice?

5. Review the questions that may thicken Blake's theme for his life story. Choose a question to ask him, or come up with your own. Explain how you intend to use your question and what you hope to accomplish.

Part Three

GOD'S STORY

9

Reading the Bible

No one is present as I sit down to read Scripture and prepare my youth lesson. I select my preferred translation of the Bible, open it and choose the book and passage to interpret. I read the passage several times to decide where I want to begin and end my reading. I write down my thoughts and insights. For hours I read and reread, write and rewrite, until I craft a lesson that will aid my youth in their Christian formation. To state the obvious, I am the one who reads, writes and interprets the Scripture for my youth lesson. Yet what looks so obvious is what blinds me.

I had accepted this individualistic approach to Scripture as a natural fact for most of my life. Reading Scripture was always a matter of my own individual interpretation, and the extent of my questioning was always, "How do I read Scripture?" You could imagine my perplexity when fourteen-year-old Anna asked me, "How do we read Scripture?" Although she was referring to herself and other youth collectively, her question now resonates with me. How do *we* read Scripture? I am the only one physically present, but am I alone? No, a host of relationships and stories form and shape my understanding and interpretation of Scripture.

A breadth of relationships frames how we each read God's Word. Everyone, including spouses, children, friends, parents, colleagues, youth group members, former professors and more, influences us when we open the Bible. How could I begin to separate all the relationships that generate my particular interpretations of Scripture? "My reading" is impossible to distinguish from "our relationships." What remains when I remove all my relationships? It's like trying to eliminate dandelions by blowing away all their seed heads. The seed heads are gone, and we ignore how dandelions were formed in the first place. The relationships I co-create and the stories generated from those relationships are lodged within my Scripture reading in ways that I may never fully recognize.

Let's face it: our readings of Scripture are deeply biased. Biases are not

THE CRITIC'S VOICE

Criticism
I am well aware of my biases. I unpacked my theological suitcase and examined my biases in seminary.

Response
I have yet to see an admissions catalog invite students to come and explore the biases of their school or faculty. The biases that students explore are usually their own, and rarely are students encouraged to contemplate the biases of their school or professors. Unfortunately, many youth ministers do not attend to their biases when they leave seminary or divinity school because, for them, the process has been completed. Consequently, an irony surfaces. Unaware that they examined their biases from the biased position of their school and faculty, most students possess even more biases than when they began their degree.

Here are some things to ask about your seminary or divinity school: What is the geographic locale? How diverse is the faculty in the following areas: ethnic, economic, gender, academic training and denomination? Are the academic and denominational affiliations of the faculty and the school closely aligned? The less diverse and more closely aligned academic and denominational affiliations are, the more biased the school will be in perpetuating its own views rather than exploring a wide range of perspectives and voices.

If the school is in the South, consists of white, middle-class males and the professors' degrees and education are closely aligned with their school's denominational affiliation, this school is much more likely to perpetuate unexamined biases of youth, God and Scripture.

necessarily good or bad. They are like noses; we all have them. But just like the noses on our faces, they can be difficult to see. When we do not recognize our biases in reading Scripture and treat them as ultimate truth, we eliminate others' biases. This limits new forms of understanding and manufactures division that hinders relational growth.

I believe that how we read the biblical texts shapes our understanding of God and Jesus as well as how we live our faith. Therefore it is vital for youth pastors to explore their biases in reading Scripture. With the multitude of biblical interpretations available today, we should be openly discussing our biases and questioning the way in which we read and present Scripture to our youth.

In this chapter, I will navigate through some of the biases we have inherited from our church experiences and academic training. Then I will suggest a Christian reading of the Scriptures as a story that culminates in the life story of Jesus. All kinds of interpretive maneuvers may be used with the text when the Bible is not read as a story. However, when Christians read the Bible as a narrative whole, they limit biases to the story's progression and overarching themes.

INHERITING A FRAMEWORK

Tanner shares his Bible with his friend Zack. He points to the words and slowly says, "For God so loved the world that he gave his only son that whoever believes in him will not perish but have everlasting life." Tanner looks at Zack to make sure he's following along. I look at Tanner and notice he is in the book of Ezekiel, and the Bible is upside down. Tanner just turned five, and he hasn't learned how to read.

Children learn a multitude of concepts, doctrines and dogmas before they have the ability to read. Many learn associations with the Bible, such as the Bible is "God's Word," "truth," "inerrant," "the Christian roadmap," "God's love story to us" and "Holy Word." When children reach an age when they can read the Bible, they are already predisposed to a particular tradition that provides a specific framework for how to approach and read it. They have been told certain stories and given certain meanings to certain words before they can read the words in the Bible for themselves. Children have no choice in the matter; they understand the Bible, God, church and Jesus in certain ways and do not question their constructed reality for years to come, if at all.

If children, teenagers and adults read the Bible, it is typically a Bible that a family member has given them or a Bible that their church uses. Rarely will a youth (or many adults) question the biblical translation she has inherited. The only difference for many is that some Bibles are easier to read than others.

My wife noticed a student reading her Bible at a local coffee shop. Intrigued that the student was actually reading her Bible, she asked her what translation she was reading. The student looked puzzled by the question, so my wife asked, "Is your Bible the NIV, CEB, KJV, NASB, *The Message* or another?" The student closed her Bible, looked at the spine and said, "It is the *holy* Bible."

If students and adults are unaware of different translations of the Bible, they may be surprised to learn that there are at least ten different Christian Bibles: Roman Catholic, Greek and Slavonic Orthodox, Georgian Orthodox, Ethiopian Orthodox, Coptic Orthodox, Armenian Apostolic Orthodox, Syriac Orthodox, Church of the East (Nestorian), Eastern Orthodox, Anglican and Protestant. The Ethiopian Orthodox contains eighty-one books that are considered to be written by "God who is the author of the Old and New Testaments containing nothing but perfect truth in faith and morals."[1] The other Christian Bibles do not contain as many as the Ethiopian Orthodox, and the Protestant Christian Bible has the least with sixty-six books. Which Christian Bible is the right Bible? Of course, it is usually the one we have inherited as *the* Christian Bible.

Before I was exposed to textual criticism and different Christian Bibles, the issue of reading the Bible was simplified to my choice of translation, the quantity of material read and its application in the life of the believer. I seldom questioned the formation and compilation of the Bible or the presuppositions I had inherited from my relationships. I assumed the Bible I used had existed always in the same structure (just a different language). As a childhood pastor of mine used to say, with his hand clutching a King James Version Bible, "God said it, they wrote it down, and here it is." Contrary to my former pastor's sincere conviction, when I began my undergraduate studies, I discovered that the process and formation of the biblical canon was much more complicated.

THE ACADEMIC FRAMEWORK

My understanding of Scripture shifted with the force of the San Andreas Fault line when I began my academic training in religious studies. I learned that we do not have any of the original writings penned by the authors. The best discovered texts are copies of copies of copies that are in some cases hundreds to thousands of years removed from the original writings.[2] Added to this complication is the fact that there are very few complete manuscripts. In other words, not only are no Scriptures translated from a document written directly by the author, but the oldest discovered writings are fragments of larger works.

Then I began studying biblical Greek. I expected to prove the accuracy of the New Testament through it, but instead I uncovered more unsettling results. I learned that among the five thousand or so Greek documents (fragmented and full) known of the New Testament, no two agree in all particulars.[3] Scholars disagree concerning which manuscripts should be dated more closely to the originals.[4] Many stylistic changes—additions, deletions, unintentional repetitions and harmonization—occur in the transmission of the text.

In addition, New Testament scholars have to consider that the original writings, even if they were discovered, were compiled twenty to forty years or more after many of the events they describe.[5] And it's not like the four Gospels record things differently because they simply have four different interpretations like four people witnessing the same event. Instead the Gospel writers intentionally change their material to suit their audience and message.[6]

Although many Christians are not familiar with these changes, most English translations note major textual variants or simply omit verses not found in the earliest manuscripts.[7] For example, Luke 17:36; Mark 9:44, 46; and John 5:4 are omitted from NIV, NRSV, NLT, NJB and ESV, while other versions note these textual additions. Many other passages involve the addition of several verses, such as the longer ending of Mark (Mk 16:9-20) and the *pericope* of the woman caught in adultery in John 7:53–8:11. If the Gospel of Mark ends in 16:8, the meaning takes on a completely different tone. Of course, still more questions arise concerning Scripture, such as authors quoting or referring to nonbiblical sources as if they were Scripture[8] and discrepancies in the biblical text.[9]

The complications that surface in attempting to find the reading closest to the original text precede the host of issues raised by higher criticism that surface in the process of interpreting a text.[10] An awareness of this hermeneutic, coupled with knowledge of the ramifications related to the existence of different biblical canons that emerged from the second century forward, are a sample of the complex issues involved in biblical interpretation.[11]

I had a growing distrust in the Bible and its formation. The more familiar I became with biblical Greek, the more I was shocked to see how different scholars translated the Scriptures, divided the text and added particular headings to fit their theological biases. I could look at the scholar who was translating the text, and, based on their academic institution, I could predict how they would render a passage. For instance, it is not an accident that translations that divide Ephesians 5:21 from 5:22 with a subheading are translated by more conservative scholars than those who place the subheading before Ephesians 5:21.

Below are examples of differences that occur when certain schools of thought translate biblical passages and the implications of these translations that lead to major interpretive differences. Should the husband and wife be mutually submissive to one another? Should this set the framework for marriage? Or does the mutual submission belong to the previous section addressing the body of Christ?

New American Standard Bible:

[19]speaking to one another in psalms and hymns and spiritual songs, singing and making melody with your heart to the Lord; [20]always giving thanks for all things in the name of our Lord Jesus Christ to God, even the Father; [21]and be subject to one another in the fear of Christ.

Marriage Like Christ and the Church

[22]Wives, be subject to your own husbands, as to the Lord.

New King James Version:

[19]speaking to one another in psalms and hymns and spiritual songs, singing and making melody in your heart to the Lord, [20]giving thanks always for all things to God the Father in the name of our Lord Jesus Christ, [21]submitting to one another in the fear of God.

Marriage—Christ and the Church

[22]Wives, submit to your own husbands, as to the Lord.

Contemporary English Version:

[19]When you meet together, sing psalms, hymns, and spiritual songs, as you praise the Lord with all your heart. [20]Always use the name of our Lord Jesus Christ to thank God the Father for everything.

Wives and Husbands

[21]Honor Christ and put others first. [22]A wife should put her husband first, as she does the Lord.

New Revised Standard Version:

[19]as you sing psalms and hymns and spiritual songs among yourselves, singing and making melody to the Lord in your hearts, [20]giving thanks to God the Father at all times and for everything in the name of our Lord Jesus Christ.

The Christian Household

[21]Be subject to one another out of reverence for Christ.
[22]Wives, be subject to your husbands as you are to the Lord.

The Message:

[19-20]Sing songs from your heart to Christ. Sing praises over everything, any excuse for a song to God the Father in the name of our Master, Jesus Christ.

Relationships

[21]Out of respect for Christ, be courteously reverent to one another.
[22-24]Wives, understand and support your husbands in ways that show your support for Christ.

The New Jerusalem Bible:

[19]Sing psalms and hymns and inspired songs among yourselves, singing and chanting to the Lord in your hearts, [20]always and everywhere giving thanks to God who is our Father in the name of our Lord Jesus Christ.

The Christian Household

[21]Be subject to one another out of reverence for Christ. [22]Wives should be subject to their husbands as to the Lord.

Let's pretend for a moment that none of these textual issues exist. What do we do with the Bible we have? We read it, right? Back to Anna's question: "How do we read Scripture?" The act of reading Scripture has its own complications, because reading Scripture is an interpretive act. I used to think interpretation meant uncovering the text's meaning, which led to understanding, and application meant applying this meaning and understanding to my life. I now see understanding, interpretation and application as a unified process.[12] The act of interpreting involves simultaneous understanding and application.

Interpretation, application and understanding as a unified process become evident in how we read Scripture, where we begin and end our reading, and the speed, tone and body language we use when reading it. I witnessed two people preach the Sermon on the Mount. Both had memorized the passage and used the same translation. One recited the sermon as if Jesus were scolding and condescending to his listeners. The other person spoke as if Jesus were encouraging and compassionate. They were the same Bible, the same passage, but two different experiences of Jesus. Youth ministers' and/or the community's choice of biblical texts and the manner in which they are read play a central role in how youth interpret, understand and apply Scripture.

THE AUTHORITY OF SCRIPTURE

With all of the known textual variants, such as additions, deletions, duplications and discrepancies, should the Bible be deemed authoritative? This question haunted me throughout my undergraduate program. I felt that my entire faith foundation had collapsed. Once again, consider the evidence: The New Testament is based on an event that occurred almost two thousand years ago, and all that scholars have are copies and many fragmented copies of witnesses' testimonies that at best date two hundred years from the time of the witnesses' actual recording of the event. The authors may not have been eyewitnesses (most probably were not). And, in the case of the Gospels, the authors wrote thirty-five to forty years after Jesus' ministry.[13] Is the evidence reliable enough to deem Scripture authoritative?

Like many well-meaning Christians, when my view of Scripture was called into question (although at the time I felt it was the Bible that was being called into question), I attempted to find ways to elevate its authority.

Looking back, I see that I was more fixated on my Bible and its accuracy and precision than on the God conveyed in the Scriptures and at work in the world today. Like many evangelical Christians, I was like a man traveling through a desert who becomes dehydrated. About to give up, he sees a sign with an arrow that reads, "Water this way." In utmost joy and excitement, the man clings to the sign and celebrates his discovery for hours. Eventually, he dies holding the sign. Neither the sign nor the message could provide the man with salvation. The Bible is an instrument of the Spirit and community of God, and it points toward God. It is no more God than the sign is water.

The authority of the Bible as the authorization of the community. If the Bible is authoritative, what makes it authoritative? The words printed on the pages, the binding and the covers are not intrinsically authoritative. In one home, the Bible may be revered and respected and given a place of prominence in family communication. In another home, the Bible may be propped under a table leg to provide balance. In which home does the Bible have authority? People may assert that the Scriptures have authority in both homes, but only one home acknowledges it in practice. Perhaps the latter family buys a new table and decides to burn the Bible with their trash. Has the Bible lost or gained any authority? If the Bible is printed in a foreign language on fuzzy pink paper with a thin paperback cover that looks like a romance novel, would it lose its authority? Is reading the Bible what makes it authoritative?

The biblical story becomes authoritative when faith communities deem it authoritative.[14] Even if people claim, theologically, that the Bible is authoritative because it is God's Word, practically it still does not become authoritative for a community unless the community agrees and acknowledges it as so. Similar to the geocentric model of the world that the early church supported with Scripture,[15] the authority of this worldview ceased to exist when people began agreeing that the sun did not rotate around the earth. The view that the earth rotates around the sun may have been true the whole time, but the authority of that truth did not become real for that community until the people recognized it as so. Those who claim that Scripture is authoritative apart from the community of faith learned to voice this claim from within a particular community of faith.

How can a community of faith view the Scripture as authoritative when it contains so many textual variants? When reading the portrayals of God in the Old Testament and New Testament, it would be presumptuous to expect a text that would be precise and accurate and that would have one distinct way of viewing God and the world in which we live. If Jesus himself rarely gave explicit answers in his own ministry, why do we expect the Bible to be clear and perfect in its formation?

In addition, Jesus entrusted and depended on the disciples, in spite of their fallibility, while he was physically present with them to proclaim the gospel. Why would it be any different with those who wrote the Scriptures? Could God be so powerful and great that God humbly uses people and their fallibilities? God is hardly confined by God's own greatness. God is also free and powerful enough to be limited by our finiteness.

A greater humility and interdependence arises when people have to wrestle with the interpretation of Scripture. Some assume that if God was really involved in the formation of the biblical text, discrepancies and variants would not pop up like weeds. This position says more about modern assumptions of God (that is, God can be experienced or revealed only through precision and accuracy, much like a supercomputer) than about the character and relational agency of God as revealed in biblical text.

Rodney Clapp makes a provocative but helpful statement in *A Peculiar People*: "It is a protestant conceit that the welfare of the church depends upon the welfare of print."[16] He further illustrates how Christians have diminished their dynamic Bible into a static text by dissecting and deconstructing words into abstract beliefs and propositions, instead of focusing on the power of the word as spoken and performed.[17] If all printed Bibles disappeared tomorrow, the community of faith would have to rely on one another to share and live their biblical stories and on the Spirit to affirm them.

Being aware of the process through which the Bible became canonized, we should hesitate to hew words into ammunition for defending our faith. If people's faith is based on an inerrant Bible, knowledge of textual variants could hinder that faith. For others, such awareness can inspire more humility and curiosity in how they approach the Bible.

From errancy and inerrancy toward inheritancy. The authority and power of Scripture resides in the community's acknowledgement of God's authority to speak through the biblical text. Bibles are inherited from earlier faith communities that deemed these writings authoritative for the life of their church.

Every year that I teach at Gardner-Webb University, I have several students who hold to the view of an inerrant biblical text and students who believe the Bible is an errant text. If we press certain issues and topics, the class becomes gridlocked in debate, and each side feels the necessity to defend its view. I, too, have waved the flag of errancy and inerrancy of Scripture. Regardless of the side I took, I felt the pressure to defend my view. In fact, our view of Scripture is sometimes used as a litmus test.

Instead of using the terms *inerrancy* or *errancy* to describe Scripture, could we move in the direction of Scripture's *inheritancy?* If so, we may be able to find more common ground in how we preserve and share the biblical story with our Christian brothers and sisters. This idea allows people to recognize the biblical text as an inheritance from previous Christian communities, and it emphasizes the value of relationships (including spiritual relationship) that form our understanding of Scripture.

Inheritance stories fascinate me. People may inherit the same objects (money, jewelry, cars, land, houses), but they interact and react differently with the items according to the stories attached to them. The inherited object means nothing by itself. A million dollars means nothing; it is paper with ink. Unless you live in a society that deals in such currency and you share its value, a million-dollar inheritance may fulfill your lifelong dreams. The worth and meaning of *any* object comes from our relationships and the stories that we tell (or that have been told) about it.

The same is true with the Bible. The Bible itself means or says nothing on its own. What does a Bible say to someone who can't read? Or what does it say to a person who has inherited the assumption that the Bible has no worth or merit? The Bible becomes meaningful because we have an inheritance (how to read it, how to understand it, how to live it out) that tells us something about the Bible and its value.

As with any inheritance, it is important that we are aware of the relationships and stories that surround biblical meaning and interpretation. Do we share this inheritance? Do we withdraw from society and keep it to ourselves? What stories do we maintain or change according to how Scripture is to be read or understood? If we share our inheritance and want others to share it, how do we ensure that they understand its worth? All of these questions will be answered according to how we inherit the Scripture as well as our community's understanding of it. What biases and assumptions will we retain or alter? How will we pass our inheritance of scriptural interpretation down to our children?

It is important to be aware of textual variants, but we can question the Bible so much that we muzzle it. Just as we can scrutinize and analyze people's sayings to nonsense, we can do the same with the Bible.

When we move to discussing the biblical text as an inheritance, we are able to sidestep the debate and work on finding creative ways to preserve and share the biblical story. After all, major differences in people's views of Scripture may not be resolved through obsessing over the differences. I could never see the full portrait of the biblical story, because I kept getting caught up in the details and minuscule brush strokes of the biblical portrait. Eventually, the brush strokes gained depth, color and brilliance when I stepped back with my community of faith and saw the painting as a whole. When we bracket our differences and liberate the stories to speak in all of their richness and diversity—textual variants and all—we may find commonality.

Scripture as story. The Christian Scriptures consist of narratives, poems, songs, legal texts and more—and they convey a central story when read as a whole. The compilation of the Bible was not accomplished according to its historical, chronological writing, but was arranged according to the overarching stories told within faith communities. Although the Bible consists of many nonnarrative materials, its congruity emerges through the narrative framework. The overall form of the Bible, preserved and enacted by the faith community, lends itself to be read in a particular way.

The overarching form of the narrative and nonnarrative passages tell of God's actions in the world as experienced by faith communities. Together they portray a coherent and communal understanding of the witness of the texts. If God is a relational agent who acts throughout history as revealed in Scripture, the narrative form is required as an indispensable hermeneutic. Therefore, to say "biblical story" is to say that the Bible as a whole renders and is governed by a particular story.

Of course, some passages of Scripture do not contain narratives. Yet they can't be properly understood apart from their storied context. When people agree that a deep structure undergirds the Scriptures, the parts and functions of Scripture are gathered and gain meaning and strength from this narrative. Although the Bible does not tell a single story or possess the kind of coherence a modern author may give, it nevertheless has remarkably unifying sections and themes that articulate its overarching story.

This hermeneutical approach does not require blending individual narratives and nonnarratives so that the uniqueness of each is lost. People could weave the Gospels into one narrative account in which the uniqueness and diversity of each is disregarded in order to harmonize the portraits of Jesus.[18] This type of harmonization is evident in the church every Christmas season. The unique birth stories of Jesus found in Matthew and Luke render two distinct portraits of Jesus that would be obscured if these stories were blended. Not only would the distinctiveness of the separate accounts be diminished, but an altogether new version of the story would be authored that is foreign to the biblical canon.[19] The cohesion of the biblical story lies in preserving the diversity within the biblical narratives and nonnarrative material.

THE PARADIGMATIC STORY OF THE BIBLICAL STORY

Losing sight of the form and function of the biblical story leads to all sorts of ways to interpret the Scriptures. After all, if the Bible is not read as story, there is no progression of God's revelation, no unfolding themes, no place for Christian identity formation,[20] no participatory role in God's redemptive mission[21] and no way to avoid being swept away by competing stories.[22] All texts may hold equal weight and importance, and, most disturbingly for Christians, Jesus would not be the center of God's revelation. But when people read the Bible as an *all-encompassing* story, they discover a climax that carries the interpretive weight of the grand biblical story: the life, ministry, death and resurrection of Jesus.

As a follower of Christ, I believe the fullness of the revelation of God is found in Jesus Christ. We know what God is most like from the identity of Jesus as portrayed in the biblical narrative. This is important when it comes to interpreting Scripture, because numerous portraits of God appear in the Old and New Testaments. A huge difference occurs if our understanding of God is framed by the Levitical codes or by the ministry, death and resurrection of Jesus. For instance, in John 8:5, the Pharisees present Jesus with Levitical law that commands them to stone a woman caught in adultery (Lev 20:10). Jesus does not abide by that law. Instead, he reminds the Pharisees that they all participate in the destruction of relationships.

Understanding Jesus as God's central revelation establishes the interpretive framework through which all Scripture is viewed. Scholars describe the unity of the biblical story, which culminates in the life and ministry of Christ as the "narrative unity,"[23] the "emerging pattern,"[24] the "coherent story,"[25] the "canon within the canon"[26] and the "paradigmatic narrative."[27] After his resurrection, Jesus interprets his own life as fulfilling everything written about him in the law of Moses, the Prophets and the Psalms (Luke 24:27, 44-45).

The life, ministry, death and resurrection of Jesus need to illuminate our understanding of the whole drama (back to front). Inversely, to understand the life, ministry, death and resurrection of Jesus, we must have an understanding of the "long history of God's self-revelation to Israel" (front to back).[28] This view is particularly helpful because many people miss the significance of the biblical story climaxing in Christ, and therefore give Old Testament passages and the ministry of Christ equal interpretive weight. This is not to neglect the Old Testament, but to see its progression and culmination fulfilled in Christ.

Consider a story I share with youth discipleship majors: With the death of his brother, a Middle Eastern man named Kadar inherited leadership of the powerful Al-Azza tribe. The Al-Azza were devout God-followers, and they believed God appointed Kadar as their leader. To show their loyalty to God and Kadar, they agreed to kill anyone who disobeyed him. With power and religion at his side, Kadar followed a vision from God to conquer and destroy the neighboring tribal cities.

Instead of trying to live among the people in peace, Kadar was convinced that God said to destroy all of the tribes of this productive land (including their women, children, animals and homes). The neighboring tribes feared the Al-Azza, and they did not want to fight them.

The only time God showed emotion was when one of Kadar's soldiers kept loot for himself. Since God told the Al-Azza tribe to destroy everything, God became angry. The soldier confessed his wrongdoing, and Kadar and his soldiers used him for target practice until he was dead. After the soldier was brutally murdered, God's anger ceased, and the Al-Azza tribe regained God's blessing to continue their killing spree.

Kadar continued to believe that God fought with them, and he had natural disasters to prove it. As they approached one of the largest tribal cities of the land, they witnessed a horrific storm overtake the city, killing many of its soldiers and wiping out its defenses. Al-Azza leveled the city and finished what they knew God had begun.

Tribe after tribe, the Al-Azza people destroyed everything until all of the land was theirs. They praised God and his servant Kadar for their victories. This is the story that the Al-Azza tribe continues to tell to this day about God's gift of their new land.

I ask my students what they think of the story, and the class unleashes a verbal assault on Kadar and Al-Azza's view of God. The condemnation mounts for a few minutes, and then I question their sharp criticism. "Aren't we limiting God when we say he would not tell a man to kill others?"

"God would not kill innocent women and children!" a student cries.

"We may think the women and children are innocent, but they may be evil," I say. "Only God really knows the future, and this must have been the only option. Kadar and the Al-Azza tribe may not be alive today to tell these stories if they had not fought for a more productive land. This is how tribes survive. Do we have any right to question God? Kadar said God told him to do it, and he had miraculous stories to prove it."

The volume in the classroom rivals the sound of a rock concert from a front-row seat. My students are appalled that I'm justifying murder in the name of God. I press them: "How do you know that God would not tell someone to murder? How do you know that God would not fight with an army and use natural disasters to destroy people (including their women and children)? September 11, the war in Iraq, Katrina, recent earthquakes and tsunamis—people make these claims every day."

Someone in the class finally says, "It's not very Jesus-like!"

I throw up my hands, "Why does Jesus matter?"

"If Jesus is God in flesh, we know that God does not murder innocent women and children."

"Unless they are not innocent and God knows that they are going to reject him in the future," I quip.

"Jesus doesn't fight anyone, and he condemns others when they take up their sword—even toward those who are rejecting him. Besides, killing innocent babies doesn't give them a choice to follow God, and I couldn't believe in that kind of God," a nineteen-year-old student says, her pierced lip protruding in a defiant pout.

"So I guess you wouldn't consider Kadar a hero of your faith or a servant of the same God you follow?" I don't have to wait for their response.

"No!" they shout.

I pause, and then open the Bible to the book of Joshua. I read through Joshua, highlighting the parallels between the stories. The students realize that this was not a modern-day story, but the story of Joshua. The only things I changed were character names, location and era. The actions of Joshua, the Israelites and God were the same. In fact, I omitted a lot of violence and brutality that God and Joshua inflicted on people.

For the first time my students are speechless. "Why is everyone silent?" I ask.

"We forgot about that story."

"Well, why aren't you responding the same way as with the modern-day story I told?"

"Because the story of Joshua is in the Bible," they say, most of them looking down at the floor.

The students' response sheds light on a particular view that most of them have inherited. They believe that everything in Scripture happened exactly the way Scripture describes. When God commands people to kill others, or when he physically tries to kill people himself (see Ex 4:24-26; Josh 10:11), we accept that this is just how it was. We leave no room for the understanding that we may have such stories to illustrate who God is *not*.

It troubles me that we allow a fair amount of latitude for the early Israelites's understanding of cosmology (how the world functions), but not for their early theology (how God functions). We do not believe that the sun stood still in Joshua 10 as it describes, because the sun never moved to begin with (it was their worldview of the earth), but we do not question their view of God.

We must not forget that Israel became a divided kingdom not just because of political differences but also because of *theological* differences. In addition, the northern kingdom and southern kingdom both go through periods of exile, and their different *experiences* weighed on their unique understandings of God. We see these differences throughout the Old Testament.

If we believe that Jesus is God's full revelation, shouldn't we react as the students did to modern stories of violence and suffering? Could we have these stories in our Bible to see how some people before Jesus missed God? They thought God was telling them to kill men, women, children, babies and animals, but we know the God we see in Jesus would never condone such behavior. Isn't this why God sent Immanuel, God with us? With all of the times they understood God, they *misunderstood* him a lot too. As

Methodist minister John Killinger states, "Jesus was God's answer to a bad reputation."

Do these stories become less authoritative or less inspired for Christians if God didn't actually say or do these things? No! We read these passages more than ever, reminding everyone of the kind of destruction and violence we can inflict in the name of God. We use these stories to show our students what God is not like and how following Jesus opposes these actions. Many Old Testament stories portray the same loving, forgiving and sacrificing God that we see in Jesus, which oppose stories like Joshua.

If our guiding hermeneutic is the life story of Christ, we can't justify oppression, neglect the poor, fuel personal vengeance, cultivate arrogance or abuse others. On the other hand, if Jesus is not the hermeneutical principle for all of Scripture, all sorts of evils may be justified in the name of Scripture and in the name of Jesus.[29] Therefore we begin with the biblical story and the centrality of the life story of Jesus, letting those narratives guide our lives.

CONCLUSION

I sit down to read Scripture and prepare my youth lesson, and I know I'm not alone. Anna's question surfaces: "How do *we* read Scripture?" A great cloud of witnesses—scribes, translators and linguists—sits with me as I select my preferred translation. I read the passage several times to decide where I want to begin and end my reading, the voices of teachers and pastors informing my preferences for dividing up the text. I write my thoughts and insights, grateful for the heritage of godly influencers who saturated my life with their biases, contexts, insights and stories. For hours *we* read and reread, write and rewrite, engaging in a kind of silent dialogue that expands across time and space until together we have crafted a lesson that will aid youth in their Christian formation.

We are deeply biased. Yet, as I mention these relational biases, I am also open to other relationships that may illuminate and generate new ways of reading the Bible. For now, I'm biased with an awareness of textual variants and discrepancies within the biblical text. I no longer exhaust my energy trying to defend the Bible because of its inerrancy or trying to find proof of the accuracy or validity of certain biblical passages. Instead, I think about how I have inherited the Bible and how I will invite youth to hear and perform its life-shaping stories. The emphasis of the accuracy and validity of the biblical stories now rests on our performance of it. In other words, we validate the story by how we live it rather than how we defend it.

The most important bias I have inherited is how I read and perform the biblical story through the stories of Jesus. This scriptural reading is a bias that I invite all youth workers to pursue. We may read Scripture in various ways, but I believe the future of the church depends on whether or not we introduce our youth to the biblical story—with an emphasis on the life stories of Jesus.

Youth ministry as a whole (minus a few recent books) has remained silent on proclaiming the Bible in its storied form. We have chopped and hacked the Bible in such a way that our prevailing cultural story carries depth and meaning for our youth. We will examine the eclipse of the biblical story in chapter 10 and look at ways to recover this narrative in our youth ministry practices.

REFLECTION QUESTIONS

1. What is your view of the Bible? List the words that you use to describe the Bible. Beside each word, write who introduced you to this understanding. Is this common language in your denomination or church?

2. Pick a passage of Scripture and create two dramatic readings of it using the same translation and passage. Create a scene with two pastors reading the same passage with very different interpretive outcomes. To make these differences occur, change your posture, facial expressions, movements, tone and voice projection with each reading. Reflect on how youth's interpretation may be affected by the way a youth pastor reads a passage.

3. Read John 7:53–8:11. Do you think any of the following titles present the thrust of the passage?: "A Woman Caught in Sin" (CEV), "The Adulterous Woman" (NASB), "A Woman Caught in Adultery" (NLT, ESV), "An Adulteress Faces the Light of the World" (NKJV), "The Woman Caught in Adultery" (NCV). What do you think these titles lead readers to focus on when reading the passage? How do you think titles like "Religious Arrogance" or "Religion Gone Sour" would shift the focus and interpretation of the passage? How do you think titles like "Freedom in Christ!" or "No Condemnation in Jesus" would shift the interpretation?

4. How can the Bible be read in a way that creates a complete contradiction to the life and ministry of Jesus? Using your Bible, justify a particular stance that contradicts Jesus' life and ministry. Explain how looking through his life and ministry would alter the interpretation of the passage you use.

5. Consider the words that you may have learned before you could read the Bible. Most children (ages four to eleven who are involved in church and/or Christian school) have a preconceived understanding of words (*Satan, hell, heaven, Jesus, God, church*) and themes (salvation, afterlife, Christian living, creation, judgment) before they ever read the Bible. What relationships shaped your understanding of these words and themes? Explain how you have reconsidered some of these words in light of reading Scripture and other relationships you have formed.

6. Pick a passage in Scripture and read it. If the act of reading is itself an interpretive act, and through the process of reading and interpreting we gain understanding, articulate how you are interpreting, understanding and applying the text at the same time you are reading it.

7. If a group of Christians proclaim to have an inerrant Bible, what does it say about other Christian Bibles from other Christian traditions (Eastern Orthodox, Catholic and Protestant)? How could the concept of the inerrancy of Scripture limit our understanding of God and hinder community? How could difficult passages and textual variants that raise more questions than answers enable authentic community?

Movements in
Youth Ministry Practices

Seventeen-year-old Natalie had never come in contact with a youth ministry. She participated in other youth functions in the area, and she wanted to know what made our youth ministry any different from those other caring youth organizations. While a multitude of similarities exist, the major difference rests in the relationships and stories that define and give life to the organization. So I told her, "We share and participate in a different story."

For Christians, the Bible provides the narrative framework that structures reality, history and purpose. As discussed in chapter 9, the relationships Christians have to each other, the way we inherit our readings of Scripture and how we pass along this inheritance is vital. Never has the time been more crucial for reclaiming the reading of the Bible as story. Unfortunately, much of youth ministry's Scripture reading shadows the biblical story and manufactures disparate scriptural references without much coherence.

In this chapter, we will examine our contribution to the loss of proclaiming the biblical narrative in our youth ministry practices. And I will propose seven movements that recover the centrality of reading the Bible as a story that culminates in the life story of Jesus and his church.

THE LOSS OF THE BIBLICAL STORY

Jesus says, "I am the way, and the truth, and the life. No one comes to the Father except through me." I had memorized John 14:6 and prepared youth lessons on this verse. Like most youth pastors, I knew it well. It wasn't until several years of practicing youth ministry had passed that I recognized I knew nothing of the verse's context. When I began asking questions, such as "Why does Jesus make this statement?" "Who is Jesus addressing?" "How is John's narrative unfolding?" and "What are some of the previous conversations and dialogues that lead to this statement?" I couldn't answer any of them.

I asked similar questions about all of the verses of Scripture I had memorized, and I continued to come up empty. I asked other youth pastors and pastors the same questions concerning their memorized verses and discovered I wasn't alone. The youth lessons, devotionals and books I received confirmed the same phenomenon. Scripture was used, but only a couple of verses, with little concerning the passage's context.

By 2009 I was convinced that the lack of biblical story among youth also applied to many of their youth pastors. To validate my assumption, I conducted surveys with youth pastors and pastors at the National Youth Minister's Convention in Columbus, Ohio (February 27–March 2, 2009). The first survey question asked youth pastors to state their favorite passage of Scripture. Most mentioned one verse. The next question asked them to rate the importance of context on a scale of 1 to 10 (10 being vitally important and 1 being not important). Everyone thought the context was extremely important or vital. The next question asked them to provide the context of their favorite passage of Scripture. Only 38 percent knew the context of the verse. I can only speculate that the youth ministers' lack of knowledge of the biblical narrative would fare worse if it were not their favorite passage.

AVOIDING SNAPSHOTS

I have a "snip-it" tool on my laptop. I can take a snapshot of anything I see on my screen and the snip-it tool formats it into a picture. No matter what I was doing before I captured the section, and no matter what I do after, I can freeze everything and save my snip-it to another location on my computer.

Youth devotionals, lessons and most youth programming are laden with snip-its of the biblical story. We have partitioned the biblical story into devotional snip-its, self-esteem snip-its, systematic theology snip-its, moral snip-its. Then our youthful snippers give the snip-its a new context based on their viewpoints.

When the majority of Christians amass snip-its without context, snip-its dissipate into the larger cultural narratives. Then the cultural narrative—with its mosaic of snip-its—shapes our lives instead of the biblical story.

In our culture, most people identify with Jesus in three stories and symbols: birth story (baby in a nativity scene), death story (crucifix) and resurrection story (empty tomb). Every Christmas baby Jesus and Santa Claus compete for attention. Baby Jesus says nothing. Saint Nick delivers the goods with a few laughs and a hearty "Merry Christmas" or "Happy Holidays." Baby Jesus doesn't even cry.

At Easter we celebrate Jesus' death and resurrection—and this story competes with a rabbit. As a child, the story of a dying man and his empty tomb didn't quite capture my imagination like a rabbit laying candy eggs. Moreover, Jesus didn't say much on the cross, and his resurrection left his speech as empty as his tomb.

In my childhood church experience, Jesus really didn't say much at all. The week after our church's nativity play and cantata, we began casting for our Easter production. When our director chose Derek to play the part of Jesus, he said, "I was just born last week; now you're going to kill me!" Jesus is born, and before he speaks, we place him on a cross to die and resurrect. The plethora of Christmas and Easter performances far outweigh performances that capture the identity of Jesus through his ministry. Has Jesus become our speechless savior?

Jesus' death and resurrection dominate most evangelical preaching. The church's creeds do not include any of Jesus' teachings or ministry. Yet what do we really know about a person, if all that is known is the stories of his birth and death? Our focus on these snip-its reminds me of the church in Laodicea. They gathered together to worship, but Jesus was standing outside their door, knocking. I can imagine this same scenario happening today. We sing songs, wear Christian T-shirts and WWJD bracelets, preach the birth of Jesus, proclaim his crucifixion and resurrection, and all the while, Jesus is knocking on the door, wanting to fellowship with us. We have left Jesus outside.

For centuries, Christians have agreed that to know God means to know Jesus. To know Jesus means to know his story—not just the beginning and ending (or three snip-its), but his *whole* story. Jesus' birth, death and resurrection gain their significance because of his action and words. Fortunately, the apostle Paul reminded the Romans that salvation is also a direct result of Jesus' life: "For if while we were enemies, we were reconciled to God through the death of his Son, much more surely, having been reconciled, will we be saved by his life" (Rom 5:10).

During Jesus' time, stories circulated of miraculous births and divine conceptions. Julius Caesar's virgin mother was said to have been impregnated by Apollo; ten thousand Jewish males were crucified; and legends circulated of resurrected gods: Osiris, Mithra, Attis, Dionysus and Adonis. However, no one has the same life story (birth, *ministry*, death and resurrection) as Jesus.

The ministry of Jesus makes his birth, death and resurrection meaningful. If Jesus had ravaged people's homes and murdered the innocent, his resurrection would provoke fear, not celebration. No personal or communal story exists with Christ without knowing the story of Christ. How well have we presented the biblical story to teens?

In 2005 a national survey of youth revealed that religion is as important to teens as their cell phones, but only under specific conditions.[1] While religion carried weight in the teens' lives, most could not say why it was meaningful, how they practiced it or why it was significant in their daily lives.[2] Perhaps even more disturbing, the survey revealed that the "God" most teenagers worshiped seemed to be a combination of a divine butler and a cosmic therapist—always on call, solving any problem, boosting self-esteem and remaining respectfully distant in the process.[3]

The Bible Literacy Project (in conjunction with Gallop) surveyed 741 Christians and more than two hundred non-Christian youth. After a survey of English teachers' assessment of students' biblical literacy as well as of students was done, the *Bible Literacy Report* stated that a vast majority of youth are not biblically literate.[4] Biblical illiteracy not only hinders youth in practicing their Christian faith; anyone serious about literature would be at a great disadvantage if they did not understand the biblical allusions. These surveys reveal the need for youth ministers to return to sharing the biblical narratives, and the necessity of teens encountering Jesus in these narratives. Proclaiming the biblical story equips students with the language to interpret and share their experiences of God. As mentioned earlier, youth can't articulate, understand and have a meaningful experience of God without God language.

I am reminded of the time one of our students, Yuri, from Ecuador, attempted to express his sincere feelings for our youth group. After saying, "I love you all," he paused and said, "I . . . " as his frustration grew. Finally, he threw up his hands and said, "You friends. I wish I had the English words to express my feelings for everyone, but I don't." Of course, his expression of his *inability* to communicate his care and concern for the group communicated volumes. However, if Yuri continued to live among English-speaking people and never learned the language of feelings and emotion, others might see him as insincere and disconnected. Would he be able to have meaningful conversations with others without using their language?

When youth do not have the words to communicate their experiences, not only will they become increasingly frustrated, but they will also use other languages and ways of seeing the world that make more sense to them. Therefore it is essential that youth ministers "re-present" and "re-tell" the thick and rich narratives of the biblical story in such a way that youth have the opportunity to frame and shape their story with God's story.

THICKENING THE PRESENTATION OF THE BIBLICAL STORY

I failed an English paper in high school on *Romeo and Juliet* because I read CliffsNotes instead of Shakespeare. My teacher gave me a second chance by altering the writing assignment. This time I had to write about all that a person misses from Shakespeare's *Romeo and Juliet* when he settles for the CliffsNotes version. CliffsNotes told me about Romeo and Juliet and their family feud, but when I read Shakespeare, I encountered Romeo, Juliet, their actions, their language and their identities. I felt their struggle, their love and the tensions that mounted within the complicated familial plot.

Ten years later I returned to this exercise. This time my text was the Bible, and I compared BrandonsNotes on the biblical story that I had proclaimed to my youth with what they missed from hearing and reading the biblical story. The results were humbling.

I can tell my youth that the disciples don't always understand what Jesus says, and they miss seeing how Jesus' kingdom is about serving and giving. There is nothing wrong with this statement, and this is basically what happens in Mark 10:32-52, below. Yet, from time to time, my youth also need to have a story to add depth to such statements. Consider how a handful of my high school youth encounter the biblical story when I didn't give them the statement about the disciples above:

I asked my youth to close their eyes and listen to Mark's portrayal of the disciples and Jesus' ministry. I read this story:

> They were on the road, going up to Jerusalem, and Jesus was walking ahead
> of them; they were amazed, and those who followed were afraid. He took the

twelve aside again and began to tell them what was to happen to him, saying, "See, we are going up to Jerusalem, and the Son of Man will be handed over to the chief priests and the scribes, and they will condemn him to death; then they will hand him over to the Gentiles; they will mock him, and spit upon him, and flog him, and kill him; and after three days he will rise again." James and John, the sons of Zebedee, came forward to him and said to him, "Teacher, we want you to do for us whatever we ask of you." And he said to them, "What is it you want me to do for you?" And they said to him, "Grant us to sit, one at your right hand and one at your left, in your glory." (Mark 10:32-37)

"Really?!" Rachel blurted out. Everyone opened their eyes.

"What do you mean, 'Really?!'?" I asked.

"Jesus is telling his closest friends about how he will be mocked, spit on, beat and killed, and it's like they don't even see him," Rachel said. "They are calling shotgun on the throne."

"Great observation!" I responded. "Mark is showing us how they don't see him, and they miss, once again, what Jesus' ministry is all about. Jesus asks the same exact question: 'What do you want me to do for you?' to someone else. And that person sees Jesus."

I continued reading verses 38-52:

But Jesus said to them, "You do not know what you are asking. Are you able to drink the cup that I drink, or be baptized with the baptism that I am baptized with?" They replied, "We are able." Then Jesus said to them, "The cup that I drink you will drink; and with the baptism with which I am baptized, you will be baptized; but to sit at my right hand or at my left is not mine to grant, but it is for those for whom it has been prepared."

When the ten heard this, they began to be angry with James and John. So Jesus called them and said to them, "You know that among the Gentiles those whom they recognize as their rulers lord it over them, and their great ones are tyrants over them. But it is not so among you; but whoever wishes to become great among you must be your servant, and whoever wishes to be first among you must be slave of all. For the Son of Man came not to be served but to serve, and to give his life a ransom for many."

They came to Jericho. As he and his disciples and a large crowd were leaving Jericho, Bartimaeus son of Timaeus, a blind beggar, was sitting by the roadside. When he heard that it was Jesus of Nazareth, he began to shout out and say, "Jesus, Son of David, have mercy on me!" Many sternly ordered him to be quiet, but he cried out even more loudly, "Son of David, have mercy on me!" Jesus stood still and said, "Call him here." And they called the blind man, saying to him, "Take heart; get up, he is calling you." So throwing off his cloak, he sprang up and came to Jesus. Then Jesus said to him, "What do you want me to do for you?" The blind man said to him, "My teacher, let me see again." Jesus said to him, "Go; your faith has made you well." Immediately he regained his sight and followed him on the way."

"OMG! The blind man is the one who sees Jesus, and the disciples are the ones who are blind," Rachel said emphatically.

Before I could respond, Tim added his interpretation: "The disciples order Jesus to do whatever they want him to do, and the blind man calls out for mercy. Jesus asks the same question to the disciples and the blind man, and we get two different responses."

"And what are they?" I asked.

"The disciples want to sit on the right and left, and the blind man addresses Jesus as his teacher and wants to see," Jaden replied.

Our conversation around this story continued for twenty more minutes. Could you imagine the depth that would be missed if all I did was supply my youth with BrandonsNotes? They encountered Jesus in Mark's story. They encountered the way he interacted with his disciples and the blind man. My youth walked away with a deeper understanding of humility and Jesus' life lesson on greatness.

If students are not given thick descriptions of this story, their personal stories (being shaped by the prevailing cultural story) will not be enriched by an alternate reality (God's story) with which to frame and story their lives. Presenting the biblical story is not about providing explanations for events that the authors did not include or searching deep behind the meaning of the words, but about re-presenting the text in vivid detail.

For example, we can talk Christology, the meaning of Jesus' life and his historical context, but youth need to hear each of the Gospel's stories, Paul's stories and stories of other New Testament authors about Jesus' ministry. A youth pastor at the National Youth Ministers convention asked me what resource I would recommend to proclaim the biblical story to our youth. "The Bible," I said. The room filled with laughter, but I was serious. We have used so many secondary sources that we do not know what the primary text says.

I began seeking alternative movements to reclaim the biblical story in youth ministry practices. After a thorough investigation of youth ministry literature, devotionals and study guides, I have traced seven movements. These movements are not about moving from wrong to right. They are guides that help remove the youth ministry rubble that has buried the biblical story.[5]

From parts of the context to the context of parts. Legos can be used to construct all kinds of structures. When we purchase new Lego sets for my son, we try to keep the parts separated from his other Legos—each set in a bag with its instruction manual. Although we can combine any Lego pieces to construct whatever we choose, the parts usually get mixed up in such a way that we can hardly return to the original structure. If we begin with the instruction guide and a picture of the whole structure, then we have a better understanding of the Lego pieces and how Lego designed them to work together.

Many times in ministry we begin with the parts of Scripture, and we combine them like Legos with other parts before we situate the parts within their context. Even worse, we sometimes pay no attention to the context; we simply hold up our parts and share what we see.

Parts of the biblical story are evident almost everywhere in America: T-shirts, bumper stickers, marquees, bulletin boards, road signs, pencils, candy, movies, Facebook posts, blogs and tweets. But when Christians who advertise these fragments of the biblical story are asked, "Can you tell me the context of that verse?" many do not know. They are also unaware whether or not the graphics and objects attached to the fragmented verse contextualize it or completely alter its meaning.

For example, a pastor was wearing a shirt with a picture of a man dunking a basketball. The verse quoted below it was Philippians 4:13. Does this image capture Paul's message to the Philippians when he said, "I can do all things through him who strengthens me"? Is the strength referring to the physical power to dunk a basketball? Or is Paul talking about strength to remain content whether he was enduring prosperity or poverty?

How many youth and adults in this minister's congregation now have the notion that Philippians 4:13 is about the kind of strength that enables one to slam a basketball through a hoop? The T-shirt graphic gives Philippians 4:13 a new context and therefore an altered interpretation and meaning for those who see the shirt.

The majority of youth lessons and devotionals rarely consider the whole context of the verses being used. Instead of rendering the passage's storied context, the verses are usually broken down into smaller parts. The idea that seems to be prevalent is that if we can break things down to their most basic parts, we will discover the meaning, and it will be easier for youth to understand. How much thickness and depth does a student or youth pastor gain, however, when he is given a verse and a five-paragraph interpretation and application of that one verse (which usually says more about the author's biases than the Scripture itself)?

Below is an example of popular youth devotionals:

Title of the youth devotional: "Jesus Loses a Friend."

Scripture: "When Jesus saw her weeping, and the Jews who came with her also weeping, he was greatly disturbed in spirit and deeply moved. He said,

---

THE CRITIC'S VOICE

Criticism

I have experienced God in devotionals that only use one verse, and they have helped me grow as a Christian. Are you saying that God can't use these devotionals?

Response

I don't limit God's work to the Bible. If God used a burning bush to speak to Moses (Ex 3:1-6) and a donkey to speak to Balaam (Num 28:21-35), then God can use anything to speak to anyone. And I believe one-verse devotionals can be great if people are already familiar with the biblical story. I am addressing the lack of Christian identity formation among our young, and I see this strongly correlated with a lack of exposure and integration of the biblical story. One-verse devotionals are not bad or wrong, but if we only covered one verse a week with our youth, it would take us over twenty-nine years to make it through the book of Genesis.

'Where have you laid him?' They said to him, 'Lord, come and see.' Jesus began to weep. So the Jews said, 'See how he loved him!'" (John 11:33-36).

Devotional: The devotional begins with a story of a teenager losing her friend in a car accident. At the end of the story, the author asks, "Does Jesus care?" The verses above were used to explain how Jesus cared deeply for his friend Lazarus and how he was greatly disturbed in spirit and deeply moved. The author emphasized the words *greatly* and *deeply* to show how Jesus was moved by the loss of his friend. The devotional concluded by encouraging teens to cast their cares on Jesus because he grieves with us too.

You may have heard sermons similar to this. The devotional is relevant and encouraging, and Scripture is emphasized throughout. Yet our youth walk away encountering an author's interpretation of a passage rather than encountering Jesus as rendered in the scriptural story. But is Jesus weeping because of the loss of his friend? The Jews certainly think so, but Jesus tells us something different.

After Jesus receives news of Lazarus's sickness, he says, "This illness does not lead to death; rather it is for God's glory, so that the Son of God may be glorified through it." Jesus waits two more days, and he tells the disciples that they are going back to Judea. The disciples question him and remind him he was almost stoned in Judea. Jesus then tells them the importance of seeing and being guided by the light of the world, and he tells them that Lazarus has fallen asleep and he will go and wake him up. The disciples don't get it, and Jesus has to tell them plainly: "Lazarus is dead. For your sake I am glad I was not there, so that you may believe. But let us go to him." And Thomas's response puts an exclamation point on the disciples' lack of faith: "Let us also go, that we may die with him."

When Jesus arrives in Judea, Martha and Mary illustrate their lack of faith in him too when they say, "Lord, if you had been here, my brother would not have died." Jesus has to remind Martha that he is the resurrection and the life, but she still doesn't place her faith in him. After Mary has a similar reaction and Jesus sees everyone crying, he cries too. Before he raises Lazurus from the dead, he prays, "Father, I thank you for having heard me. I knew that you always hear me, but I have said this for the sake of the crowd standing here, so that they may believe that you sent me."

So the struggle in John 11 is not about Jesus losing a friend, but Jesus' friends losing faith. We miss much of the biblical story in devotionals that do not focus on the whole text.

Word and etymological searches are another strategy that focuses on parts of Scripture to discover meaning.[6] Yet they are not helpful if the whole context is not considered.[7] As many are aware, words can have completely different meanings and new understandings in different contexts.[8] This type of Bible study is typified by the view that the best commentary on the Bible is the Bible. While this may be true in a sense, it is fruitless to look at how other works use certain words if the overall context is ignored.

Simply performing a word search to survey how a particular word is used in other passages may do more harm than good. Different authors (even the same author) commonly use the same word with different meanings in different contexts. Plus, most Greek and Hebrew words have several different meanings and usages. The words must first be considered and determined through an examination of their immediate storied context.[9]

Unfortunately, this type of decontextualizing happens not only with the interpretation of words, but also with themes and ideas that are unified but are never combined in the Scripture's context. For instance, 1 Thessalonians 4:16-17, Luke 17:34-36, Matthew 24:40-41 and Revelation 4:1 are often interpreted as "rapture" passages. A closer look at their context reveals that the people taken away in Matthew 24 and Luke 17 are destroyed,[10] and Revelation 4:1-2 alludes to the trumpet voice heard in Revelation 1:10-11. When the parts of the whole are viewed within their storied context, these texts can hardly be seen as referring to the same event.

From explaining the text to exploring the text. If there is one book in the Bible I want to explain to my students, it is the book of Revelation. I have read many apocalyptic works, including Revelation in its Greek form, and have lectured on Revelation at a few colleges. I want to tell my students what it says by explaining its imagery and meaning. Yet, in doing so, I would remove their *experience* of Revelation. When my youth read Revelation, they are immersed in imagery, and their imaginations are opened to a whole new reality, which would be lost if I asserted my explanations.

Most youth ministers can probably recall those *aha* moments when they wrestled with a biblical text, struggled to understand it, sought help from others (commentaries and other people) and finally grasped some understanding. Youth should be invited into this kind of meaning-making process.

Explaining Scripture does not make it more specific. The more youth ministers seek to explain the text, the more general it becomes.[11] Many ministers enter the text with an inductive process, but then turn that process of meaning making into a deductive sermon that restricts the listener from personally making meaning of the Scriptures. When youth receive propositional statements or a youth minister's interpretation of Scripture instead of engaging in a meaning-making process, their ability to apply Scripture and grow in their faith is stunted. Youth ministers and other adults would be better suited to view their role in the meaning making of Scripture as collaborative.

Graduate students of Christian religious studies have the resources of credentialed Old and New Testament professors and the ability to read the Scriptures in their original languages of Greek, Hebrew and Aramaic and access to libraries of study commentaries. And they certainly acquire the skill of exegesis. But they quickly forget that the task of exegesis is not to get to the essence of anything but to have a better understanding of the complete unit. Sadly, the influence of popular preaching and teaching with which many students have grown up often overpowers the exegetical wrestling that they acquire in seminary.[12]

Early in youth ministry, I managed to allow popular preaching and teaching to shape how I understood the apostle Paul's two names (Saul and Paul). The popular message is that God changed Saul's name to Paul after his conversion on the road to Damascus. After a thorough reading of Acts, I was shocked to discover that Saul never received a new name. After his conversion in Acts 9, he remained Saul until he encountered the proconsul, Sergius Paulus, in Acts 13:7. Luke tells us in Acts 13:9 that Saul is "also known as Paul," perhaps not to confuse the two Pauls. After Acts 13:9, Luke uses Saul's Roman name, Paul. The apostle himself said that he heard a voice in his Hebrew language, saying, "'Saul, Saul, why are you persecuting me?'" (Acts 26:14). Paul is his Roman name, and Saul is his Hebrew name.

Many times we move from living in tension with and exploring the text to finding out what the passage means and explaining it to our audience. Explaining the text is not wrong. Some explanations are needed for students to connect to the story. Unfortunately, many lessons intended for youth focus on providing an explanation of a text and fail to explore it.

When youth ministers do not allow students time to explore Scripture, youth do not grapple with the text, and their encounter with the Bible is less meaningful. Youth learn to rely on someone else's interpretation and don't become deep and thick interpreters themselves.

Creating meaning is a collaborative exercise involving connection and relationships, stemming from sharing our own stories with others.[13] Simply said, meaning making is much larger than the task of explanation. Explanation is a one-sided, teacher-to-student mode of learning that, at best, deposits meaning. Meaning making allows youth to be co-interpreters of Scripture. They become receivers of meaning but also makers as we invite them into the process.

Jesus did not explain much. He asked a lot of questions and he told many stories. His style sparked his listeners' curiosity and imagination, opening the conversation to more questions, discussions and interactions. Chapters 1 and 2 of Genesis are examples of how we've "explained away" the biblical texts in youth ministry. The antidote to explaining away the text is to explore it—and to limit preconceived conclusions.

When youth explore the biblical context, they are often surprised to discover that certain words are never mentioned in Genesis 1 and 2, words such as *Satan, devil, apple, sin* and *fall.* Of course, this analysis pales in importance when they begin to explore the differences between Genesis 1:1–2:4a and Genesis 2:4b–3:24. When they read these texts, they face many decisions about other narratives they have incorporated. Will science, theological categories and denominational influences determine their reading of Genesis 1–3? Again, it is impossible to read anything without our relational interactions biasing and shifting our perspective of certain words, phrases and meaning. However, a careful exploration of Scripture, while being aware of our traditions, may shift our perspectives and allow us to see beyond them.

If our approach to the text is one of exploration, we notice differences between Genesis 1:1–2:4a and Genesis 2:4b–3:24. If we read these passages without inserting additional information, problems arise for our current worldview. For example, water exists before God creates. Light exists before he creates the greater and lesser lights. A dome separates the waters above from the waters below, and the waters above never come back down.[14] God creates the lesser light to rule the night and the greater light to rule the day, but we know the moon only reflects light; it doesn't produce it. God creates all the animals before he creates male and female in Genesis 1. God tells the unnamed male and female that they can eat of every tree and fruit-bearing seed, with no stipulations.

If we explore Genesis 1:1–2:4a and are familiar with Genesis 2:4b–3:24, we may want to know what happened to Adam and Eve. We may also want to know why God is called "God" in Genesis 1, but "Lord God" in Genesis 2:4b–3:24. God also seems to speak the world into being in Genesis 1, but in Genesis 2:4b–3:24, the Lord God forms man from dust and breathes into his nostrils. The Lord God makes an observation: "It is not good that the man should be alone; I will make him a helper as his partner" (Gen 2:18). Many are disturbed when they discover that the Lord God does not first make a woman to be his helper; God makes animals. This is a completely different order of creating than in Genesis 1. *Of course* animals are not satisfactory: "for the man there was not found a helper as his partner" (Gen 2:20).

After the Lord God's creation of animals to be Adam's partner (misjudgment, mistake or intention?) and Adam's inability to find a suitable helper, the Lord God causes the man to fall asleep. He extracts a rib, closes the wound and forms a woman from the rib. A short explanation comes out of nowhere: "Therefore a man leaves his father and his mother and clings to his wife, and they become one flesh" (Gen 2:24). This commentary normally adds to the confusion, since no one else has yet been created.

Questions, concerns and curiosity in relation to the text allow room for community to develop. If we explain the text to preempt conflicts and tensions, we stifle youths' opportunity for developing community.[15] Why must we have set-in-stone answers or a consensus on the correct interpretations? When we reduce the thick, rich and vibrant stories to thin propositions, we stifle collaboration in communities.

From reducing the story to propositions to expanding propositions into story. The following are all propositions: God is love; Jesus died on a cross and was resurrected; Jesus is the son of God; love your enemies; bless those who curse you. No Christian would deny the importance and validity of these propositions. Yet what does it mean to say that God is love or that Jesus died on a cross and was resurrected? These statements make no sense without their storied context. Although propositions, cognition and explanation all constitute textual understanding, "they are neither the starting point nor the goal."[16]

Both young and old Christians become skilled at grasping propositions. But what have we accomplished in youth ministry when we reduce the thick and rich biblical narratives of God to mere statements? I am not suggesting that we should discard all propositions. Instead of elevating propositions to establish doctrines and orthodoxy, we can present propositions in the context of the stories from which they were formed.

With this emphasis, many may discover that their propositions gain depth and meaning when framed in light of the biblical story. Others may discover that their propositions need revision. For example, when I noticed that the proposition, "Ask Jesus into your heart as your personal savior and you shall be saved," does not exist in Scripture, [17] I began using Jesus' words in John's Gospel: "Follow me." And when I encourage youth to follow Jesus, I want them to know where Jesus' story takes them.

While modern conservatives sought to use propositional statements as their guide to truth and doctrine, modern liberals gave theological authority to an historical reconstruction of the biblical text.[18] What resulted from both approaches was a foundational approach to Scripture that moved away from reading the text as narrative. The Bible became a puzzle, and both approaches separated the puzzle and analyzed its pieces. Conservatives took out pieces and held them up to represent certain truth claims, and liberals removed pieces based on their historicity. Both approaches weaken the integrity of the whole and leave us with a pocked image. To move toward a more holistic approach to Scripture and provide youth with thick narratives of the biblical text, we need to resist the temptation to reduce the story to propositions or doctrinal truths.

From biblical authority to biblical authority in Christ. Some Christians have interpreted "biblical authority" to mean that God's Word is all factually true and should be followed as such. Proponents of this view tend to defend the Bible and often look to the Scriptures to provide precise answers to questions that the authors could never have imagined.[19]

The stories, the commandments and the poetry should all be interpreted in light of Jesus—his ministry, his message, his life, his death and his resurrection.[20] Therefore, Christians do not put to death sons or daughters when they curse their parents (Lev 20:9) or follow much of what the Torah demands of the Hebrews, because many of the stipulations differ from what Jesus required of his disciples. For process theologian John Cobb, the

Christian task in interpreting and understanding Scripture begins with Christ—not the words of Christ codified into literal and legalistic ideologies, but the way Jesus points to God's love and calls us to love God and others. He argues that many Christians have an idolatrous understanding of the Bible and have become bound to outdated notions that have nothing to do with faith in Christ.[21]

An example of biblical authority standing over and against authority in Christ can be seen in Christians who spend valuable time, energy and money fighting for and defending public displays of the Ten Commandments. Why would Christians wish to defend or promote the Ten Commandments? There are three versions of the Ten Commandments in Scripture (Ex 20; 34; Deut 5). Which one should we use? Exodus 34 differs from the similar commandments in Exodus 20 and Deuteronomy 5. In Exodus 34, God's new Ten Commandments include these directives: celebrate the Feast of Unleavened Bread; offer the firstborn of every womb to God; celebrate the Festival of Weeks; do not offer the blood of a sacrifice containing yeast; bring the best of your first fruits to the house of the Lord; and do not cook a young goat in its mother's milk.

In addition to this issue, Protestant, Orthodox, Catholic and Jewish traditions number the commandments differently. Even if we ignore the other version of the commandments (Ex 34) and continue with our traditional set, problems emerge when we compare them to Jesus' message. Jesus does not quote any of the Ten Commandments when he is asked, "Which commandment is the first of all?" (Mk 12:28). In the entire Sermon on the Mount, he mentions only three of the commandments (Mt 5:21, 27-28, 33-34). And these commandments are not quoted for followers of Jesus to live by. Instead they were incomplete, and Jesus fulfilled them (made them full and complete)—from murder to anger; from adultery to lust; from swearing falsely to swearing at all. For the Christian, the Ten Commandments are not on par with Jesus' teachings; people can follow all commandments and still abuse and take advantage of their neighbor. They can physically and verbally abuse others, and as long as they do not kill them, they will not have technically broken the Ten Commandments.

In addition to these issues, the Ten Commandments allow room for the belief that there are other gods than God[22] and that slavery and the subjugation of women is acceptable.[23] When it comes to Christian practice, some people have fixated on the right to display the Ten Commandments—a specific listing, a specific numbering—in courts of law or schools. Some evangelical Christians have relegated more authority to the Ten Commandments than to the spirit of Christ.

Scripture never points to itself as having authority, but it does point to Jesus as having all authority (Mt 28:18; Jn 17:2). When we can remove our focus that all of Scripture is equally authoritative in application and interpretation, we can reclaim the life story of Jesus as being central and paradigmatic.[24]

From the sayings of Jesus to Jesus and his sayings. As youth pastors, we call our youth to follow the teachings of Jesus, his actions and his ministry methods. But if we separate Jesus from his teachings and actions, youth can't encounter the identity of Jesus rendered in the narrative accounts. In the pulpit, we must echo not only the preaching of Jesus, but also the Jesus who preaches. Too often we extract Jesus' identity from his parables, teachings and actions. The Gospels, and thus the early church, proclaimed Jesus as the subject of his proclamations.

Many youth lessons and devotionals single out the parables Jesus told. And why not? He told incredible stories. Such lessons are "thin" because the minister becomes the teller of Jesus' parable and not Jesus. If it is an important task of youth ministry to render the identity of Jesus as portrayed in the Gospels, why tell the Gospel stories without the character of Jesus?

The stories of the early church would hardly have made any sense apart from him. The story of the good Samaritan imparts an important moral lesson, but that is all the story will convey if Jesus is excluded. Without Jesus' interaction with the lawyer, including the lawyer's question of inheriting eternal life and the story Jesus then tells to answer the lawyer's question "Who is my neighbor?" a great loss occurs. When Jesus' interaction with the lawyer is included in a sermon or youth lesson, we face issues such as how Jesus defined a neighbor, how he defined eternal life and how he reacted to one who was trying to test him (Lk 10:25-29).

As Christians we are not called to follow Jesus' storytelling method or his stories, but to follow the God-Man as he is described in the stories; thereby, we encounter him.[24] This also happens in some popular narrative preaching styles where the preacher accentuates the movements of the text instead of the one (agent and character) who moves in and through the text.[25] Theologian Charles Campbell writes, "What is important for Christian preaching is not 'stories' in general or even 'homiletical plots,' but rather a specific story that renders the identity of a particular person."[26]

The story of the prodigal son has been told from just about every perspective imaginable: the father losing his son, the son being lost, the older brother and the servant. This story typifies how ministers often make a story their own without any awareness of the one who told the story. Where is Jesus? He appears at the beginning of Luke 15 with the sinners and tax collectors. The Pharisees and scribes are complaining about the company he's keeping (Lk 15:2), to which Jesus tells a trilogy: the stories of the lost sheep, lost coin and lost son.

At the end of the first story, Jesus interjects a statement: "Just so, I tell you, there will be more joy in heaven over one sinner who repents than over ninety-nine righteous persons who need no repentance" (Lk 15:7). At the end of the second story, he makes a similar point, "Just so, I tell you, there is joy in the presence of the angels of God over one sinner who repents" (Lk 15:10). At the end of the third story, Jesus omits his statement about the joy over one sinner who repents, because the third story *is* the story of the joy over one sinner who repents. When Jesus and his interaction with the Pharisees are included, we gain deeper insight into his compassion for the outcast and oppressed. In this light, when we criticize "sinners," we take the position of the Pharisees. And like the older brother, we miss the party.

Including or excluding Jesus in this showdown with the Pharisees recasts our interpretation of the trilogy. The story of the lost son speaks volumes, but it is more transformative when we allow youth to come face to face with Jesus as he counters the blows and barbs of the scribes and Pharisees with a startling reality: joy over one sinner who repents—and the older brother who misses that joy. Without Jesus, we miss his point—and we miss the joy of repentance and forgiveness.

From framing the biblical story around youth's experience to the biblical story framing youth's experience. Youth ministers should use the language and symbols that resonate with their students in order to communicate with them. However, there is a difference between reducing a message to fit a person's frame of reference and presenting a message that opens a door to new frames of reference.

People do not reduce their language, customs or lifestyle to fit a five-year-old's way of knowing. Even though people communicate as best they can with a five-year-old so that the child may understand, they can never completely reduce the world in terms that make absolute sense to the child. Explaining the tragedy of 9/11, for example, or the death of a grandparent proves daunting, and there is not enough vocabulary to convey the totality of the loss. After playing college baseball and coaching an American Legion baseball team, I encountered something more daunting: tee-ball. I knew I was in for a complex season when I met with my players and told them to go to home because we were going to run the bases. They all dropped their heads and with their shoulders slumped began to walk to their parents.

"But we just got here," one girl said, kicking the dirt.

The only home my players knew was the one where they lived, and bases were designated spots for hide-and-seek. Instead of allowing their limited understanding of the game to dictate my coaching, I began collaborating with them, expanding on the pieces they did understand. I walked over to home plate with my tee-ball team and showed them how it was in the shape of a house. We talked about how every time they batted, they would start at the plate that was in the shape of a house, just like most mornings they begin their day at home. A new language and way of being was formed through our participation and use of tee-ball language.

We do a great disservice to our children when we reduce biblical stories to concepts they understand, or worse, simplify and alter the story to project a similar meaning with completely different characters and character actions.[27] Imagine reducing the movie *Avatar* to only what its audience knows prior to the movie. The story is extraordinary because it opens the audience's imagination to an entirely different world and perspective that transforms and shapes them.

The church does not need to translate its language entirely into the vernacular of youth. Our youth should be formed and informed by the language of the church. When we understand the biblical narrative as an optional accessory for our life story, our individual experiences tend to shape the narrative, not the other way around.[28] When we become the authority over the text, we limit and coordinate stories and theological concepts such as salvation, sin and the kingdom of God into our individual experience.

We can grossly diminish issues of racial discrimination, sexual harassment, injustice and other forms of oppression when we simplify them to issues of individual sin.[29] From this lens, we view these issues as individual problems; we assume that if we can eradicate the individual sin, the problems will go away. Once again, this line of thought underestimates the shaping power of relationships through cultural construction. Let's continue to move from an individualistic formation of youth toward the collective formation of youth in relation to adults and children as the church—the body of Christ.

From the individual interpreter to God's community of interpreted individuals. Youth ministry's communal formation through scriptural proclamation has been hindered through individualistic reductions of the biblical story. An emphasis on the meaning of the text for an individual reader encourages reading according to subjective interests.[30] To remain focused solely on the individual interpreter neglects the formation of the youth as a vital part of God's community, which is comprised of individuals who are confronted collectively by God's unfolding story. Individualism blinds us to the collective and social dimensions of life, as illustrated in the book *Habits of the Heart: Individualism and Commitment in American Life*:

> We find ourselves not independently of other people and institutions but through them. We never get to the bottom of ourselves on our own. We discover who we are face to face and side by side with others in work, love, and learning. All of our activity goes on in relationships, groups, associations, and communities ordered by institutional structures and interpreted by cultural patterns of meaning. . . . Finally, we are not simply ends in ourselves, either as individuals or as a society. We are parts of a larger whole that we can neither forget nor imagine in our own image without paying a high price.[31]

Individual interpreters are shaped and influenced by their community and are a product of their community through relational processes. Individualism leads people to believe that their ideas are unique to them and that no one else possesses their thoughts and ideas—that the self exists independently from tradition or community.[32]

Youth are not simply individual interpreters. Community influences and forms the exact methods by which people articulate their choices and interpretations. Youth do not guide their lives as Christians, but their lives, as part of the community, are interpreted and shaped by God's reality as revealed in Jesus, through the biblical stories.

For instance, Santel, an eighth-grader in my ministry, believed that when people hurt him, he should hurt them back. When he encountered Jesus' way of nonviolence and love, he first called it "stupid." He also insisted that he would never let people take advantage of him. The more Santel participated in the church body and the more relationships and stories he was exposed to that involved Jesus and Christians giving up the desire to hurt someone for the greater good of love, he understood that surrendering was the most powerful path he could choose.

Santel moved from a preoccupation with his own individual hurts to stopping the hurt he created with others. He may not have ever known such a way of life without participating in our faith community and without being shaped by Jesus' stories. The church is a particular people that is interpreted by a "constitutive narrative."[33] The biblical narratives that the community shares and explores together have a powerful way of co-shaping youth and children. When people allow the biblical story to re-narrate their life story, God's reign is revealed, and community emerges.[34]

A youth ministry that centers on ministering individually to youth may reinforce the problem of individualism. At best, this type of youth ministry falls prey to the assumption that youth ministry is primarily about ministering to youth.[35] In many youth ministry settings, the ministry exists on the church fringes. If youth are never integrated and assimilated into the larger church body, how will they ever become functioning members of any church?[36]

Community comes before the individual, and the individual is shaped through the relationships and stories of a particular community.[37] Youth and adults are predisposed to act in certain ways, pursue certain goals and avow certain tastes according to certain stories they heard growing up.[38] I am not proposing that churches ignore youth or their needs, but that we minister to them within their communal and relational context as co-agents of the church.

Faith is not limited to the individual, but rather is a journey into the practices of the church (her symbols, signs, rituals, language and stories) that help youth frame their understanding of the world in God's story.[39] Therefore, *the task of the youth minister* is not *sola* youth ministry, but serving the whole church through assimilation of youth. *The task of the church* is to help youth become a vital part of God's reign by teaching them the language, practices, traditions and customs of the body of Christ.[40]

Youth ministers can break the ice and open a conversation between adults and youth. This opening allows a way for stories to narrate the lives of the entire faith community. Shared stories provide narrative templates for youth and adults, and they can serve as interpretive guides that frame and organize the perceptions of all future stories.[41] Sharing biblical stories with a gathering of youth and adults creates and sustains the ministry through a common narrative. Alasdair MacIntyre said, "For the story of my life is always embedded in the story of those communities from which I derive my identity."[42] In other words, the tried-and-true campfire method works; when people gather to tell and hear stories, they form a bond that defines those in the circle.

CONCLUSION

Seventeen-year-old Natalie had never attended a youth ministry, and she experienced a story that was a different story from the ones she'd received from other caring and loving youth organizations. During her first Wednesday night in a small group of high school youth, she encountered Jesus and his conversation with the disciples about power and greatness (Mk 10:35-52). She was baffled with Jesus' counter-maneuver as he told the disciples that to be great, you must serve others first. The story of—and contrast between—blind Bartimaeus and the disciples (the blind man sees Jesus and cries out for mercy, while the disciples are blind as they plead for power and status) opened Natalie's eyes to a new portrait of Jesus. The stories allowed her room to put power and greatness in an entirely new frame—one shaped by Jesus and the biblical story.

REFLECTION QUESTIONS

1. Articulate how the life and ministry of Jesus make his birth, death and resurrection meaningful and how neglecting the life of Jesus denies youth a context in which to situate the significance of his death and resurrection.

2. In what ways could theology classes, biblical studies classes and preaching classes cause the fragmentation and reduction of the biblical story? How could they enhance the story?

3. Reflect on popular devotionals written today. How do many of these devotionals ignore the powerful narratives of Scripture?

4. Write examples of how you have seen the biblical story reduced to fragments and parts. Beside each of these examples, write how you think they may have altered the meaning of the biblical story.

5. Many youth lessons and devotionals seek to explain the text to students. How would you explore the text with youth without rushing into explaining it with your own biases and assumptions? How might this be more beneficial to students than explaining the text to them?

6. Write down propositions that are meaningful to you. How might you expand and frame these propositions with the biblical story to provide more meaning and depth?

7. Pick a passage from the Gospels and focus on Jesus' words. Think about how people might preach on this passage, write about this passage and live out this passage. After you have thoroughly enmeshed yourself in Jesus' words, familiarize yourself with his character. How does the Gospel author render the identity of Jesus in this passage? What are Jesus' actions, movements and interactions? Who is he interacting with, and why does he speak? After a thorough reading of Jesus' identity and character in this Gospel story, how does this give you a broader picture and add meaning to Jesus' words? How does understanding the identity and character of Jesus shift your interpretation of his words?

8. Summarize your understanding of the gospel in two or three sentences. Circle the words that are given a specific meaning in your Christian context (for example, *savior, Jesus, life*). If these words were no longer used or valued, how would you articulate your understanding of the gospel? Reflect on the importance of using Christian language to provide youth with the Christian story to form their lives.

9. What are some ways you have seen the biblical story reduced to the experiences of children or youth? How might you tell the biblical story in such a way that frames their experiences rather than reducing the biblical story to their experiences?

10. The community shapes our understandings. How might youth ministry function differently if we moved our focus from individual youth toward our relational engagements with youth through the whole body of Christ? How can this enhance the importance and value of individual youth?

11

Life Story in Christ

Every year I ask my college youth ministry class, "What is the purpose and message of a youth pastor?"

"Jesus," a student responds.

"What about Jesus?" I ask.

"To proclaim Jesus and his message," a student says, and other students nod their heads.

"What is Jesus' message? What does Jesus say is his purpose for being sent? What is the message that Jesus sends his disciples out to proclaim?"

Silence. When I encourage them to voice their ideas, they say things like "Jesus' primary purpose for being sent is to

> . . . forgive our sins.
> . . . save us from hell.
> . . . so we can ask him into our hearts as our personal savior.
> . . . show us the way to God.
> . . . get us into heaven with him.
> . . . enter into a relationship with us.
> . . . love God and neighbor."

Although some of these answers may be a part of Jesus' message, they are not his primary purpose for being sent. After asking this question for several years to Christian discipleship majors and exhausting the majority of their responses, I discovered many of them did not know what Jesus claimed to be his primary message and reason for being sent. If youth pastors are going to proclaim anything about Jesus, we should know and understand Jesus and his central message.

THE CENTRAL STORY

Jesus proclaims the good news of the kingdom of God, and he sends his disciples out to do the same (Mt 10:5-15; Lk 9:1-6). In Luke 4:43, Jesus says, "I must proclaim the good news of the kingdom of God to the other cities also; for I was sent for this purpose." The Synoptic Gospels all emphasize the kingdom of God as central in the proclamation of Jesus: "From that time Jesus began to proclaim, 'Repent, for the kingdom of heaven has come near' (Mt 4:17). Mark 1:14-15 states, "Now after John was arrested, Jesus came to Galilee, proclaiming the good news of God, and saying, 'The time is fulfilled, and the kingdom of God has come near; repent, and believe in the good news.'"

The terms *repentance, gospel* or *good news (euanggelion)* and *kingdom* were all familiar, highly charged political terms to Jesus' audience. *Good news* or its plural, *good tidings*, were proclaimed in the pronouncement of Caesar Augustus with his birth and reign.[1] It would not have been uncommon to hear someone proclaim, "The time is here, the kingdom (or empire) of Caesar is at hand; repent and believe in the gospel." However, such proclamations would be made only when a new and contrasting reign and rule was established. Jesus' proclamation of repentance, coupled with the kingdom of God being at hand, would have raised the suspicion and curiosity of all within earshot.

Rome declared that it had brought good news to all people as the Romans established *Pax Romana* (Roman Peace). Yet they achieved said "peace" through war, crucifixions and heavy taxation. Jesus proclaimed a different kingdom, a different gospel, than the one established by Caesar and his puppet king, Herod.

How do we know that Jesus proclaiming God's reign is not the same as Caesar's reign and rule? John doesn't use the term "kingdom of God" as much as the Synoptic Gospels do, but the importance and uniqueness of the kingdom appears in Jesus' conversations with Nicodemus and Pilate (Jn 3:1-5; 18:33-37). Jesus' language to Nicodemus reveals that no one can *see* or *enter* the kingdom of God without being born again and without being born of water and Spirit. Jesus' proclamation of the kingdom is something that can be seen and entered, but it takes a new way of living and seeing. Jesus' kingdom proclamation had spread far enough that Pilate's first question to Jesus was, "Are you King of the Jews?" (Jn 18:33). Jesus answered

Pilate's question with a question: Had Pilate concluded that Jesus was king of the Jews or did he get the idea from others?

"I am not a Jew, am I?" Pilate shot back. "Your own nation and the chief priests have handed you over to me. What have you done?"

Jesus answered, "My kingdom is not from this world. If my kingdom were from this world, my followers would be fighting to keep me from being handed over to the Jews. But as it is, my kingdom is not from here."

We learn that the world's violence does not dictate this kingdom. We know from the Gospel of John that Jesus' kingdom is such a paradigm shift that it requires a rebirthing to learn how to talk, walk and live within God's new reign.

We also know that Jesus' kingdom is distinct from Caesar's and Herod's because of Jesus' use of the word *repentance*. For youth who feel abandoned, who do not feel that they belong, who long to connect, inviting them into God's relational reign requires repentance. In many youth ministry circles, the word *repentance* is popularly known as "taking a turn" or "a 180 from sin." This idea assumes repentance is only about sin, when it ought to include the portal to God's kingdom through it. We can become obsessed with managing our sins instead of trying to see and enter God's relational reign. Beginning with individual sin is like focusing on the wrong turns and dead ends in a maze and not looking ahead to how we can live without being entrapped. In youth ministry we tend to get more caught up in managing sins—which often are defined by the church we attend—than living and loving in the kingdom of God.

The kingdom of God is mostly concerned with relationships: our relationship with God and our relationship with others. Within this framework, sin can be relinquished from the realm of rules and regulations and best understood as hindering relationships. From time to time, youth want me to give them a quick checklist of sins. I receive questions like, "After people turn twenty-one, is it a sin to drink?" And with most of their questions I have a similar response: "It depends on our relationships." Drinking responsibly after age twenty-one may not hinder anyone's relationship until he is drinking around a recovering alcoholic. The sin is not alcohol; it is the neglect of the relationship. Eating a cheeseburger appears innocent until we do so in front of a starving child. With this understanding of sin, we are less likely to limit sin to originating or being contained within the individual.

THE CRITIC'S VOICE

Criticism

What about the body of Christ?

Response

I've found individualism so pervasive among my youth that no matter how many times I present relational lessons on the kingdom of God and body of Christ, they continue to frame their understanding within their individualistic view of culture. The relational reign of God is reduced to how God "relationally" reigns in them, and participation in the body of Christ is always about their part.

This reduction of the kingdom of God and body of Christ is precisely what Paul was confronting in the Corinthian church. I found that I couldn't just talk about the kingdom of God and body of Christ; I had to help them see the relational aspect of both messages. By the time youth reach college age, they have an extensive language about their part or gift in the body of Christ. When we begin with the kingdom of God and the body of Christ within that kingdom, we may gain an altogether different portrait.

Therefore, we can address the larger relational picture where sin lurks most.

Repentance is about turning from patterns of living that distort our genuine humanity.[2] Jesus' proclamation of the good news of the kingdom of God, coupled with repentance, was as shocking and transformative as hearing the words, "We are sinking," on the *RMS Titanic*. In order to see the gravity of their situation, those on board the *Titanic* had to repent; they had to take on a whole new way of seeing their ship. The *Titanic* was no longer a vessel of luxury and enjoyment; it was now a hazard that threatened their lives. Yet when first confronted with those words, some passengers couldn't physically see the ship sinking, so they hesitated to board the life boats.

Jesus announces the good news of the kingdom of God; similar to passengers on the *Titanic*, those who do not repent will miss seeing what is in

> *As Paul reminds the local Corinthian church, we are never to forget that we are always an extension or part of the body of Christ. We are not simply born with gifts; our gifts emerge from our participation in the body of Christ. We may have a wonderful singing voice, but not until we begin participating within the body do we learn whether or not our singing is needed to help the body of Christ become more like Christ. Through participation within the body, we may discover gifts that God bestows on us through our relationships.*
>
> *A student, Adam, went overseas with his gifts of preaching and teaching, only to discover his Western style of communicating from the pulpit is not valued in Eastern cultures. Adam's gift shifted to singing for children in a village who needed an encouraging song.*
>
> *Our spiritual gifts emerge from—and are sustained in—relationships. I am not an ear because I bring my "earness" to the body; I am an ear because of the body. We may have the gift of singing, speaking, listening and so on in one body of believers, but that gift may not be needed in the next body in which we participate. We may develop a new gift that we never knew we had.*

their midst. The word *repentance* combines return from captivity (exile) and new vision.[3]

The kingdom of God is not an individual kingdom or located "within" a person. Jesus told the Pharisees the kingdom was upon them (Lk 11:20) and in their midst (Lk 17:20). Some scholars have translated the "among you" or "in your midst" in Luke 17:20 as "within you." With such a translation and our ever-increasing individualism, God's vast and expansive kingdom is reduced to being inside the person.

As Baptist minister Walter Rauschenbusch noticed long ago, God's relational reign "has been dropped as the primary and comprehensive aim of Christianity and personal salvation has been substituted for it . . . pushing out of sight the collective idea of the kingdom of God on earth."[4] If we begin with the individual and personal salvation as our starting points for ministry, the kingdom of God will be secondary to the individual. When we make salvation about something contained within the individual, we have turned it into a possession. Repentance should usher in a kingdom of living in relationship with God and others, not in our private kingdoms and queendoms.

THE KINGDOM MANIFESTO

In the Sermon on the Mount, Jesus proclaimed that everyone should strive first for the kingdom of God and his righteousness.[5] "But strive first for the kingdom of God and his righteousness, and all these things will be given to you as well" (Mt 6:33). The entire Sermon on the Mount can be understood as Jesus' kingdom manifesto concerning what life looks like for participants in the kingdom of God.[6] He stood up and poured verbal blessing on those who were the poor in spirit, meek, mourners, merciful, peacemakers, persecuted, pure in heart, reviled and accused (Mt 5:1-11). He changed the focus from murder to anger and slanderous words (Mt 5:21-22); from conflict and lawsuits to reconciliation (Mt 5:23-26); from adultery to how we survey others (Mt 5:27-30); from divorce to faithfulness (Mt 5:31-32); from lying to honesty (Mt 5:33-37); from vengeance to sacrificial love and justice; from loving neighbor and hating enemies to loving neighbor *and* enemies (Mt 5:43-48); from public displays of giving, praying and fasting to private and humble spiritual disciplines (Mt 6:1-8); from concerning ourselves with possessions on earth to focusing in our relationship with God (Mt 6:19-24). Jesus said worrying about tomorrow limits us, and he encouraged us to seek the kingdom first (Mt 6:25-34). Jesus modeled not only how to live but also how to pray: for God's kingdom to come and his will to be done *on earth* as it is in heaven. At the end of the Sermon on the Mount, Jesus reminded his listeners that his words were not lip service, but they were practices on which we build our lives.

The kingdom of God is an interactive process between the human and divine.[7] Believing and participating in the kingdom of God means believing and participating in the way of Jesus. It means encountering the life story of Christ and answering his call when he says, "Follow me," loving and serving the way he loved and served. The kingdom of God is an invitation for others to come and see how we live following the spirit of Christ and then live like us—a true communal program.[8]

And the community that Jesus established is one of mutuality and equality from the bottom up, in contrast to the hierarchically structured Roman society.[9]

LIFE STORY IN CHRIST

The evolving story of self is guided by some kind of culturally interpretive framework—whether or not one is aware of it.[10] As mentioned in chapter 4, interpretation precedes experience. Youth learn to classify, differentiate, organize and arrange their life story according to the classifications, differentiations and causal and thematic coordinations that they have learned from others.

Assuming that wholeness and love for all humanity are important attributes to acquire, what story will youth or adults use to help them live a whole and complete life? What does it mean to be fully human? Inhuman? What do the terms *wholeness* and *human* mean? People's definitions of these terms and answers to these questions vary according to the stories they have used to frame their understanding of the world. Learning to coordinate with others through culture's stories enables youth to think about such questions and ultimately discover ways to articulate their understanding of such concepts in their own life stories. To pose the question another way, "What stories will youth turn to that will allow them to structure and link their life story in a way that promotes wholeness and love for all humanity?"

The ultimate symbol of interpretation that governs all experiences for the Christian community came not through writings, language or speech, but in flesh. "Christ, who, though he was in the form of God, did not regard equality with God as something to be exploited, but emptied himself" to co-exist and co-construct with other human beings.[11] Christ humbled himself and entered humanity through relational constraints. God allowed his identity through Jesus to depend on humans and their proclamation of his good news and kingdom.

Youth ministry should be about providing youth with the framework that enables them to story their identity in Christ, so that the love of God as revealed in Jesus becomes the integrative, configuring interpretive tool in molding their identity. The incarnation is central. God did not proclaim his kingdom simply through stories or some kind of inner revelation that youth have not grasped, but by emptying himself and becoming the living, transformative, paradigmatic practice of love.

A paradigmatic narrative incorporates powerful storied events (paradigmatic events and symbols) that should shape reality for both youth ministers and their youth. It should become the main narrative that forms and structures all of our other narratives.[12] From this perspective, we exist as an extension of God's relational and creative activity. In this paradigm, God's relational activity with humanity is always first. To be Christian means to be in relationship with God through Jesus.

REPENTANCE FROM INDIVIDUALISM

The narrative construction of the self is essential for establishing meaning and direction in a person's life.[13] Personal narratives risk solidifying a boundary between the self and others, as each person may understand his story as a separate and individual journey.[14] As a faith community, Christians do not establish separate journeys, but rather journey together as one. The Christian's life is not her own, but she submits her life story to the greater life story in Christ. As Dietrich Bonhoeffer stated, "'We with Christ'—for Christ is Emmanuel, 'God with us.'"[15]

When people choose to follow Jesus, they are confronted with his identity, recorded in the biblical stories. Christians allow the stories of Jesus to form and frame their lives as they enter a faith relationship, trusting and participating in the Christian community that has preceded them. In essence, they trust the Spirit of God to continue forming them through the stories that have formed others.

Like the disciples, when people are confronted with the identity of Christ, there is always the calling to follow. "If anyone would come after me, he must deny himself and take up his cross daily and follow me. For whoever wants to save his life will lose it, but whoever loses his life for me will save it. What good is it for a man to gain the whole world, and yet lose or forfeit his very self?" (Lk 9:23-25 NIV 1984).

The flow of the biblical narratives reveals that the individual becomes a self only by accepting the divine invitation to love and be responsible for the human other.[16] Therefore, the self is one "who discovers itself through losing itself in and with and for the other."[17]

Martin Luther King Jr. told a story about asking a student to find a quotation that expressed his feelings toward the struggle for racial reconciliation. The student typed the following quotation and left it on King's desk:

> I sought my soul, but my soul I could not see,
> I sought my God, but he eluded me,
> I sought my brother, and I found all three.[18]

The author of 1 John penned a similar statement:

> We love because he first loved us. Those who say, "I love God," and hate their brothers or sisters, are liars; for those who do not love a brother or sister whom they have seen, cannot love God whom they have not seen. The commandment we have from him is this: those who love God must love their brothers and sisters also. (1 Jn 4:19-21)

People have a plethora of life stories from which to form and revise their life story. The Christian message proclaims that there is one life story that directs us toward what it means to be human: the life story of Jesus Christ. As Gerard Loughlin says,

> Christian truth has never been a matter of matching stories against reality. It has always been a life story that comes first, against which all other things are to be matched. This life story is what 'truth' means in Christianity. . . . The story is imagined for us before it is re-imagined by us: the story is given to us.[19]

Structuring our life according to the life of Jesus creates a new narrative. Our new identity is formed as Jesus invites us to participate in the community of God. This community shapes personal identity and contributes to the "formation of the self by mediating a communal narrative—a history."[20] Furthermore, one of youth ministry's ongoing tasks is to help youth construct personal identities "according to the paradigmatic narrative of the Christian faith community, with its expectant anticipation of the eschatological future."[21] Through "storying" to youth the paradigmatic narrative of Jesus, they are presented with an opportunity to become, at least partially, the embodiment of Jesus' narrative, which constitutes their relational identities in Christ (see Eph 1:7-13). As Kenda Dean states,

> Normally, an adolescent takes in her representation of the other and eventually makes it her own. But imitating Christ does not make Jesus part of her; she becomes part of him. The Christ-event transforms adolescents into people who actually do "have it together" as they repent and identify with Jesus

Christ instead of with the piecemeal fragments of consumer culture. . . .

Strictly speaking, the Christian view of self is not unitary anyway; Christian identity is irreducibly relational, involving the persons of the Trinity as well as the individual and the individual's community identifications.[22]

Youth construct their identity in Christ by allowing him and his story to construct their identity. Thus the paradigmatic narrative of Jesus provides the thematic and causal connections of youth's life narratives, which shifts from an anthropocentric narrative with cultural themes to a christocentric narrative with christological themes.[23] Here youth find their identity and humanity through the life, passion, resurrection and ongoing ministry of Jesus.

Paul's encounter with the risen Lord shifted his understanding of life in God to life in God through Christ. An event that was interpreted by Paul as an execution was restoried as a revelation.[24] This revelatory encounter with the spirit of Jesus brought Paul face to face with the Savior's true identity. For Paul, Jesus was no longer an executed criminal, but the one through whom people would gain life and a deeper understanding of God.

Answering Jesus' call to follow him, Paul had to die to his old identity and its way of life, and rise to a new identity, a new life.[25] The themes of God's love through Christ restructure and restory those identities. In a fragmented and individualistically driven society, most youth who restory their lives in Christ will discover a more holistic way of living. The narratives of Christ and the Christian community are opposed to many of the popular narratives of society. As Borg and Crossan state,

> But life "in Christ" for Paul was not primarily about a new personal identity for individuals. Paul's understanding was very different from a widespread understanding of the role of "religion" and the purpose of "spirituality" in modern Western culture, where they are often thought of as primarily private, individual matters, even though many Christians would say that being Christian also means being part of a church. For Paul, life "in Christ" was *always* a communal matter. This was not simply because "it's important to be part of a church," but because his purpose, his passion, was to create communities whose life together embodied an alternative to the normalcy of the "wisdom of this world."[26]

The kind of love that Christ modeled and Paul lived out identifies and stands against systems of oppression and domination. In Jesus' demonstration and approach to people, love and justice can't be separated. "Justice without love can be brutal, and love without justice can be banal. Love is the heart of justice, and justice is the social form of love."[27]

Jesus, Paul and other Christians were not executed for saying, "Love one another," but because their "love one another" extended to the unacceptable, the outcasts, the nonreligious, the enemies. Paul recognized that the Christian struggle was not against individuals (enemies of flesh and blood), but "against the rulers, against the authorities, against the cosmic powers of this present darkness, against the spiritual forces of evil in the heavenly places" (Eph 6:12). Martin Luther King Jr. offered a similar sentiment when speaking to an audience of young men and women, reminding them that their battle was not against individuals:

> This was always a cry that we had to set before people that our aim is not to defeat the white community, not to humiliate the white community, but to win the friendship of all of the persons who had perpetrated this system in the past. The end of violence or the aftermath of violence is bitterness. The aftermath of nonviolence is reconciliation and the creation of a beloved community. . . .
>
> Then we had to make it clear also that the nonviolent resister seeks to attack the evil system rather than individuals who happen to be caught up in the system. And this is why I say from time to time that the struggle in the South is not so much the tension between white people and Negro people. The struggle is rather between justice and injustice, between the forces of light and the forces of darkness. . . .
>
> And so at the center of our movement stood the philosophy of love. The attitude that the only way to ultimately change humanity and make for the society that we all long for is to keep love at the center of our lives.[28]

Accordingly, when a youth learns the story of God's love through Jesus, his life stories are chapters in God's metanarrative. This is not just a story that the youth tells, but one in which the youth lives and participates. Jesus becomes the form of the church as its members, including youth and children, collectively embody the stories of Jesus. As Ray Anderson states,

> The form of Christ in the world thus becomes the paradigm for the church in the world. This form is not a principle or style to be adopted by an already existing institution, nor is it a "shape" determined by the need of the world. Rather, it is conformity to Christ who is in the world as one who shares in

human solidarity as the incarnation of God in human flesh. The form of the church is thus incarnational; not another incarnation, but a continuation of the one incarnate life of God in the form of Jesus Christ.[29]

As the Gospel of John declares, "The Word [God's word, God's story] became flesh." The church becomes an embodiment of the story of Christ by following after his story that was before them, is now with them and extends in front of them through his resurrected spirit. To the extent that Christians are able to take the form of Jesus in the world, they bring wholeness to all of God's creation. This means pointing to the "human" by whom all humanity needs forming.

Youth ministry can play a major role in healing teenagers who are victims of societal pressures of neglect and abandonment. It can be a collaboration with teenagers in becoming functioning members of the larger church body. Some wounds are deep, and even the best therapists can't create a healing communal atmosphere in their one-on-one sessions. The church is a community that functions as an agent within the reign of God, where youth should be able to find belonging, encouragement, support, appreciation and respect.

Jesus' gospel of the kingdom of God emphasizes the importance of relationships and inclusion. The only people not included are the ones that exclude themselves by being exclusive toward others and rejecting the love of God that we see in Christ. Nevertheless, the kingdom of God continues to advance and continues to love—even those who reject the King's inclusive love.

Jesus said people will know that we are his disciples by how we love one another. Do people know we are Jesus' disciples? Is the church tattooed with God's love? Or do we deter them from anything "Jesus" through how we abuse and argue with one another?

If Jesus' central proclamation is the creation of a kingdom community, it is problematic for Jesus' disciples to restrict his message to an individual focus. Archbishop Desmond Tutu and Douglas Carlton Abrams wrote a children's book that captures the essence of the kingdom of God in what they call "God's Dream":

> Dear Child of God . . . Do you dream about being free to do what your heart desires? Or about being treated like a full person no matter how young you might be? God dreams about people sharing. God dreams about people caring. God dreams that we reach out and hold one another's hands and play

one another's games and laugh with one another's hearts. But God does not force us to love one another. Dear Child of God, it does happen that we get angry and hurt one another. Soon we start to feel sad and very alone. Sometimes we cry, and God cries with us. But when we say we're sorry and forgive one another, we wipe away our tears and God's tears too. Each of us carries a piece of God's heart with us. And when we love one another, the pieces of God's heart are made whole. God dreams that every one of us will see that we are all brothers and sisters . . . even if we have different mommies and daddies or live in different faraway lands. Even if we speak different languages . . . have different eyes or different skin. Even if you are taller and I am smaller . . . Dear Child of God, do you know how to make God's dream come true? It is really quite easy. As easy as sharing, loving, caring. As easy as holding, playing, laughing. As easy as knowing we are family because we are all God's children.[30]

Under God's reign and rule, youth learn that they matter. They are the greatest in the kingdom of God![31] They have an incredible opportunity as part of the body of Christ to surrender to God's reign and rule through loving, sharing, caring and establishing a new culture. As the cliché goes, "This is easier said than done." But this cliché fails to account for the fact that what people say shapes what they do. Perhaps a better way of articulating cultural transformation in youth ministry is to say, "This is as easy as what is said and what is done."

CONCLUSION

A youth pastor wanted to know what God's kingdom would look like if it existed in her youth ministry environment. What differences would exist between living in God's relational reign and living in the absence of it? One night she dreamed God showed her the difference. God placed a door in front of her and said, "Beyond this door you will experience the absence of my relational reign." The youth pastor expected to see an environment of torment: flames, disaster, evil. To her surprise, the room looked like a high school cafeteria. The tables were covered in food. All the youth were sitting around their tables, and adults were sitting at a separate table.

As she approached the tables, she noticed that everyone was malnourished, yet they held long forks in their hands. The only way they could pick up food was with these forks, and they could hold the forks only at the bottom. One teen had managed to pick up food with his fork, and he was trying over and over again to get the food into his mouth, but the fork was too long. The adults had the same problem. As she stood by the table, she heard those sitting around the table cursing God. "Why did you create me this way? I hate my body! I hate the wretched people you have placed me with. You put all of this food in front of us, but we can't feed ourselves."

The youth pastor continued to hear the groans of those who hated themselves, their bodies, their environment, their situation and, most intensely, God. She could not take it anymore. The suffering was too immense. Why would God do such a thing to them? She begged to see God's kingdom.

God placed another door in front of her. She opened the door and was shocked. It was the exact same cafeteria with the same food on the tables. As she walked inside, she heard music and saw people dancing. Everyone was well nourished. A group of children and adults were creating their own music with objects in the room, and they were singing and dancing. Not far from the exuberant dance floor were others laughing, playing games and sharing stories. The room was filled with praise for God and his creation.

How could this be? Everything in the cafeteria was the same, but the youth and adults had constructed a completely different environment. She began to cry. "I don't get it. What makes the youth and adults in this cafeteria so different? I want this in our church."

She noticed a few teens taking a break to eat. She rushed to their table. Slowly, she saw what made all the difference in their world: One youth picked up food with his fork, extended it across the table and fed his neighbor. His neighbor reached across the table with her fork and fed him.[32]

The exact same situation and environment can be either a heaven or a hell on earth, depending on how we view our relationships and what we do with them. If we begin with our individual selves, we are not able to feed ourselves. If we begin with the individual other, we may feed the other and starve ourselves. If we begin with relationships, we sustain one another. What we do with each other matters. The more we recognize this, the more we will discover our continuous connectivity *and* the power of God's love in our relationships with our youth.

REFLECTION QUESTIONS

1. How does beginning with the kingdom of God help us move beyond individualism?

2. How can understanding repentance as doing a 180 from sin limit the depth of how Jesus' audience would have understood it?

3. Articulate your understanding of the kingdom of God and how it affects your youth ministry practices.

4. Consider how Paul's encounter with Jesus altered his entire life story. Write about some of the things Paul had to revise in his life story when he encountered Jesus as Lord.

5. The conclusion consists of a parable about the kingdom of God and how the same environment can be transformed with the love of God. What might your youth ministry look like if your youth embraced relationships and God's love in this way?

Relational Responsibility

I arrived at the church ten minutes before our youth ministry meeting. Many of the students were waiting in the parking lot, hanging around their cars and socializing. The serene picture of relationships forming came to a halt with squealing tires, smoke and the aroma of burned rubber. David, a senior in our youth ministry, was making donuts with his car while other church members were witnessing his lack of concern for our newly painted parking lot. Children were waiting for him to finish so they could cross the parking lot to the playground. When David decided he had only so much rubber left on his tires, he pulled back to his usual parking spot, got out of his car and smiled in admiration of the black cloud he'd left behind.

What would you say or do if you were the youth pastor?

Who is responsible for the reckless driving? David, who was driving the vehicle, right? A few years before, I would have thought so. I was taught to view human action and behavior as the result of individual choices and decisions. If I would have arrived at the church ten minutes later, I would have asked, "Who is responsible for the black donuts on our newly paved parking lot?" In asking this question, I would have been looking for the individual to blame for his or her poor choice. I would have approached David in a loving way and talked with him about his poor decision. I would have told him to clean up the parking lot and to apologize to the church members who were present (including the youth).

From years of youth ministry experience, I know this approach would have allowed David to think about what he did and would have reduced the chances of him doing it again. He would have thought about how he did not consider that the church had just paid thousands of dollars to repave and paint the parking lot. He would have thought about how irresponsible he had been with his car and how he had put others at danger—especially the children and himself. I would have addressed these things because they would have been the natural response that my individualistic tradition insists on. In essence, I would have tried to fix David's internal workings (his thoughts) so that his outward actions would be appropriate.

This was youth ministry before I practiced relational responsibility. Relational responsibility begins with an emphasis on relationships first. What are the relational dynamics that formed David, and how do they intersect with the relationships of those who were present (including me)? Would David have burned donuts without anyone around? How much thinking did David really do before he performed such actions?

I attempted an exercise in relational responsibility. I playfully asked David, "Why would you do such a thing?"

"I don't know. It just seemed like fun," David said, as he patted the hood of his car.

I turned the question to his friends: "Why would David burn donuts on our newly painted parking lot?"

His brother replied, "He was showing off for the girls."

"Aha." I turned to the group of girls that David was attempting to impress, and I asked them why they shouldn't be blamed for David's actions.

"Someone did not do a good job communicating to him that girls are not impressed or amused by such antics," Emily said.

I turned back to David. "Should I blame your parents for not telling you that girls are not impressed by such things?"

Before he had a chance to respond, I asked, "Or should I blame myself? I should have told you that doing donuts in our newly paved and painted parking lot is not permitted. Wait a minute! It's not my fault either; it's the church's fault. We have a 'No skateboarding' sign, but we do not have a 'No donuts in the parking lot' sign." David and a few students laughed.

"What about the children?" I asked in a more serious tone.

"What children? I didn't see any kids around." David frowned.

"There were children near the sanctuary who were trying to cross the parking lot to the playground. Fortunately, they decided to wait, because you couldn't see them. But I assumed that you were just trying to keep them from the playground because you wanted the swings all to yourself."

David laughed and said, "I do enjoy the swings, but I really didn't see the kids."

"Okay, David, be honest. Why did you do it?" I asked.

"Well, I can't really do anything else in my car," he said. I looked at David's beat-up, rundown car, and I looked around at all the newer cars surrounding it.

"You're right, David. If anyone is to blame, it's your car. If your car could go faster, you would be speeding; if your car could go zero to sixty in four seconds, you would race; if your car was new and sportier, you could just let it sit while others admired it. But no, your car is none of those things, and your car demands some kind of unique attention."

Through playing my silly blame game, David and several of our youth were able to see a lot of other relational factors and stories involved in a split-second decision. David and I continued our conversation, centered on the relationships that had helped lead to his decision and created a scene in our church parking lot.

I never had to address this issue with David again. And David, without being prompted, offered to apologize to the children and adults, and he offered to clean up the marks. And a few of our youth offered to help him.

I didn't seem to take David's action too seriously, did I? What if David was intoxicated while he was spinning donuts? What if the car he was driving was stolen for drug money? And what if it had been my car? Would I have taken these situations more gravely? Would I have scolded and condemned David for his behavior? Obviously, when illegal activity is involved, certain actions must take place, but my attention would continue to be on our relationships.

My approach to most problems in youth ministry has changed because of how I understand responsibility and how we shape each other in the moment of our interactions. To me, responsibility used to mean taking problems seriously and holding the individual accountable. However, when I begin with relationships and the life story of Jesus, I gain a different picture of responsibility.

BEYOND INDIVIDUAL RESPONSIBILITY

Responsibility in the Western world has rested primarily on the shoulders of the individual. In academic training and the American justice system, responsibility has been understood to be related to individual choice.[1] If a problem occurs with our youth, we usually search for the individual who is responsible. When behavior outside the normal conventions for a youth-ministry environment occurs, most pastors look for the people who are at fault, those who can be blamed—as if blame can be clearly delimited amid a sea of relationships and relational influences. If youth ministry is to practice living in the kingdom of God and being the body of Christ in the midst of God's relational reign, responsibility is shared and communal.[2]

This is not an invitation for the individual to be responsible to his or her relationships. It's an invitation to recognize our connection in the ongoing process of relational formation. The night David tested his car's limits, I was intent on remembering that my actions with him and my youth were constructing our stories. I was able to keep our relationships at the center of our discussion. The move was not from blaming one person to blaming several, but rather to recognizing that more factors were involved than individual choice and decision, and we were all connected.

Discussing and emphasizing the relational responsibilities youth and adults have toward each other does not disregard the action of the individual. When we allow space for a broader and deeper understanding of responsibility, we share responsibility for the behavior of youth and love and encourage each other to stem negative behavior.

Relational responsibility helps youth comprehend their actions and the actions of others. It also generates a broader emphasis on how our choices are constrained within particular frameworks and how those choices affect and influence others. This form of responsibility is much more effective than the traditional modes of individual blame and punishment. The emphasis moves from the individual to a communal sharing of responsibility and action.

In ministry, we talk frequently about loving, helping and caring for others. There was a time when I did such a thing, and I almost destroyed myself. I have also loved and cared for myself to the neglect of others. What happens when we begin with the kingdom of God as our framework for love? What happens when our love and focus is placed on the relationship and not on one individual or the other? What happens when we see God in our relational connectivity?

Paul expressed this responsibility to others in God's kingdom by

THE CRITIC'S VOICE

Criticism

What about Christian accountability partners? Isn't that being relationally responsible?

Response

Accountability partners can focus on their responsibility for their relationship to each other and God. However, the way some view accountability may hinder relationships rather than help them. What is the purpose of an accountability partner? The general response is "holding someone accountable to their walk with God." The accountability partner focuses on whether or not the other person is carrying out spiritual disciplines (such as prayer and reading the Bible). And the person takes action when his partner fails.

I appreciate the story of the paralytic who is lowered through the roof by his friends. "When Jesus saw their faith*, he said to the paralytic, 'Son, your sins are forgiven'" (Mk 2:5, emphasis added). The man's friends were not holding him accountable for sins. They saw beyond his condition, and they took on a shared responsibility for him.*

What if we moved our focus from sin and accountability to love and encouragement? I love the title of the parenting book Why Can't You Catch Me Being Good? *by Edythe Denkin. Denkin illustrates how focusing on the bad does not encourage a child to overcome it. However, if we focus on the good that they do, they will be less likely to do the bad. As discussed earlier, it does not help our youth to focus on their problems; it helps when we find ways to empower them and thicken their narratives with the life story of Jesus.*

Perhaps we can change the name from "accountability partners" to "encouraging partners." Thereby the person moves from "holding" one "accountable" to co-creating an encouraging relationship that motivates both partners to deepen their relationship with God and others.

reminding his readers to be aware of the things that destroy relationships and lead to dissension:

> We do not live to ourselves, and we do not die to ourselves. If we live, we live to the Lord, and if we die, we die to the Lord; so then, whether we live or whether we die, we are the Lord's. . . . Let us therefore no longer pass judgment on one another, but resolve instead never to put a stumbling block or hindrance in the way of another. If your brother or sister is being injured by what you eat, you are no longer walking in love. Do not let what you eat cause the ruin of one for whom Christ died. . . . For the kingdom of God is not food and drink but righteousness and peace and joy in the Holy Spirit. The one who thus serves Christ is acceptable to God and has human approval. Let us then pursue what makes for peace and for mutual upbuilding. (Rom 14:7, 13-15, 17-19).

And again in Galatians:

> For you were called to freedom, brothers and sisters; only do not use your freedom as an opportunity for self-indulgence, but through love become slaves to one another. For the whole law is summed up in a single commandment, "You shall love your neighbor as yourself." If, however, you bite and devour one another, take care that you are not consumed by one another. Live by the Spirit, I say, and do not gratify the desires of the flesh. Now the works of the flesh are obvious: fornication, impurity, licentiousness, idolatry, sorcery, enmities, strife, jealousy, anger, quarrels, dissensions, factions, envy, drunkenness, carousing, and things like these. I am warning you, as I warned you before: those who do such things will not inherit the kingdom of God. By contrast, the fruit of the Spirit is love, joy, peace, patience, kindness, generosity, faithfulness, gentleness, and self-control. There is no law against such things. (Gal 5:13-23)

For Paul, the body of Christ is so connected and interdependent that there is no dismissal of others—regardless of their status or stature. When one hurts, everyone hurts. When one rejoices, everyone rejoices.

> For just as the body is one and has many members, and all the members of the body, though many, are one body, so it is with Christ. For in the one Spirit we were all baptized into one body—Jews or Greeks, slaves or free—and we were all made to drink of one Spirit. . . .
>
> That there may be no dissension within the body, but the members may have the same care for one another. If one member suffers, all suffer together with it; if one member is honored, all rejoice together with it. (1 Cor 12:12-13, 25-26)

Relational reflections. Youth and youth pastors are so inundated with individual actions that we miss the stories that grip and paralyze us every day. In taking relational responsibility, we recognize that stories and relationships are with us everywhere we go—even when we are alone. We carry negative conversations with us; youth ministry can be a place where these stories are addressed and re-authored before they become debilitating. To illustrate, let's take something as innocent as a mirror.

I positioned myself in a local mall by a department store that had a mirror-like surface on the outside of it. My goal was to record my observations of those who walked by the mirror. I was surprised to record that every teenager and adult who walked by the mirror looked at themselves. It was as if the mirror called their name. One by one, male and female, black, white, Latino, young and old, all walked by the mirror and looked—some staring the entire five-foot distance. Although most looked and continued walking, some stopped to adjust their outfit, hair, glasses, makeup or shoes.

We have mirrors in our restrooms, on our doors, in our vehicles, in our pockets, in our purses, in our wallets and on our walls. Although mirrors have multiple uses, there is one use that has gripped us all: surveillance. We look into the mirror and gaze over our bodies, looking for anything that might be out of place or not quite right: hair, clothing and body.

How is it that we have managed to use mirrors in this way? There is nothing about a mirror that says we have to use them to look at ourselves or survey our bodies. When I stand in front of a mirror, no one else is present. When I ask myself what I am looking for, I know it is anything out of place from a certain way I am taught to define beauty. When I ask why I scrutinize myself in this way, my relationships and stories are the culprit. The following poem unveils the illusion of individualism:

My Mirror, Mirrors We

Mirror, mirror, on my wall,
have you manipulated all?
Looking into you I see
no one's there, only me.
So I make my choice to change;
my face, my body, I arrange.

I feel that there are others there,

but all I see is my own stare.
You show, I look, it is me.
Isn't this reality?
How'd I learn to look into your gaze?
Will I ever outgrow this phase?
How does everyone seem to fall
deep into your seductive call?

I try not to look with my eyes,
because when I do, you scrutinize.
How did I come to use you this way?
Every time I wake, you say,
"Look in my gaze and you will find
changes needed to be divine."

But when I close my eyes I see,
relationships reflecting back at me.
Mirror, mirror, you're still there.
You're not the only thing we share.

I evaluate people as they evaluate me.
From this scrutiny can we be free?
Mirror, mirror on the wall,
You're not the culprit after all.

Young children are fascinated by mirrors, but they do not use them to evaluate their bodies negatively. We are not born with a trait that tells us how to use a mirror. When youth and adults stand in front of a mirror, it may not take long before internalized conversations of guilt, perfection, fear, hopelessness and other problems emerge.[3] Some of these voices may have existed for a long time, and some are probably still influential. Negative internalized conversations may be related to panic attacks, depression, anorexia, violence and so on. The vast majority of our youth carry internalized conversations of guilt, shame and inadequacy, and they reach the point where they don't care. Here are some quotes from youth:

- I don't care if I end up paralyzed from a speeding accident; my life is already full of paralysis.

- I don't care if my parents get mad at me; my parents already hate me.

- I don't care about success; my life is already a failure.

- I don't care if drugs damage my brain; I have been told my brain is already damaged.

- I don't care if I get pregnant; my baby will love me.

- I don't care if a guy is using me for sex; it's the only usefulness I have experienced.

- I don't care if I lose my life; I have never found it.[4]

How do we treat such problems with our youth?

ADDRESSING SERIOUS PROBLEMS WITHOUT TAKING THEM TOO SERIOUSLY

Bethany, a former student in my youth discipleship class at Gardner-Webb University, called me in a panic. "I just received a text message from one of my youth. She has been super depressed lately, and now she says she is praying that God will take her life. What do I do? What do I say? I know we talked about this in class, but I can't remember anything right now."

"Well, Bethany," I responded, "You should have taken better notes, because I can't remember anything either."

"Really?" she asked.

"I am kidding."

"Oh my gosh!" she responded. "I thought you were being serious."

"No," I assured her. "But as serious as your situation is, I need you to take it less seriously for a moment. I feel your anxiety seething through the phone."

Bethany chuckled. "Yeah, I am freaking out. I have never had this happen before."

"Can we talk about your 'freaking out' for a moment before we address interacting with your youth?" I asked. She agreed, and for the next fifteen to twenty minutes I explored and probed Bethany's anxiety in responding to her youth. Where did she think her "freaking out" was coming from? What stories was she playing over and over that kept her from helping her youth? How could we revise those stories so she could feel more adequate about addressing her youth's problem? Together we discovered that Bethany's life story and interaction with her youth was being crippled with a larger narrative of fear—in particular, her fear of failure.

Many times when youth pastors are faced with serious problems, we react out of fear rather than love. Fear can fuel defensiveness, criticism and feelings of inadequacy. As John says, "There is no fear in love, but perfect love casts out fear; for fear has to do with punishment, and whoever fears has not reached perfection [completion] in love" (1 Jn 4:18). I have had my share of fears that I have reacted from: fear of not having the right response, fear of youth going astray, fear of not being a good minister.

Out of our own fear, we often counter stories that we do not want our youth acting out. We offer a rebuttal to their stories, and we give them a new story according to how we think they should live. Much of our language and the way we approach our students' problems adds more deficits to their already depleted sense of self.

Most of our youth approach us from a space of vulnerability. We should handle everything they say with great compassion and concern, not criticism and condemnation. What would you say if a youth told you she hated God and no longer wanted anything to do with church or Christianity? How would you respond if a youth said he no longer trusted the Bible? What if a youth said she no longer trusted you?

If we are fearful, we tell her she shouldn't think that way (emphasizing her "faulty thinking"). We tell him he shouldn't act that way (emphasizing his poor performances). We tell her she shouldn't believe that way (emphasizing her lack of faith). Then we tell them what to think, how to act and what to believe. Our youth deserve more attention to their problems than quick and easy rebuttals like these.

We should be patient and relax about—although not ignore or dismiss— most of our youth's problems. We should exercise caution in how we react; if we react too strongly to some problems, it may give the problems more power over our youth's lives. Families tend to focus on the child's problems, so their stories become saturated with the problem. A story that describes a child in a negative way tends to shape that child's thoughts and behaviors unfavorably. When we treat a problem as major, we concentrate too much of our time, energy and focus on it. There may be better ways to address and treat the problem.

We downloaded the movie *Zathura* for our seven-year-old. It is a PG movie, and I had watched it several times before we downloaded it for him. Somehow a curse word slipped through my radar, and my wife overheard it. Since he had seen the movie several times, we decided not to remove it. Instead we stressed not to repeat the bad word. We were stern and serious, and we told him that he could get in big trouble for repeating that word to any of his friends at school.

The next day, my son, being a responsible seven-year-old, decided he would share our words of wisdom with a friend who had also seen the movie. He told his friend the bad word and that he shouldn't say the word, because they could get in serious trouble if they did. The friend understood the seriousness of the word, and he felt that my son's concern should be shared with his other classmates so that they would not say the bad word either. Half of the kids in the first grade responsibly shared the bad word that most of them did not know so that no one would say it.

We were mortified when Kaden's teacher told us what happened. Next time we may not take such a situation as seriously.

Therapists Jennifer Freeman, David Epston and Dean Lobovits state,

> The price of choosing seriousness for us as therapists may be the dampening of our own resources, such as the ability to think laterally, remain curious, be lighthearted enough to engage playfully . . . and have faith that the situation is resolvable. Lacking these, we may have our wits dulled . . . or become overwhelmed. What happens when we engage our imagination, humor, and resourcefulness in opposition to the deadly seriousness of problems? We believe this leads to the rise of inspired problem-solving and the downfall of serious problems. Weighty problems seem to have a knack for convincing caretakers that it's time to quit playing around and get down to business. However, a serious approach may exclude or alienate children [and youth] and work to the advantage of the problem.[5]

Jesus faced serious problems during his life, and I am amazed at how unseriously he responded. A woman was about to be stoned, and Jesus doodled (Jn 8:8). The disciples approached him with important questions, and he told stories. A fierce storm on the lake frightened the disciples, and Jesus snoozed (Mk 4:35-41; Mt 8:23-27; Lk 8:22-25). When Jesus faced death before Pilate, he refused to give him a direct answer and asked Pilate a question instead (Jn 18:34). Brothers argued over their inheritance, and Jesus told a horror story of a farmer's possessions eating him alive (Lk 12:13-21).

Being blind, paralyzed, lame, mute or outcast were all considered serious issues during Jesus' time. These were understood to be the direct result of sin—the person's sin or their parents' sin. Jesus did not take this view of sin as serious at all. He reacted strongly against it and empowered the outcasts through touching and forgiving them, never condemning. A woman with a sketchy reputation entered a Pharisee's home where Jesus was invited for table fellowship. She washed Jesus' feet, dried them with her hair and continued to kiss his feet. This would be a *serious* problem for any minister in a public setting. Jesus commended the woman in the midst of ridicule from his host, forgave her sins and told her to go in peace (Lk 7:36-50).

A man was blind. Jesus spit on clay and put it on his eyes and told him to go take a bath (Jn 9:6-7). Jesus instructed people to give up their cloak when others sued or stole from them (Mt 5:40), which left them naked to expose the evil of their persecutors. Jesus faced the near-fatal illness of his friend Lazarus, and yet he waited two days to go to him (Jn 11:1-6). Jesus didn't take these problems nearly as seriously as I would have. Yet he did not neglect the problems either.

After Bethany revised her story of failure with the story of being God's beloved, her anxiety drastically decreased. She was able to focus on how she could love her youth during this difficult time, and once her imagination was set free from the bondage of fear, we were able to come up with some concrete ways that she could respond:

1. Simply being available and present would speak volumes to this young girl, who feels that no one cares and her life does not matter.

2. Being vulnerable with her and saying, "I don't know" would be okay. When we are vulnerable with our youth we provide them with an example of how to be open, honest and authentic in their relationships.

3. Bethany should allow her space to talk about her pain without countering it. Giving her a voice to express her feelings of insignificance gives her a sense that she matters and is worthy enough to sit with in her pain.

4. Bethany should listen to her whole story, exploring her life story with her and discovering her themes of her life and how she is connecting her negative stories. Bethany should find out where in her relationships and stories she began to feel inadequate or not worthy enough to live.

5. Bethany should identify who is her youth's supporting cast (family members, friends, teachers, coaches, etc.). Whose voice matters to her and why? Bethany would help her to see how interconnected she is with everyone and how they depend on her just as much as she depends on them.

6. Bethany would help her youth explore how she could revise her story with the life story of Jesus. What stories can she relate to in the Bible where women may have felt similar to her? How did Jesus respond? How can that story speak to her?

Bethany contacted me a week later to report the incredible transformation that had taken place in this young girl's life. Not only did her questioning and exploring her youth's story help both Bethany and the youth, but her youth told her that she was able to help her friend in a similar way, asking some of the same questions and hearing her story.

REVISING THE LIFE STORIES OF YOUTH

Problems come in many forms, and they can profoundly shape youth. As mentioned earlier, many of us walk around with an internalized negative conversation. What happens when youth allow problem-saturated stories to structure their life stories? Their lives become problematic, and they become less than the whole human beings God created them to be.

Narrative therapy has identified the power of story and how problem stories can dominate a person's life. Certain themes spoken by adults or peers (such as, "you're stupid") may be the message around which a person structures his life. In narrative therapy, problem-saturated narratives are uncovered and externalized. The problem is named, and the youth begins to restory his life with the help of a therapist. If the problem is stealing, then stealing is given a name by the youth.

Once I had a student who named her tendency to steal "Swiper." We explored how Swiper started ruling her life story and how she could stop Swiper from dominating it. Externalizing the problem in such a way enables youth to understand that the problem is not inherent within them, and that God did not create them this way. Therefore it can be overcome the same way it began—through relationships and stories. As Michael White often says, "The person is not the problem, the problem is the problem." With this approach, the problem is contextualized, and separation occurs from the dominant story in a way that invites resolution. Students can shift from being ensnared by the problem story to active participation in re-authoring the story.

Focusing on the problem as part and parcel of the individual reinforces the problem. In youth ministry, we focus on how God has not created us to live problem-saturated lives.[6] In helping our youth separate from their problems, we live the life story of Jesus through how we gently and lovingly guide them, reminding them of their worth and dignity in Christ.

If we do not address problem stories and negative labels with our youth, they may never share their hurtful labels and stories with anyone else. And they risk holding onto these negative labels for the rest of their lives.

I asked everyone in our congregation to write down a hurtful name they were called in childhood. We spent several minutes talking about our participation in harmful speech, and we worked through restorying the hurtful name and our view of the person who said it to us. Our focal passage was 2 Corinthians 5:11-19, and my sermon was on becoming a new creation through the ministry of reconciliation.

I was overwhelmed with the number of senior adults who could vividly remember hurtful names that were given to them in childhood. Eighty-year-old Bridget Berryhill approached me with her piece of paper in her hand. With tears flowing down her cheeks, she extended her slip of paper to me and said, "Thank you. For seventy years I have held onto this name, and it has bothered me until today. Now I can finally let go." And she did. She dropped it in my hand, gave me a hug and walked away. I opened the paper, and she had crossed out the hurtful name: "Midget Bridget." She had written her new name below it: "Legit Bridget." I laughed, smiled and cried at the same time.

Objectification. One of the most dangerous overarching stories that Jesus struggled against, and one that youth ministers should too, is the problem of objectification, in which people are treated as less than persons created and loved by God. Whenever people view others or themselves as less than precious children of God, they are engaging in objectification. Allowing the Spirit of God to form their life stories in conjunction with Jesus' life story enables youth to begin seeing the world and others with God's love, which means treating others as full human beings. Many internalized conversations of guilt and failure come from objectification.

People today are labeled by their profession ("He is a youth minister"), their roles ("She is a mother"), their education ("He didn't graduate high school"), their social positioning ("She and her family are all rednecks"), their religious affiliation ("He is a Muslim") and so on. Obviously, people are more than the labels we attach to them. Most problems in youth ministry stem from labels that people have storied into their lives—stories that have ensnared them so that every future story they tell is negatively impacted by them. Albert Nolan wrote,

> Our problem is that the ego treats everyone, even those who are close to us, as objects. The ego sees them as objects to be used, to be possessed, to be accommodated and cultivated or to be hated and rejected. They may be the objects of interest or not; they may be seen as sex objects or even as objects to be pitied, charity cases. But what the self-centered ego never sees them as is subjects, that is to say, as persons. Jesus loved his neighbor as himself, as another self. In fact he identified himself with other human beings.[7]

Jesus values the wholeness and sanctity of all humanity. His story treats everyone as God's beloved child and offers wholeness for everyone. Jesus does not ostracize those who strive against the wholeness of humanity and creation—those who attempt to dominate, those who treat others as objects. He loves them openly through their rejection of God's love, patiently waiting for them to come to their senses and to come home to the Father—knowing the painful reality that they might not.

Objectification is a dominant problem in society because it is engrained in ancient Western dichotomies such as good/evil, respect/disrespect, pretty/ugly, male/female, normal/abnormal, winner/loser.[8] These classifications bear their mark in every conversation between youth and adults, helping to craft youth's identities. Youth ministers should be aware of these classifications and be careful not to reinforce and reproduce the social differentiations that objectify youth and treat them as less than children of God.

Amy tagged me and about twenty youth in our youth ministry in a Facebook photo from a recent trip. Since the picture showed up on my Facebook timeline, I saw that several adults from our church had clicked that they "liked" it. The first comment was from a random guy that attempted to hit on Amy by writing, "When you want a real man instead of those dweebs, hit me up." It didn't take five minutes before forty comments were added, and several of my youth launched a full-fledged assault on this guy for "dissing" them and their friends.

This guy objectified my youth, and my youth retaliated with the same objectification, just with different words. Interestingly, a few years ago, I would have scolded my youth because of their behavior and language, and I would have also participated in the objectification.

Objecting to objectification. The objectification of people runs deep in human history. Through the biblical narratives, we can see how people were objectified in Jesus' place and time. Lepers were considered unclean, women did not have a voice, and the condition of the blind was considered a result of parental sin. Objectification has not disappeared, but it has become more subversive. Ironically, it has become part of many therapeutic and religious processes. The very institutions that most people perceive as existing to help are in fact preventing them from becoming fully functioning human beings.

However, both the church and the therapeutic community have an opportunity to reverse this process through careful discourse. How youth ministers address their youth, call on their youth, talk about their youth and confront what their youth call each other during their time together has major implications.

I met with a few of my youth in a coffee shop a few days after the Facebook posting. Within a few minutes, one of them brought up the post. "That was crazy how that guy had to put down everyone, trying to flirt with Amy."

"That was creepy, not crazy," Amy said, shuddering.

I asked my youth how they felt about his comments and how they felt about their own. The consensus was that the guy's comments were ridiculous, and he deserved the backlash he received.

"What about the guy's comments were ridiculous?" I asked.

"He put us down, and he doesn't even know us."

"So it's okay to put someone down if you know them?"

"No, but it is even worse if you have no idea who they are."

"Did anyone know this guy?"

"No, he just came out of nowhere. He was friends with Greg, so I accepted him as a friend," Amy said.

I remained silent for a moment, and one of my students said, "Oh crap! We did the same thing he did, didn't we?"

I used this opportunity to talk about how we treat people like objects by labeling them, "dissing" them, criticizing them and not taking the time to see them as human beings just like us. We talked about ways that they had been treated like objects on Facebook. I told them how a few years before I would have criticized them for their responses to this guy. I asked, "If I did criticize you for your responses, what would I have done?"

"You would have done the same thing this guy did to us and we did to him."

"How do we stop objectifying people when they objectify us? Did Jesus get objectified?"

"All the time."

"How so?"

"He was called a drunkard, and the Pharisees were constantly on his back because he hung out with the wrong crowd."

"What did he do?" I asked.

"He didn't retaliate; he loved."

"What did he do with people who were objectified?"

"He loved them too."

We talked about several of Jesus' encounters with people who were objectified, and we shared the importance of loving people in order to stop the vicious cycle of objectification.

This conversation would have never taken place if I was concerned with individual responsibility. Moving to relational appreciation and responsibility provided space where a deeper reflection and articulation of actions and the life story of Jesus could take place.

Youth ministers are not therapists, but we have an incredible opportunity to be therapeutic. We can help youth restructure their life stories in ways that weaken the problem stories that dominate their lives. Countering the problem stories with other stories youth have neglected or forgotten weakens those stories and provides youth with a thicker understanding of identity. For Christians, the form of life of the Christian community and the life story of Christ combat problem stories. We allow Christ's spirit and life story to be our guide to restructuring and rethinking our current relationships, according to his love and life. His stories can help restructure youth's stories in a way that enables them to withstand crippling stories.

Restructuring and restorying involves much more than individual decisions. For the local church and its youth ministry, it becomes a way of being and doing for the whole body. The collective body of Christ seeks ways to explore and practice the communal narratives of Scripture.

CONCLUSION

By the time youth graduate from high school, they have been subjected to highly complex societal systems of manipulation and conditioning that carry distinct stories and produce "normalization."⁹ This process takes many forms, but it can be seen and heard in youth's stories. Youth can walk into any store that sells magazines and see an aspect of the normalization process, which reminds them there is a norm, a way they are supposed to look, talk and walk in society.

There is no denying that today's youth have been subjugated by societal narratives that rip richness from their life, take them hostage, blind them with illusions and oppress them. In contrast, Jesus said, "The Spirit of the Lord is upon me, because he has anointed me bring good news to the poor. He has sent me to proclaim release to the captives and recovery of sight to the blind, to let the oppressed go free, to proclaim the year of the Lord's favor" (Lk 4:18 19).

Relational responsibility in youth ministry means combating society's oppressive stories with the paradigmatic narrative of Jesus, which narrates the richness of life, the way out of captivity and the removal of society's blinding powers. This narrative of relational responsibility gives hope, love and freedom in the midst of oppression.

Jesus was aware of the various power structures of his day because he was engaged with the sociocultural life of the people. In many ways, he was a product of his sociocultural life. He was aware of the various roles that people played, aware of the difference between the kingdom of God and the populist understanding of God, and aware of those who were in a dominated or dominant position. Jesus spoke the language of the people, and he was cognizant of how his society and culture functioned. For this reason, he was able to address past issues that formed the present society and point to a *telos* (an end goal) that could change the present circumstances. Jesus' life and death indicate solidarity with humanity, and his resurrection is our new life. Jesus illustrates a God who suffers with the suffering, who is present and who loves all.

REFLECTION QUESTIONS

1. How might relational responsibility, as presented in this chapter, bring youth groups and churches closer together?

2. Give an example of a problem that became worse because it was taken too seriously. How could the problem have been handled differently?

3. Write injurious names that have been given to you throughout your life. How have these names shaped you? What has your reaction to these names been? Have you created stories about your life according to these names? Do any of these names continue to hinder your engagement with others? How have you used these same names toward others?

4. Take a good look in the mirror. What do you usually look for? How can you see yourself differently?

5. What are some ways you or your youth have been objectified?

6. What are some ways you can combat society's oppressive stories of our youth? Instead of telling youth they shouldn't think, act or believe certain ways, how could we address serious issues with them without demeaning them?

Conclusion

Books, like stories, have an ending. This is not because there is anything inherent within a book or story that provokes closure, but because we expect some type of conclusion. A book's conclusion must coordinate with the culturally accepted conventions of good writing. And anything out of the ordinary may throw the book, its author and its content into question.

As currently understood, books without some sense of closure may be considered incomplete. However, from a social constructionist understanding, conclusions provide a false sense of completion. If you are willing to accept the invitation to relational narrative youth ministry practices, this book will not end with the conclusion or its last sentence. As with the endings of the Gospels, the conversation only begins, and the story continues in the lives of its participants.

Stories do have social endings. These social endings are not determined by their conclusions. The ultimate ending of a story is when it no longer has any use in relationships. When this happens, the story ceases to exist, because it is no longer meaningful and it has no socially forming role. The biblical story forms Christians.[1] Without it, there would be no Christianity.

I recognize that the limitations of this work are enormous. I have intentionally left out topics because there is not enough room. Perhaps at the top of the list of additional topics are specific ways the concepts can be applied in a youth ministry setting. My goal is to begin the conversation, but there is much to be explored in developing specific practices. The theological praxis of relational narratives could also be more thoroughly examined—especially in regard to social justice and environmental responsibility. God's revelation and the role of the Holy Spirit would also be a fruitful topic of further investigation. I hope I have raised enough questions related to current youth ministry practices that an alternative space for new conversations will emerge and new youth ministry practices will be implemented.

God's story, as revealed in Christ, opens youth to a new way of living and relating. When youth's imaginations are engaged and their thoughts begin to stir with the reading or hearing of a story, the words, sentences and paragraphs become a real world in which they begin to envision a new reality. When a story unfolds in this way, its co-constructors are never the same. Some form of their experience and some aspect of their perception are altered so that their eyes see the world from a new perspective.

Once invited into a story, people choose whether or not it is worth incorporating into their world—or in the case of God's story, worth allowing their world to become a part of it. This book has been formed from an active participation in the life story of Christ, his kingdom and his body, the church. It seeks to be a testimony to God's story as it recognizes that stories live on in their participants.

An invitation is extended to you to join this movement, beginning with relationships and stories in ministering to our youth. Presuming your acceptance of the invitation, this book will end the way it began—with an invitation to more.

This is not the end of the story.

Afterword

As Brandon McKoy opened this inspiring work, "Even when a story reaches its last sentence, its impact continues in the lives of those who have participated in its reading, telling and living." These words drew me into fond reverie, as I returned to warm memories of Brandon's participation in the home workshops Mary and I conduct in social constructionist thought. The intense sharing that had taken place during those hours did not terminate with his departure. Indeed, within this work those searching dialogues are now revitalized. And this new life is not simply a replica of the past; it is a multi-hued transformation. The abstract ideas we shared there—on socially constructed worlds, narrative, the primacy of relationship, multiple being, the co-construction of meaning and the like—here now acquire living flesh. As the ideas are settled into the context of youth ministry, with all its abundant and complex challenges, they acquire new and unimagined potentials. We find the ideas playing out concretely in the lives of Angela, Blake, Lisa, Todd, and a host of other young people, and in Brandon's life as well—both in his recollections and in his professional actions. And we see how the ideas can deeply enrich the potentials of the youth minister—and possibly all of our potentials for living our daily lives. Here indeed is a transformation of what took place in those workshops. I imagine here a form of resurrection—in rebirth, a transcendence.

I am also moved into further dialogue by this innovative work. So often I simply wish to respond in affirmation: "Yes, yes," "Right on target," "Brilliant!" But there are moments as well in which I want to take the conversation further. I want to ask, for example, about the narratives of resistance that we so often encounter among youth, the tales they secretly tell to each other that ensure they are all unified against the "system"—the school, parents, even the law. How should we access and respond to these narratives as they function both to divide and unite?

I wonder as well, what we should do with the unarticulated worlds of many youth—not their narratives but their lack of narrative engagement. Their silence is also a language, but how shall we coordinate with such a language in such a way that more promising futures may emerge?

And finally, how are we to relate beyond the coordination of speaking and listening? To be sure, these verbal exchanges are enormously important, but the relational practices that foster such sharing, and are in turn invited by them, deserves expanded attention. There are some good conversations invited here.

I also emerge from this text inspired by the relationship into which Brandon has invited me. Now I am the learner! He develops ideas in this text that to my knowledge are nowhere to be found in the voluminous literature on narrative and associated practices of therapy and mediation. There are volumes available on narrative reconstruction, for example, but Brandon introduces the novel idea of helping youth to imaginatively extend the future trajectory of their narrative accounts. What happens if the story goes on in this or that way? In imagining future outcomes, Brandon writes, one may "overcome complacency, apathy and indifference," and grow with the possibility of envisioning "God's future reality." Brandon goes on to show how biblical stories, and most especially the story of Jesus, can be folded into and enrich the stories that youth tell about themselves. Here too is a creative contribution to our understanding of narrative and its practical potentials. Rather than treating the personal narrative as solidified and intact, Brandon asks us to consider ways in which stories can be reformed in the context of reading or listening to other stories. The possibilities here are fascinating.

Finally, I must express my deep appreciation for Brandon's extending the implications of my work into the domain of religion. My writings on social construction and relational being are largely secular. And as many religiously faithful readers discover (and Brandon points out), these ideas can form a bracing challenge to their faith. My writings were never intended to destroy people's beliefs so much as to generate a shared consciousness in the ways in which we all participate in the making of these beliefs. Informed by this consciousness, the hope is to soften the boundaries of difference, to recognize the vulnerabilities in our beliefs, and encourage mutual appreciation for the many forms of understanding available to us. All may potentially enrich the human condition.

Brandon has realized these potentials in his writing, and has invited the secular and sacred to sing together. I am touched and inspired by the resulting harmonies, and shall carry them with me into future relations.

Kenneth J. Gergen

Notes

Introduction
[1]Chris A. M. Hermans, "Social Constructionism and Practical Theology: An Introduction," in *Social Constructionism and Theology*, ed. C. A. M. Hermans et al. (Leiden: Brill, 2002).

Chapter 1: The Way We See It
[1]Albert Nolan, *Jesus Today: A Spirituality of Radical Freedom* (Maryknoll, NY: Orbis, 2006), p. 162.

[2]I will use several terms, such as *co-action* here, that may be unfamiliar to the reader. The English language does not have many words that represent how we simultaneously take action with others. We chop up our actions into individual causes and effects. Language like *co-action, coordinate, co-construct* and *collaborate* will suffice to represent such actions.

[3]Kenneth J. Gergen, *Relational Being: Beyond Self and Community* (New York: Oxford University Press, 2009).

[4]I adapted this story from Leviticus Rabbah 4:6.

[5]If you are not familiar with practical theology, I want to offer a simple and straightforward definition. Theology is the combination of two Greek words, *theos* (God) and *logos* (word). Literally translated it can mean "God words" or "words about God." When we talk about God, we are doing theology. Combining the words *practical* and *theology* gives our "God words" a context: practice. Therefore, practical theology is concerned with Christian action—namely, how we put our God talk into action and how our action changes our God talk. Practical theology is concerned with the mundane, not with abstract philosophical problems. Theologians may entertain and write books on the omniscience of God, but a practical theologian is interested in what kinds of practices emerge from understanding God as omniscient. Simply put, practical theology is theological reflection within everyday life. In addition, if we do not separate God from our relationships but believe God is actively involved in our relationships, then any kind of action and talk can be considered practical theology. My hope is to have people reflect on how our talk and actions convey God's love to others in how we interact and form communities.

[6]Nancey C. Murphy, *Bodies and Souls, or Spirited Bodies?*, Current Issues in Theology (New York: Cambridge University Press, 2006), p. 33.

[7]Kenneth J. Gergen, *An Invitation to Social Construction*, 2nd ed. (London: Sage, 2009), p. 11.

[8]Ibid.

[9]Marie Wachlin and Byron R. Johnson, *Bible Literacy Report: What Do American Teens Need to Know and What Do They Know* (Front Royal, VA: Bible Literacy Project, 2005). See also Christian Smith and Melinda Lundquist Denton, *Soul Searching: The Religious and Spiritual Lives of American Teenagers* (Oxford: Oxford University Press, 2005).

[10]Smith and Denton, *Soul Searching*, p. 133.

[11]Clifford Geertz, *The Interpretation of Cultures: Selected Essays* (1973; repr. New York: Basic Books, 2000).

[12]Gergen, *Social Construction*, p. 44.

[13]Ibid., p. 87.

Chapter 2: The Inadequacies of Individualism

[1]Kenneth J. Gergen, *An Invitation to Social Construction*, 2nd ed. (London: Sage, 2009), p. 87.

[2]Kenneth J. Gergen, *Relational Being: Beyond Self and Community* (New York: Oxford University Press, 2009), p. 15.

[3]Catrina Brown, "Discipline and Desire," in *Narrative Therapy: Making Meaning, Making Lives*, ed. Catrina Brown and Tod Augusta-Scott (Thousand Oaks, CA: Sage, 2007), p. 106.

[4]These social distinctions form the stories that youth tell about themselves. For most youth, there is no other way to perceive the world than through these labels. In a society that is becoming faster-paced, these distinctions and labels will only become worse because they are quick and easy ways to classify, categorize and story understandings of self and others. Unfortunately, most adults are not aware of the dangers of these classifications, and they reinforce them through adult-run programs. When youth become adults, they generally repeat the pattern.

[5]I believe that what little help comes from self-esteem talk has more to do with an attentive relationship than the topic of conversation.

[6]One study examined suicide incidence data from 1965–1985 within thirty-three nations (including the United States). Individualism was found to be a strong positive correlate to suicide. Individualism was defined as a "people's self-perception that they are autonomous personalities not defined by, or merged into, collective familial or social groups." The United States and Australia were high on individualism, while countries like Columbia and Venezuela were low. The study found that the higher the individualism, the higher the suicide rate. Floyd Webster Rudmin, Marcello Ferrada-Noli and John-Arne Skolbekken, "Questions of culture, Age and Gender in the Edidemiology of Suicide," *Scandinavian Journal of Psychology* 44 (2003): 374.

[7]During Jesus' time people didn't have our Western understanding of self. Jesus is calling his audience away from their allegiances with their family and friends and into an allegiance of following him and participating in God's kingdom.

Chapter 3: Relational Being

[1]Michael White, *Maps of Narrative Practice* (New York: Norton, 2007), p. 137.

[2]The *Diagnostic Statistical Manual* is the mental health counselor's Bible for diagnosing and coding clients. Insurance companies require a classification for reimbursements, and they want to know what their money goes toward. Deficit classification has been long scrutinized by many scholars. Unfortunately, many of these articles are unknown to the general public who use the "professional" language of deficits and disorders. A growing number of psychiatrists, psychologists and counselors are taking a stand against such classifications and labeling. See Tom Strong et al., "Counsellors Respond to the Dsm-Iv-Tr," *Canadian Journal of Counselling and Psychotherapy* 46, no. 2 (2012). Even the former chair of the *DSM-IV* speaks out against the forthcoming *DSM-V.* See Allen Frances, "DSM 5 will further inflate the ADD bubble," weblog comment, August 1, 2011, psychologytoday.com/blog/dsm5-in-distress/201108/dsm-5-will-further-inflate-the-add-bubble. Ethan Watters, *Crazy Like Us: Globalizing the American Psyche* (New York: Free Press, 2010); Philip Cushman, *Constructing the Self, Constructing America: A Cultural History of Psychotherapy* (New York: Perseus, 1995); Kevin Aho and Charles Guignon, "Medicalized Psychiatry and the Talking Cure: A Hermeneutic Intervention," *Human Studies* 34 (2011): 293-308.

[3]White, *Maps of Narrative Practice*, p. 25.

[4]Some therapists are seeing the crippling effects of such language and refuse to use the labels with their clients. Although insurance requires the diagnostic labels according to the *Diagnostic Statistical Manual,* they only use them to properly code, not with their clients.

[5]John Winslade and Lorraine Smith, "Countering Alcoholic Narratives," in *Narrative Therapy in Practice: The Archaeology of Hope*, ed. Gerald Monk et al.(San Francisco: Jossey-Bass, 1997), p. 163.

[6]For a search engine of psychiatric side effects, see www.cchrint.org/psychdrugdangers. This website includes two search engines: an international search engine for warnings and studies on psychiatric drugs, and a search engine for adverse reactions reported to the U.S. Food and Drug Administration's Medwatch.

[7]Kenneth J. Gergen, "Therapeutic Challenges of Multi-Being," *Journal of Family Therapy* 30 (2008): 335-50.

[8]Ibid.

[9]Ibid.

[10]Kenneth J. Gergen, *Relational Being: Beyond Self and Community* (New York: Oxford University Press, 2009), p. 34.

[11]Kenneth J. Gergen, "Meaning as Co-Created," in *Constructing Worlds Together: Interpersonal Communication as Relational Process,* ed. Kenneth J. Gergen, Stuart M. Schrader and Mary Gergen (Boston: Pearson, 2009).

[12]James Day emphasizes several benefits of social construction in religious development and pastoral theology. See James M. Day, "Religious Development as Discursive Construction," in *Social Constructionism and Theology*, ed. C. A. M. Hermans et al., Empirical Studies in Theology (Leiden: Brill, 2002), pp. 83-85; and Kenneth J. Gergen, *An Invitation to Social Construction,* 2nd ed. (London: Sage, 2009), p. 98.

Chapter 4: The Reality and Not-So-Reality of Our Life Stories

[1]Derek Edwards, Malcolm Ashmore and Jonathan Potter describe how realists use their absolute hard cases, such as death and furniture, to position themselves against relativism. In attempting to do so, realists miss how they are utterly dependent on the acknowledgement and agreement of an audience that adheres to their objectivist assumptions. As the authors state, "Reality can serve as rhetoric for inaction (*be realistic . . . face the facts . . . come off it . . . you can't walk through rocks . . . you can't change reality, human nature, market forces . . . it's just the way things are . . . life isn't fair*). It is a familiar kind of argument against change, against action, against open-ended potentiality of any kind. Reality is given, perceived, out there and constraining. Arguably, it is for relativists and constructionists that the good life is to be lived and made, as and in accountable social action including that of social analysis; rather than to be taken as given, ruled out as impossible or, as disengaged objective analysts, passively observed and recorded. At the very least, realism has no exclusive claim upon the pragmatics of making a better world." "Death and Furniture: Arguments Against Relativism," in *Social Construction: A Reader,* ed. Mary Gergen and Kenneth J. Gergen (Thousand Oaks, CA: Sage, 2003), p. 235.

[2]Kenneth J. Gergen and Mary Gergen, *Social Construction: Entering the Dialogue* (2004; repr. Chagrin Falls: Taos Institute Publications, 2008), p. 16.

[3]Ludwig Wittgenstein, *Philosophical Investigations,* trans. G. E. M. Anscombe, 3rd ed. (Upper Saddle River, NJ: Prentice Hall, 1958), p. 11e.

[4]Pierre Bourdieu, *Science of Science and Reflexivity,* trans. Nice Richard (2004; repr. Cambridge: Polity, 2006), pp. 95, 116.

[5]Special thanks to Ken and Mary Gergen for this creative game.

[6]Ralph Strauch, *The Reality Illusion* (Pacific Palisades, CA: Somatic Options, 2000), p. 40.

[7]Ludwig Wittgenstein, *Tractatus Logico-Philosophicus,* trans. D. F. Pears and B. F. McGuiness (London: Routledge Classics, 2001), p. 68.

[8]The Western understanding of private experience that is rampant in many theological and psychological circles is a good example. Private experience relies on the central metaphor of *the mind as a mirror* that defines the world as "out there," with its contents reflected by experience "in here." A person's perception of his mirrored world becomes distorted when the metaphors begin to be questioned. As Gergen states, "You can begin to realize that the idea of experience as an 'in here' is a metaphor when you stop to locate what precisely is in versus out. Where does the outside stop and the inside begin, on the skin or the surface of the retina, in the receptor nerves, or perhaps the cortex? Consider: if you removed everything we consider 'outside' from experience (for example, everything 'in the physical world'), would there be anything left over we could identify as experience; and if you removed everything we call inside, would there be any 'objects of experience' still remaining? When we try to tease apart what is inner versus outer, we enter a thicket of ambiguity." *An Invitation to Social Construction,* 2nd ed. (London: Sage, 2009), p. 35.

[9]Jerome S. Bruner, "Life as Narrative," *Social Research* 71, no. 3 (2004): 708.

[10]David Yamane, "Narrative and Religious Experience," *Sociology of Religion* 61, no. 2 (2000): 171-89.

[11]The same is true with religious experience, as George Lindbeck has observed: "Instead of deriving external features of a religion from inner experience, it is the inner experiences which are viewed as derivative. . . . Human experience is shaped, molded, and in a sense constituted by cultural and linguistic forms. There are numberless thoughts we cannot think, sentiments we cannot have, and realities we cannot perceive unless we learn to use the appropriate symbol systems." *The Nature of Doctrine: Religion and Theology in a Postliberal Age* (Philadelphia: Westminster Press, 1984), p. 34.

[12]In tests of children two to three years of age, they remembered events (six to twelve months prior) when shown a picture, but they could not translate that event into any new words they had acquired since the event. The researchers discovered that "there was not a single instance in which a child used a word or words to describe the event that had not been part of his or her productive vocabulary at the time of encoding. . . . The results . . . yielded no evidence whatsoever that children could translate preverbal (i.e. nonverbal) attributes of their memory representations into language." Gabrielle Simcock and Harlene Hayne, "Breaking the Barrier? Children Fail to Translate Their Preverbal Memories into Language," *Psychological Science* 13, no. 3 (2002): 229.

[13]Clifford Geertz, *The Interpretation of Cultures: Selected Essays* (1973; repr. New York: Basic Books, 2000), p. 46.

[14]Jerome S. Bruner, *Making Stories: Law, Literature, Life* (New York: Farrar, Straus and Giroux, 2002), p. 86.

[15]Edward Sapir, "The Status of Linguistics as a Science," *Language* 5, no. 4 (1929): 209.

[16]There are several theological models that begin with individual experience, and they do not take into consideration the person's social influences. The minister walks through a theological model with a certain situation, asking questions and theologically reflecting on the outcome. Most theological models do not take into consideration that the minister's view of God and theology (shaped by his/her social influences) will largely determine the outcome.

Chapter 5: Life Stories

[1]Tilmann Habermas and Susan Bluck, "Getting a Life: The Emergence of the Life Story in Adolescence," *Psychological Bulletin* 126, no. 5 (2000): 749.

[2]Although I am influenced by the work of Habermas and Bluck, I find their work limiting since they begin with the individual and focus on the coherence of the life story in the mind. Coherence "in the mind" is not so much that people think "rightly" but that their thinking coheres with society's understanding of "right and orderly thinking." Therefore, I replace coherence with *coordination* to emphasize the relational component of telling a life story. No one simply tells a story; we are dependent on the cultural understanding, interest, response and questions of the other(s) as we share and form our story.

[3]Clifford Geertz, *The Interpretation of Cultures: Selected Essays* (1973; repr. New York: Basic Books, 2000), pp. 49-51.

[4]*Beverley Hillbillies,* season 1, episode 3.

[5]Paul Ricoeur, *Figuring the Sacred: Religion, Narrative, and Imagination,* ed. Mark I. Wallace, trans. David Pellauer (Minneapolis: Fortress, 1995), p. 309.

[6]Alasdair MacIntyre, "The Virtues, the Unity of a Human Life, and the Concept of a Tradition," in *Why Narrative?: Readings in Narrative Theology,* ed. Stanley Hauerwas and L. Gregory Jones (Eugene, OR: Wipf and Stock Publishers, 1997), p. 99.

[7]Kenneth J. Gergen, *Realities and Relationships: Soundings in Social Construction* (Cambridge, MA: Harvard University Press, 1994), p. 208.

[8]Ibid.

[9]Ibid., p. 209.

[10]Gergen, *Social Construction,* p. 92.

[11]Ibid., p. 92.

[12]Ibid.

[13]Annette Bohn and Dorthe Berntsen, "Life Story Development in Childhood: The Development of Life Story Abilities and the Acquisition of Cultural Life Scripts from Late Middle Childhood to Adolescence," *Developmental Psychology* 44, no. 4 (2008): 1136-38.

[14]Tilmann Habermas and Cybele de Silveira, "The Development of Global Coherence in Life Narratives across Adolescence: Temporal, Causal, and Thematic Aspects," *Developmental Psychology* 44, no. 3 (2008): 709.

[15]Bohn and Berntsen, "Life Story," p. 1136.

[16]Dan P. McAdams, "The Problem of Narrrative Coherence," *Journal of Constructivist Psychology* 19 (2006): 115.

[17]Ibid., pp. 111-12.

[18]We are also constrained by the amount of time we exhaust sharing parts of our life story. Spending ten minutes on my birth story and two minutes on the rest of my life may not coordinate well unless I have a significant and unique birth story to share.

[19]Peter L. Berger and Thomas Luckmann write, "The temporal structure of everyday life not only imposes prearranged sequences upon the 'agenda' of any single day but also imposes itself upon my biography as a whole. Within the co-ordinates set by this temporal structure I apprehend both daily 'agenda' and overall biography. Clock and calendar ensure that, indeed, I am a 'man of my time.' Only within this temporal structure does everyday life retain for me its accent of reality." *The Social Construction of Reality: A Treatise in the Sociology of Knowledge* (New York: Anchor Books, 1966), p. 28.

[20]Jay Griffith writes about different times: "Come with me to visit the Karen, a hill-tribe in forests of Northern Thailand, and see how such a forest can be teeming-full of times. Or to Indonesia on the night of the 'little pig moon.' Or to the Andaman forests and smell your way through the scent-calendar. See cow-time and bee-time, coconut clocks, Watermelon months and the month of the Snowblind. See how the seas and oceans are full of time, culturally and physically. . . . There are thousands of times, not one. To say any one time is *the* time is both untrue and highly political." *A Sideways Look at Time* (New York: Penguin, 2004), p. 4.

[21]Even if I say, "When the grass begins to turn green," I am temporally locating an event according to seasonal change.

[22]Susan Bluck and Tilmann Habermas, "Extending the Study of Autobiographical Memory: Thinking Back About Life across the Life Span," *Review of General Psychology* 5, no. 2 (2007): 140.

[23]Anne McKeough and Randy Genereux noticed a 59 percent difference between children at age 10 and adolescence at age 17 in utilizing interpretive flashbacks. There was a 23 percent increase between the ages 10 and 12 and a 28 percent increase between the ages of 12 and 14. "Transformation in Narrative Thought During Adolescence: The Structure and Content of Story Compositions," *Journal of Educational Psychology* 95, no. 3 (2003): 545.

[24]McAdams, "Narrrative Coherence," p. 115.

[25]Habermas and Silveira, "Global Coherence," p. 710.

[26]Tilmann Habermas and Christine Paha, "The Development of Coherence in Adolescents' Life Narratives," *Narrative Inquiry* 11 (2001): 35.

[27]Habermas and Silveira, "Global Coherence," p. 719.

[28]Bohn and Berntsen, "Life Story," p. 1136.

[29]Susan Bluck and Tilmann Habermas, "Extending the Study of Autobiographical Memory: Thinking Back About the Life across the Life Span," *Review of General Psychology* 5, no. 2 (2001): 141.

[30]Habermas and Bluck, "Getting a Life," p. 758.

[31]Susan Bluck and Tilmann Habermas, "The Life Story Schema," *Motivation and Emotion* 24, no. 2 (2000): 133.

[32]Kate C. McLean, "Stories of the Young and the Old: Personal Continuity and Narrative Identity," *Developmental Psychology* 44, no. 1 (2008): 256.

[33]Bohn and Berntsen, "Life Story, " p. 1136.

[34]Bluck and Habermas, "Life Story Schema," p. 132.

[35]Habermas and Silveira, "Global Coherence," p. 719.

[36]Habermas and Bluck, "Getting a Life," p. 759.

[37]Dan P. McAdams, "The Psychology of Life Stories," *Review of General Psychology* 5, no. 2 (2001): 106.

[38]Bluck and Habermas, "Life Story Schema," p. 132.

[39]Kenneth J. Gergen, *An Invitation to Social Construction*, 2nd ed. (London: Sage, 2009), p. 39.

[40]Kenneth J. Gergen, "The Acculturated Brain," *Theory and Psychology* 20, no. 6 (2010).

Chapter 6: Childhood Foundational Elements for Adolescents

[1]Dan P. McAdams, *The Stories We Live By: Personal Myths and the Making of the Self* (New York: Guilford Press, 1993), p. 40.

[2]Clifford Geertz, *The Interpretation of Cultures: Selected Essays* (1973; repr. New York: Basic Books, 2000), p. 81.

[3]Maia Szalavitz and Bruce D. Perry, *Born for Love: Why Empathy Is Essential—and Endangered* (New York: HarperCollins, 2010), p. 52.

[4]Ibid., p. 40.

[5]See dyadic relationships in Urie Bronfenbrenner, *The Ecology of Human Development:*

Experiments by Nature and Design (Cambridge, MA: Harvard University Press, 1979).

[6]Bruce Perry, "Applying Principles of Neurodevelopment to Clinical Work with Maltreated and Traumatized Children," in *Working with Traumatized Youth in Child Welfare*, ed. Nancy Boyd Webb (New York: Guilford Press, 2006), p. 40.

[7]Ibid.

[8]John Bowlby, *A Secure Base: Parent-Child Attachment and Healthy Human Development* (New York: Basic Books, 1988), p. 11.

[9]McAdams, *Stories*, p. 47.

[10]Szalavitz and Perry, *Born for Love*, pp. 87-88.

[11]Ludwig Wittgenstein used the metaphor "language-games" as a way to illustrate how certain usages of words and the meanings we attach to them can be understood only according to the "rules" of the specific "game" in which they are used. Thought and language do not offer pictures of the world, but they are the agreed-upon rules for the specific game being engaged. *Philosophical Investigations*, trans. G. E. M. Anscombe, 3rd ed. (Upper Saddle River, NJ: Prentice Hall, 1958), p. 20e. See also pp. 5e, 11e, 31e, 39e, 44e, 61e.

[12]McAdams, *Stories*, p. 55.

[13]David Elkind, *The Hurried Child: Growing Up Too Fast Too Soon*, 3rd ed. (Cambridge, MA: Da Capo Press, 2007), p. 120.

[14]Lev Vygotsky, *Thought and Language*, trans. Alex Kozulin (Cambridge, MA: MIT Press, 1986), p. 222.

[15]Ibid.

[16]Vygotsky and his colleagues asked preschoolers to play a game. They informed the preschoolers that the names for a cow and a dog were going to be switched. The preschoolers could not switch the names without carrying over the animals' attributes. Some preschoolers said things like, "If it's called cow, it has horns. That kind of dog has got to have little horns." Ibid., p. 223.

[17]At age four and a half, she was able to adjust to the game and understand I was switching the names; she picked up on the game within a few minutes of playing.

[18]Vygotsky, *Thought and Language*, p. 223.

[19]McAdams, *Stories*, p. 35.

[20]Ibid., p. 55.

[21]Ibid., p. 58.

[22]Ibid., p. 67.

[23]Ibid., p. 69.

[24]Elkind, *Hurried Child*, p. 127.

[25]McAdams, *Stories*, p. 77.

[26]Ibid., p. 36.

[27]Vivien Burr, *Social Constructionism*, 2nd ed. (New York: Routledge, 2004), p. 33.

[28]Ibid.

[29]W. Lance Bennett and Martha S. Feldman illustrated this by asking people to tell a story of an actual occurrence or fabricate a story. Evaluators judged stories as being true based on the stories that were most closely associated with a well-formed narrative. *Recon-*

structing Reality in the Courtroom (New Brunswick, NJ: Rutgers University Press, 1981).

[30]Kenneth J. Gergen, *An Invitation to Social Construction*, 2nd ed. (London: Sage, 2009), p. 38.

[31]Robyn Fivush and Katherine Nelson, "Parent-Child Reminiscing Locates the Self in the Past," *British Journal of Developmental Psychology* 24 (2006): 235.

[32]Ibid., p. 237.

[33]Ibid.

[34]Ibid., p. 240.

[35]Jennifer G. Bohanek et al., "Family Narrative Interaction and Children's Sense of Self," *Family Process* 45, no. 1 (2006): 41.

[36]Tilmann Habermas and Christine Paha, "The Development of Coherence in Adolescents' Life Narratives," *Narrative Inquiry* 11 (2001): 35.

[37]Ibid., p. 36.

[38]Dan P. McAdams, "The Psychology of Life Stories," *Review of General Psychology* 5, no. 2 (2001): 105.

[39]Fivush and Nelson, "Parent-Child Reminiscing," p. 235.

[40]Lisa M. Tillmann-Healy, "A Secret Life in a Culture of Thinness," in *Social Construction: A Reader*, ed. Mary Gergen and Kenneth J. Gergen (Thousand Oaks, CA: Sage, 2003), p. 80.

[41]Elaine Reese and Robyn Fivush, "The Development of Collective Remembering," *Memory* 16, no. 3 (2008): 204.

[42]Robyn Fivush, Elaine Reese and Catherine A. Haden, "Elaborating on Elaborations: Role of Maternal Reminiscing Style in Cognitive and Socioemotional Development," *Child Development* 77, no. 6 (2006): 1581.

[43]Ibid.

[44]Fivush and Nelson, "Parent-Child Reminiscing," p. 241.

[45]Ibid., p. 240.

[46]Katherine Nelson and Robyn Fivush, "The Emergence of Autobiographical Memory: A Social Cultural Developmental Theory," *Psychological Review* 111, no. 2 (2004): 500.

[47]Fivush and Nelson, "Parent-Child Reminiscing," p. 242.

[48]Vygotsky, *Thought and Language*, pp. 86-87.

[49]Geertz, *Interpretation of Cultures*, p. 81.

[50]The importance of being able to restructure and reevaluate one's past narratives in a more positive manner is illustrated by a study conducted of children who experienced post-traumatic stress from a category 4 hurricane. Jessica McDermott Sales et al. asked children three and four years old to recall their experience of Hurricane Andrew, which had destroyed their homes. Six years after the initial study, they conducted a follow-up with forty-two of the original one hundred participants when they were nine to ten years old. They found that the children who were more stressed initially named more negative emotions, recalled less information overall and used fewer cognitive processing words as they recalled their experience of the hurricane. This study suggests that the children were still trying, six years later, to process and understand the stressful event. Children who used more positive emotion words and included

more information overall had a reduction in post-traumatic stress in comparison to those initially recorded. These results illustrate that evaluative and orienting information in the content of children's narratives is related to their well-being. "Children's Narratives and Well-Being," *Cognition and Emotion* 21, no. 7 (2007): 1429. Therefore, Sales found, the ways in which preschoolers learn to cope with stressful events, through recall with a caregiver, continue to be influential into elementary school. "Stressing Memory: Long-Term Relations among Children's Stress, Recall and Psychological Outcome Following Hurricane Andrew," *Journal of Cognition and Development* 6, no. 4 (2005): 533.

[51]Fivush et al., "Children's Narratives," p. 1429.

[52]Jessica McDermott Sales and Robyn Fivush, "Social and Emotional Function of Mother-Child Reminiscing About Stressful Events," *Social Cognition* 23, no. 1 (2005): 85.

[53]Ibid.

[54]Marshall P. Duke, Amber Lazarus and Robyn Fivush, "Knowledge of Family History as a Clinically Useful Index of Psychological Well-Being and Prognosis: A Brief Report," *Psychotherapy Theory, Research, Practice, Training* 45, no. 2 (2008): 268.

[55]Rudi Dallos, "Attachment Narrative Therapy: Integrating Ideas from Narrative and Attachment Theory in Systemic Family Therapy with Eating Disorders," *Journal of Family Therapy* 26 (2004): 47.

[56]Kate C. McLean, Monisha Pasupathi and Jennifer L. Pals, "Selves Creating Stories Creating Selves: A Process Model of Self-Development," *Journal of Personality and Social Psychology Review* 11, no. 3 (2007): 266.

[57]Amy Bird and Elaine Reese, "Emotional Reminiscing and the Development of an Autobiographical Self," *Developmental Psychology* 42, no. 4 (2006).

[58]McLean, Pasupathi, and Pals, "Selves Creating Stories, " p. 266.

[59]Ibid., p. 262.

[60]Robyn Fivush, "Remembering and Reminiscing: How Individual Lives Are Constructed in Family Narratives," *Journal of Memory Studies* 1, no. 1 (2008): 55-56.

[61]Perry, "Applying Principles," p. 45.

[62]Perry also discusses the problem with artificial light (video gaming, movies and other technological avenues that have replaced face-to-face relational contact) and insists that the brain is not well designed for such activities, and they may contribute to emotional, social and physical health problems. Ibid., pp. 44-46.

[63]Ibid., p. 46.

Chapter 7: Relationships and Stories in Middle School

[1]The word *adolescence* comes from the Latin verb *adolescere*, which means "to grow up."

[2]Jeffrey Arnett's argument is strong and plausible concerning the importance of removing the term *adolescence* as a reference to those eighteen to twenty-five and referring to this age group exclusively as emerging adulthood. However, it is ironic that he is the sole editor of the *Journal of Adolescent Research* (note *Adolescent* in the journal name), which published more articles on emerging adulthood in 2007 than adolescence. Their September edition published exclusively emerging adulthood articles

(six). And the trend to split publication between emerging adulthood (eighteen to twenty-five) and adolescence (ten to eighteen) continues. In practice, it gives the impression that emerging adulthood is a phase within adolescence, but Arnett is adamant that adolescence is a precursor to emerging adulthood and that they are two distinct phases between childhood and adulthood. Jeffrey Jensen Arnett, "Emerging Adulthood," *American Psychological Associates* 55, no. 5 (2000): 469-80.

[3]For example, see Jeffrey Arnett. *Adolescence and Emerging Adulthood: A Cultural Approach*, 4th ed. (Upper Saddle River, NJ: Prentice Hall, 2010); Paul Kaplan, *Adolescence*, ed. Kerry Baruth, Bess Deck, Caryn Yilmaz, Aileen Mason and Liliana Ritter (Boston: Houghton Mifflin, 2004); Richard M. Lerner, *Concepts and Theories of Human Development*, 3rd ed. (Mahwah, NJ: Lawrence Erlbaum Associates, 2002); John W. Santrock, *Adolescence*, 12th ed. (Boston: McGraw-Hill, 2008); Laurence D. Steinberg, *Adolescence*, 8th ed. (Boston: McGraw-Hill Higher Education, 2008).

[4]Laurence Steinberg, former president of Society for Research on Adolescence, is passionate about his suspicion of "emerging adulthood," as he states, "despite the popularity of this [emerging adulthood] in the mass media, there is little evidence that this is a universal phase of life or that the majority of young people are in some sort of psychological or social limbo (Shanahan, Porfeli, Mortimer, and Erikson, 2005). . . . If you want to speak to an emerging adult in the U.S., you are better off looking on either of the coasts than in the middle of the country." *Adolescence*, ed. Steinberg Laurence, 8th ed. (Boston: McGraw-Hill Higher Education, 2008), pp. 7, 99. For Steinberg and others who do not consider emerging adulthood a valid phase, childhood ends in adolescence and adolescence ends in adulthood.

[5]William Kessen, "The American Child and Other Cultural Inventions," in *The Critical Middle School Reader*, ed. Enora R. Brown and Kenneth J. Saltman (New York: Routledge, 2005), p. 58.

[6]Kenneth J. Gergen, *Relational Being: Beyond Self and Community* (New York: Oxford University Press, 2009), p. 54.

[7]John J. Conger, *Adolescence and Youth: Psychological Development in a Changing World*, 2nd ed. (Scranton: HarperCollins, 1977), p. 103.

[8]Arnett, *Adolescence and Emerging Adulthood*, p. 32.

[9]Our notions of beauty and our physiological reactions to it are also socially constructed. In other cultures, notions of beauty are quite different. Nigerian women are traditionally fattened up before their wedding to appear more attractive and healthy to their future husbands. And tribes around the world that have not been Westernized do not see nakedness as a sexual stimulant.

[10]For instance see the following books' and articles' bibliographies: Barbara Strauch, *The Primal Teen: What the New Discoveries About the Teenage Brain Tell Us About Our Kids*, 2nd ed. (New York: Bantam Doubleday Dell, 2004); Laurence Steinberg, "A Social Neuroscience Perspective on Adolescent Risk-Taking," *Developmental Review* 28 (2008): 78-106; and David Walsh, *Why Do They Act That Way: A Survival Guide to the Adolescent Brain for You and Your Teen* (New York: Free Press, 2004).

[11]Laurence Steinberg suggests that "heightened risk taking in adolescence is likely to be

normative, biologically driven, and, to some extent, inevitable." "Risk Taking in Adolescence: New Perspectives from Brain and Behaviorial Science," *Current Directions in Psychological Science* 16, no. 2 (2007): 58. Sociologist and researcher Mike Males counters Steinberg, who claims the brain influences behavior. Males's critique is helpful as he illustrates his proficiency in countering poor quantitative research with better quantitative research data. However, he lacks qualitative analysis in most of his research and builds his arguments purely on quantitative analysis that may reveal more dangers to the discourse of "the inadequacies of the teenage brain." (For a brief but helpful critique of Males's methodology, see Chap Clark, ed., *Hurt: Inside the World of Today's Teenagers*, Youth, Family, and Culture Series [Grand Rapids: Baker Academic, 2004], pp. 41-43). Males considers Steinberg's work to reflect "minimum subject experiments maximally interpreted," and he criticizes Steinberg and others for neglecting the socioeconomic issues at hand. "Does the Adolescent Brain Make Risk Taking Inevitable?: A Skeptical Appraisal," *Journal of Adolescent Research* 24, no. 1 (2009): 4. Furthermore, Males concludes that biological determinism threatens "the well-being of young people" and further removes "integrating the diverse capacities of older and younger thinking." Ibid., p. 18.

[12]Kenneth J. Gergen, "The Acculturated Brain," *Theory and Psychology* 20, no. 6 (2010): 795-816.

[13]Ibid.

[14]Gergen, *Realities and Relationships*, p. 22.

[15]Ibid., pp. 101-5.

[16]Michael Robbins, *Conceiving of Personality* (New Haven: Yale University Press, 1996), p. 67.

[17]Ibid.

[18]Ibid., p. 66.

[19]Kessen, "The American Child," p. 63.

[20]Kathy Weingarten, "From 'Cold Care' to 'Warm Care': Challenging the Discourses of Mothers and Adolescents," in *Narrative Therapies with Children and Adolescents*, ed. Craig Smith and David Nylund (New York: Guilford Press, 1997), p. 310.

[21]Cigdem Kagitcibasi, "Autonomy and Relatedness in Cultural Context: Implications for Self and Family," *Journal of Cross-Cultural Psychology* 36 (2005): 405.

[22]Ibid., p. 416.

[23]Gergen, *Relational Being*, p. 33.

[24]Kenneth J. Gergen, *An Invitation to Social Construction*, 2nd ed. (London: Sage, 2009), p. 112.

[25]While early adolescence has been noted as the beginning of a rapid decline of parental involvement, the decline is not solely related to adolescents separating from their parents. One study illustrates that the changes in middle school also become difficult for the parents to navigate and requires more time, energy and investment than the simplistic structure of elementary school. See Nancy E. Hill and Diana F. Tyson, "Parental Involvement in Middle School: A Meta-Analytic Assessment of the Strategies That Promote Achievement," *Developmental Psychology* 45, no. 3 (2009).

[26]Gergen, *Social Construction*, p. 113.

27Ibid.

28David Elkind's imaginary audience and personal fable are particularly helpful in understanding early adolescent identity formation and development. Instead of viewing the imaginary audience and personal fable within the framework of cognitive egocentrism, I reconceptualize these theories within the context of relationships and language. Therefore, I move from individual cognitive distortion to the social roles of adolescence and the stories they tell.

29David Elkind has influenced my understanding of "perceived audience" with his notion of the "imaginary audience." *The Hurried Child: Growing Up Too Fast Too Soon*, 3rd ed. (Cambridge, MA: Da Capo Press, 2007), p. 134. However, his focus on the audience being "imaginary" is problematic. It is my belief, in conjunction with recent research, that the imaginary audience is not so imaginary, and early adolescents construct such an audience because of real social pressures. See Lesa Rae Vartanian, "Adolescents' Reactions to Hypothetical Peer Group Conversations: Evidence for an Imaginary Audience?," *Adolescence* 36, no. 142 (2001); Joanna H. Bell and Rachel D. Bromnick, "The Social Reality of the Imaginary Audience: A Grounded Theory Approach," *Adolescence* 38, no. 150 (2003); and Luc Goossens et al., "The Imaginary Audience and Personal Fable: Factor Analyses and Concurrent Validity of the 'New Look' Measures," *Journal of Research on Adolescence* 12, no. 2 (2002).

30David Elkind, "Egocentrism in Adolescence," *Child Development* 38, no. 4 (1967): 1030.

31Ibid.

32Generally, when people are asked who they have had conversations with today, they only give an account of "real" conversations. However, if they are pressed further (and if they are comfortable enough with the relationship), they may admit to having other conversations. They may have had a conversation with the president, appeared on the *Late Show with David Letterman*, performed a concert and meditated with the Dali Lama through the course of their day. These imagined conversations are called "social ghosts." Mary Gergen writes about social ghosts, claiming that these imaginary relationships occur throughout a person's life. See "Social Ghosts: Others Within," in *Constructing Worlds Together: Interpersonal Communication as Relational Process*, ed. Kenneth J. Gergen, Mary Gergen and Stuart M. Schrader (Boston: Pearson, 2009).

33This is not to suggest that some of their friends will not make fun of them because they do not have a cell phone, certain clothes and so on; they will. Due to their heightened sensitivity of self (produced by their social and cultural interactions), their perception of others is often heightened and exaggerated (according to the perspective of most adults), but not imaginary.

34Tilmann Habermas and Susan Bluck, "Getting a Life: The Emergence of the Life Story in Adolescence," *Psychological Bulletin* 126, no. 5 (2000): 749.

35Annette Bohn and Dorthe Berntsen, "Life Story Development in Childhood: The Development of Life Story Abilities and the Acquisition of Cultural Life Scripts from Late Middle Childhood to Adolescence," *Developmental Psychology* 44, no. 4 (2008): 1146.

36Habermas and Bluck, "Getting a Life, p. 755.

37Tilmann Habermas and Christine Paha, "The Development of Coherence in Adolescents' Life Narratives," *Narrative Inquiry* 11, no. 1 (2001): 36.

[38]Habermas and Bluck, "Getting a Life," p. 755.

[39]Dan P. McAdams, "The Psychology of Life Stories," *Review of General Psychology* 5, no. 2 (2001): 106.

Chapter 8: The Life Story in Midadolescence

[1]James Lock, "Acting Out and the Narrative Function: Reconsidering Peter Blos's Concept of the Second Individuation Process," *American Journal of Psychotherapy* 49, no. 4 (1995).

[2]See Jennifer G. Bohanek, Kelly A. Marin and Robyn Fivush, "Family Narratives, Self, and Gender in Early Adolescence," *The Journal of Early Adolescence* 28, no. 1 (2008); and Jeffrey J.Wilson et al., "Verbal Abilities as Predictors of Retention Among Adolescents in a Therapeutic Community," *Child Psychiatry and Human Development* 36, no. 4 (2006).

[3]John Stewart and Carole Blake, "Focus On 'Ours,'" in *Constructing Worlds Together: Interpersonal Communication as Relational Process*, ed. Kenneth J. Gergen, Mary Gergen and Stuart M. Schrader (Boston: Pearson, 2009), p. 129.

[4]Ibid.

[5]Kenda Creasy Dean, "Ascension Deficit Disorder," in Andrew Root and Kenda Creasy Dean, *The Theological Turn in Youth Ministry* (Downers Grove, IL: InterVarsity Press, 2011), p. 204.

[6]Dan P. McAdams, "The Problem of Narrrative Coherence," *Journal of Constructivist Psychology* 19, no. 2 (2006): 115.

[7]Tilmann Habermas and Cybele de Silveira, "The Development of Global Coherence in Life Narratives across Adolescence: Temporal, Causal, and Thematic Aspects," *Developmental Psychology* 44, no. 3 (2008): 710.

[8]Tilmann Habermas and Christine Paha, "The Development of Coherence in Adolescents' Life Narratives," *Narrative Inquiry* 11 (2001): 35.

[9]Habermas and Silveira, "Global Coherence," p. 719.

[10]Annette Bohn and Dorthe Berntsen, "Life Story Development in Childhood: The Development of Life Story Abilities and the Acquisition of Cultural Life Scripts from Late Middle Childhood to Adolescence," *Developmental Psychology* 44, no. 4 (2008): 1136.

[11]Habermas and Paha, "Development of Coherence," p. 38.

[12]Bohn and Berntsen, "Life Story Development, p. 1136.

[13]Ibid.

[14]Susan Bluck and Tilmann Habermas, "Extending the Study of Autobiographical Memory: Thinking Back About the Life across the Life Span," *Review of General Psychology* 5, no. 2 (2001): 132.

Chapter 9: Reading the Bible

[1]See www.ethiopianorthodox.org/english/canonical/books.html.

[2]For a discussion of the changes in the many copies of the New Testament manuscripts, see Bart D. Ehrman, *Misquoting Jesus: The Story Behind Who Changed the Bible and*

Why (New York: HarperSanFrancisco, 2007), pp. 51-62.

³Bruce Metzger, *A Textual Commentary on the Greek New Testament*, 2nd ed. (D-Stuttgart: Deutsche Bibelgesellschaft, 1998), p. 10*.

⁴The earliest complete or nearly complete manuscripts of the New Testament are the Codex Sinaiticus and Codex Vaticanus, which are four hundred years removed from the original manuscripts. See *Dictionary of New Testament Background*, s.v. "Textual Criticism."

⁵Although I am trying to stress the distance from the actual event that occurred to the writings of the Gospel, I am not assuming that the Gospel writers wrote as eyewitnesses or gathered eyewitness accounts simply to record history. They were telling their story in certain ways with certain slants on events to relate to their audience. I am not interested in separating the Jesus of faith from the Jesus of history. I believe this is a moot point. See Craig Evans, *Fabricating Jesus: How Modern Scholars Distort the Gospels* (Downers Grove, IL: InterVarsity Press, 2006), and Richard Burridge, *Four Gospels, One Jesus? A Symbolic Reading*, 2nd ed. (Grand Rapids: Eerdmans, 2005).

⁶A helpful exercise is to purchase a Bible with the Gospels in parallel, and color code materials that are similar, different, removed, added, and changed to fit the authors' themes within their Gospel.

⁷Most translations note textual variants, except the KJV. The scholars who compiled the KJV had access to some of the same textual variants that we have today, but they decided not to include them in the printings for the people.

⁸Numbers 21:14 (Book of the Wars of the LORD); Joshua 10:13; 2 Samuel 1:18 (Book of Jashar); 1 Kings 11:41 (Book of the Acts of Solomon); Joshua 24:26 (book of the law of God); Esther 10:2 (annals of the kings of Media and Persia); Malachi 3:16 (book of remembrance); Jesus may have been quoting the Wisdom of God in Luke 11:49 and Matthew 23:29-36. Paul used the Wisdom of Solomon in Romans 1:18-3:20, and he cites well-known pagan sources (Epimenides and Arastus) in the Athens speech in Acts 17:28. Epimenides is quoted in Titus 1:12; and Jude 14 comes from 1 Enoch 1:9.

⁹Genesis 1:1-2:4a: God creates in six days, speaking his creation into being. Animals are created before man on day five, and God creates male and female on day six. Genesis 2:4b-3:24: The Lord God creates man from dirt and because he recognizes "it is not good for man to be alone" (Gen 2:18), he creates a "helper suitable for him"—animals. Animals do not work for the man, so God creates woman from man's rib. 1 Samuel 16:14-23: Saul knows David very well, and in 1 Samuel 17:55-58 Saul does not recognize David. 1 Chronicles 21:1: Satan rises up against Israel and incites David to take a census of Israel. 2 Samuel 24:1: The Lord incites David to count Israel and Judah. Genealogies of Jesus differ in Matthew 1 and Luke 3. Even if the Gospel authors are trying to trace Jesus' lineage from Mary (Lk 3) and Joseph (Mt 1) as some say, the lineage of David changes in the listings. Angels in Jesus' tomb: Matthew 28:5 has one angel; Mark 16:5 has one angel; Luke 24:4 has two angels; and John 20:12 has two angels. The *Skeptics Annotated Bible* is a source that illustrates a modern-literal interpretation of the Bible. Its authors list four hundred contradictions found within Scripture. Although I do not agree with their interpretive method, this is a good illustration of the

problems that arise when one subscribes to a modern interpretation of the Bible. See "Skeptics Annotated Bible," http://skepticsannotatedBible.com/contra/by_name.html (accessed February 5, 2009).

[10]Many textual criticisms discussed in the academy lead to different ways of interpreting and understanding the Scriptures: historical criticism, source criticism, social-scientific criticism, form criticism, redaction criticism, structural criticism, rhetorical criticism, canonical criticism, narrative criticism, feminist criticism, ideological criticism, postmodern criticism, reader-response criticism, audience criticism, psychoanalytic criticism, poststructuralist criticism and so on. For more information see Richard N. Soulen and R. Kenall Soulen, *Handbook of Biblical Criticism*, 3rd ed. (Louisville: Westminster John Knox, 2001). For postmodern methods of criticism, see Elizabeth A. Castelli et al., eds., *The Postmodern Bible: The Bible and Culture Collective* (New Haven: Yale University Press, 2001).

[11]For a discussion concerning the many biblical canons that emerged, see Harry Gamble, "Canonical Formation of the New Testament," in *Dictionary of New Testament Background*, ed. Craig A. Evans and Stanley E. Porter (Downers Grove, IL: InterVarsity Press, 2000).

[12]Hans-Gorg Gadamer states, "Understanding always involves something like applying the text to be understood to the interpreter's present situation. . . . This is not to return to the pietist tradition of three separate 'subtleties,' for, on the contrary, we consider application to be just as integral a part of the hermeneutical process as are understanding and interpretation. . . . This implies that the text, whether law or gospel, if it is to be understood properly—i.e., according to the claim it makes—must be understood at every moment, in every concrete situation, in a new and different way. Understanding is always application." *Truth and Method*, trans. Joel Wensheimer and Donal Marshall, 2nd ed. (2004; repr. New York: Continuum, 2006), pp. 306-10.

[13]Bart D. Ehrman, *Jesus, Interrupted: Revealing the Hidden Contradictions in the Bible (and Why We Don't Know About Them)* (New York: HarperOne, 2009), p. 23.

[14]Gerard Loughlin states, "The story that the Bible tells is given . . . through the Church's ruled reading of the Bible as Scripture. It is the story and the communal aspect of the story as constituting and constituted by the Church." *Telling God's Story: Bible, Church and Narrative Theology* (Cambridge: Cambridge University Press, 1996), pp. 62-63.

[15]The following are ways the Scripture was used to prove that the earth was the center of the universe and everything revolved around it: Proof that the sun moves around the earth: Joshua 10:12-13; Psalm 19:4-6; Ecclesiastes 1:5-7. Proof that the earth/world does not move: 1 Chronicles 16:30; Psalm 93:1; Psalm 96:10. If God created the earth to move, he wouldn't have set it on a foundation: 1 Samuel 2:8; 2 Samuel 22:16; Job 38:4-6; Proverbs 8:27-29; Isaiah 48:13. Proof that the earth is flat: if the earth is round, all of it cannot be seen from the same vantage point: Job 28:24; Daniel 4:10-11; Matthew 4:8; Isaiah 40:22; Revelation 1:7. If the earth was really round, it wouldn't have an end: Deuteronomy 28:64; Job 37:3; Psalm 22:27; 46:9; 48:10; 59:13; 61:2; 65:5; Isaiah 41:9; Jeremiah 51:16; Daniel 4:10-11. If God created the earth round, it would not have corners: Isaiah 11:12; Ezekiel 7:2; Revelation 7:1. The popular quoted passage of Psalm 103:12 that claims

God has removed our transgressions "as far as the east is from the west" wouldn't make
sense on a round planet. Our transgressions would eventually meet again. If we believed the earth was flat, then east and west would never meet.

[16]Rodney Clapp, *A Peculiar People: The Church as Culture in a Post-Christian Society*
(Downers Grove, IL: InterVarsity Press, 1996), p. 133.

[17]Ibid., pp. 133-39.

[18]See Tatian, *The Earliest Life of Christ Ever Compiled from the Four Gospels, Being the
Diatessaron of Tatian*, trans. J. Hamlyn Hill (Piscataway, NJ: Gorgias Press, 2001).

[19]See Ehrman, *Jesus, Interrupted*, pp. 73-76.

[20]Joel Green, "Narrating the Gospel in 1 and 2 Peter," *Interpretation* 64, no. 4 (2006): 266.

[21]Michael W. Goheen, "The Urgency of Reading the Bible as One Story," *Theology Today*
64, no. 4 (2008): 475.

[22]Ibid., p. 478.

[23]Mark Ellingsen, *The Integrity of Biblical Narrative: Story in Theology and Proclamation*
(Eugene, OR: Wipf and Stock, 2002), p. 22.

[24]William Placher, *Unapologetic Theology: A Christian Voice in a Pluralistic Conversation*
(Louisville: Westminster/John Knox Press, 1989), p. 126.

[25]Richard Bauckham, "Reading Scripture as a Coherent Story," in *The Art of Reading
Scripture*, ed. Ellen F. Davis and Richard B. Hays (Grand Rapids: Eerdmans, 2003), p. 38.

[26]John Howard Yoder, "The Use of the Bible in Theology," in *The Use of the Bible in Theology: Evangelical Options*, ed. Robert K. Johnston (Eugene, OR: Wipf and Stock, 1997),
p. 111.

[27]Stanley Grenz and John R. Franke, *Beyond Foundationalism: Shaping Theology in a
Postmodern Context* (Louisville: Westminster John Knox, 2001).

[28]Davis and Hays, *Art of Reading Scripture*, p. 2.

[29]Placher, *Unapologetic Theology*, p. 161.

Chapter 10: Movements in Youth Ministry Practices

[1]Christian Smith and Melinda Lundquist Denton, *Soul Searching: The Religious and
Spiritual Lives of American Teenagers* (Oxford: Oxford University Press, 2005), p. 130.

[2]Ibid., p. 131.

[3]Smith and Denton refer to this as "Moralistic Therapeutic Deism." See ibid., pp. 162-71.

[4]"The teachers defined biblical literacy as basically consisting of five components: (a)
knowing the book the Bible, (b) being familiar with common Bible stories, (c) being
familiar with popular Bible characters, (d) being able to recognize common biblical
phrases, and (e) being able to connect that knowledge to references in literature."
Marie Wachlin and Byron R. Johnson, *Bible Literacy Report: What Do American Teens
Need to Know and What Do They Know* (Front Royal, VA: Bible Literacy Project, 2005),
p. 19.

[5]For the purpose of our analysis, these movements have been separated. However, in
practice, they are integrated.

[6]*Etymology* is a linguistic term referring to the earliest understanding of a word and its
usage. In other words, we trace the history and application of certain words and ex-

amine how they function in earlier contexts to provide a more coherent understanding of how the word may be used in the context being read.

[7]James Voelz states, "Etymology and/or general meaning are no key to the meaning of words as used at a given context at a given point in time." *What Does This Mean? Principles of Biblical Interpretation in the Post-Modern World*, 2nd ed. (Saint Louis: Concordia, 2003), pp. 92-93, 110-11.

[8]We only have to think back to the changes that have occurred with the word *bad*. *Bad* used to have a negative connotation, but now it can also have a positive connotation in certain contexts.

[9]For an example of a word that can have different meanings within the same writing see the word *law* in W. Gutbrod and H. Klenknech, νόμος, in *Theological Dictionary of the New Testament*, ed. Gerhard Kittle (1967; repr. Grand Rapids: Eerdmans, 1995).

[10]In Matthew 24, Jesus tells of those who are taken away by the flood waters during the days of Noah to introduce those who are taken away from being in the field and grinding. In response to Jesus saying they will be taken from bed, from grinding and from the field, the disciples ask, "Where?" Jesus responds, "Where the corpse is, there the vultures will gather." To be taken away is not a good thing; it entails death and destruction.

[11]Charles H. Cosgrove and W. Dow Edgerton, *In Other Words: Incarnational Translation for Preaching* (Grand Rapids: Eerdmans, 2007), p. 13.

[12]For example, see Barbara Brown Taylor, "Caution: Bible Class in Session," *Christian Century* 119, no. 23 (2002); Anna Carter Florence, "Put Away Your Sword! Taking the Torture out of the Sermon," in *What's the Matter with Preaching Today?* ed. Mike Graves (Louisville: Westminster John Knox, 2004); and Gary M. Burge, "The Greatest Story Never Read: Recovering Biblical Literacy in the Church," *Christianity Today* 43, no. 9 (1999).

[13]Kenneth J. Gergen, *An Invitation to Social Construction*, 2nd ed. (London: Sage, 2009), p. 97.

[14]Look up in the sky on a clear day. It looks like a clear dome is holding back water. The ancient Hebrews believed that it would not rain until God opened the floodgates in the dome (see, for example, Gen 7:11; 8:2).

[15]See chapter 9, endnote 15 for a sample of biblical passages that illustrate ancient cosmology. They believed the earth was flat, the sun and moon moved across the dome of the earth, and the earth did not rotate.

[16]Cosgrove and Edgerton, *In Other Words*, p. 15.

[17]The closest Scripture we have to this statement is Romans 10:9: "because if you confess with your lips that Jesus is Lord and believe in your heart that God raised him from the dead, you will be saved. For one believes with the heart and so is justified, and one confesses with the mouth and so is saved."

[18]Henry Knight, *A Future for Truth: Evangelical Theology in a Postmodern World* (Nashville: Abingdon, 1997), p. 98.

[19]William Stacy Johnson, "Reading the Scriptures Faithfully in a Postmodern Age," in *The Art of Reading Scripture*, ed. Ellen F. Davis and Richard B. Hayes (Grand Rapids:

Eerdmans, 2003), pp. 110-19. See also Stanley Grenz and John R. Franke, *Beyond Foundationalism: Shaping Theology in a Postmodern Context* (Louisville: Westminster John Knox, 2001). p. 34.

[20]I am not suggesting that Jesus should be irresponsibly inserted back into the Old Testament when the authors were unaware of Jesus from Nazareth.

[21]John B. Cobb Jr., *The Process Perspective: Frequently Asked Questions About Process Theology*, ed. Jeanyne B. Slettom (St. Louis: Chalice Press, 2003), p. 77.

[22]"You shall have no other gods before me" (Ex 20:3). This does not mean the god of money, greed, sloth and so on. These are other gods that were worshiped in their polytheistic culture. The Ten Commandments do not say there are no other gods, but that other gods should not be first.

[23]The tenth commandment is directed toward men who are not supposed to covet their neighbor's belongings. Those belongings include their house, slave, wife, ox, donkey and so on. This commandment is not addressed to women, because they are listed and understood as property.

[24]Grenz and Franke state, "The Bible narrates the primary paradigmatic events that shape the identity of the Christian community, for as a people of the book, Christians comprise a fellowship of persons who gather around the story of Jesus Christ. As such, the Bible is the instrumentality of the Spirit. By orienting our communal and personal present on the basis of the past and in accordance with the vision of the future disclosed in the texts, the Spirit appropriates the biblical narrative to create in and among us a new world. And as we inhabit that world, we become the contemporary embodiment of the paradigmatic biblical narrative." *Beyond Foundationalism*, p. 80.

[25]Ronald Thiemann, *Revelation and Theology: The Gospel as Narrated Promise* (Eugene, OR: Wipf and Stock, 1985), p. 88.

[26]Charles Campbell and Mark Ellingsen both illustrate how these narrative approaches focus more on plot and story in general than on the character of Jesus. Charles L. Campbell, *Preaching Jesus: New Directions for Homiletics in Hans Frei's Postliberal Theology* (Grand Rapids: Eerdmans, 1997), p. 169; and Mark Ellingsen, *The Integrity of Biblical Narrative: Story in Theology and Proclamation* (Eugene, OR: Wipf and Stock, 2002), p. 57.

[27]Campbell, *Preaching Jesus*, p. 192.

[28]Narrative therapist Michael White builds on the work of Lev Vygotsky in developing his concept of scaffolding. For him, the zone of proximal development cannot be traversed without another providing manageable steps through conversation so that learning and development occurs. *Maps of Narrative Practice* (New York: Norton, 2007), pp. 275-76.

[29]Thiemann, *Revelation and Theology*, p. 85.

[30]Michael O. Emerson and Christian Smith, *Divided by Faith: Evangelical Religion and the Problem of Race in America* (New York: Oxford University Press, 2000), pp. 77-78.

[31]Grenz and Franke, *Beyond Foundationalism*, p. 109.

[32]Robert Bellah et al. acknowledge that religious individualism is not to be rejected but transformed by connecting it to the public realm. *Habits of the Heart: Individualism*

and Commitment in American Life (Berkeley: University of California Press, 1985; repr., 2008), p. 248.

[33]Grenz and Franke, *Beyond Foundationalism*, p. 207.

[34]Ibid., p. 226.

[35]Ibid., p. 235.

[36]Kenda Dean emphasizes that "youth ministry is primarily about the church's witness to the self-giving love of God." Youth ministry contextualizes this story for youth, but it also teaches us to be the church for all people. *Practicing Passion: Youth and the Quest for a Passionate Church* (Grand Rapids: Eerdmans, 2004), p. 14.

[37]At the same time, if the church does not make it a focus to integrate its young through adding elements that they can relate to, it will be difficult for any youth pastor to assimilate youth into the larger church body.

[38]Campbell, *Preaching Jesus*, p. 222.

[39]Pierre Bourdieu, *The Logic of Practice*, trans. Richard Nice (Stanford: Stanford University Press, 1990), p. 54.

[40]Campbell, *Preaching Jesus*, pp. 232.

[41]For a practical and theological understanding of how to assimilate youth into the larger church body, see Chap Clark's funnel of programming in his "The Myth of the Perfect Youth Ministry Model," in *Starting Right: Thinking Theologically About Youth Ministry*, ed. Kenda Creasy Dean, Chap Clark and David Rahn (Grand Rapids: Zondervan, 2001), pp. 118-24.

[42]Edward Bruner, "Ethnography as Narrative," in *The Anthropology of Experience*, ed. Victor W. Turner and Edward M. Bruner (Urbana: University of Illinois Press, 1986), pp. 146-47.

[43]Alasdair MacIntyre, *After Virtue*, 3rd ed. (Nortre Dame: University of Nortre Dame Press, 2007), p. 221.

Chapter 11: Life Story in Christ

[1]John Dominic Crossan, *God and Empire: Jesus against Rome, Then and Now* (New York: HarperOne, 2007), pp. 147-48.

[2]N. T. Wright, *Simply Christian: Why Christianity Makes Sense* (New York: HarperSanFrancisco, 2006), p. 208.

[3]Marcus Borg, *Jesus: Uncovering the Life, Teachings, And Relevance of a Religious Revolutionary* (New York: HarperCollins, 2006), p. 220.

[4]Paul M. Minus, *Walter Rauschenbusch: American Reformer* (New York: Macmillan, 1988), pp. 88-89.

[5]Anthropologist Michael Wesch conducted a study on the effects of media in society through the venue of YouTube. See "An Anthropological Introduction to Youtube," www.youtube.com/watch?v=TPAO-lZ4_hU (accessed March 5, 2009). Within this "networked individualism" of YouTube, Wesch and his team discovered a "cultural inversion" between what people expressed and what they actually valued: persons expressed individualism but longed for community; they expressed independence but longed for relationship; they expressed commercialization but longed for au-

thenticity. Some found community, relationships and authenticity through YouTube, but the vast majority were still searching. Although the majority of YouTube users were twenty- to thirty-year-olds, Wesch's analysis could be another indication that those young adults have not experienced authentic and communal relationships through their adolescence and that they continue to search for those relationships through mediums such as YouTube. At the very least, this study should lead us to question the church and its role in relation to those who are seeking relationships, community and authenticity. Jesus' proclamation of the kingdom of God is not just concerned with community, relationships and authenticity, but with authenticity in community and relationships. There are many relationships and communities formed, but they are quite different from Jesus' proclamation and establishment of the kingdom of God.

[6]Brian McLaren, *The Secret Message of Jesus: Uncovering the Truth That Could Change Everything* (Nashville: Thomas Nelson, 2007), pp. 117-28.

[7]Crossan, *God and Empire,* p. 116.

[8]Ibid., p. 117.

[9]Ibid., p. 118.

[10]Dan P. McAdams et al., "Continuity and Change in the Life Story: A Longitudinal Study of Autobiographical Memories in Emerging Adulthood," *Journal of Personality* 74, no. 5 (2006): 1.

[11]Or as Paul says, "taking the form of a slave, being born in human likeness" (Phil 2:6-7).

[12]Stanley Grenz and John R. Franke, *Beyond Foundationalism: Shaping Theology in a Postmodern Context* (Louisville: Westminster John Knox, 2001), p. 80.

[13]Kenneth J. Gergen, *Realities and Relationships: Soundings in Social Construction* (Cambridge, MA: Harvard University Press, 1994), p. 187.

[14]Kenneth J. Gergen, *Relational Being: Beyond Self and Community* (New York: Oxford University Press, 2009), p. 176.

[15]Dietrich Bonhoeffer, *The Cost of Discipleship,* Touchstone First Edition (New York: Simon & Schuster, 1959), p. 240.

[16]Mark I. Wallace, "Losing the Self, Finding the Self: Postmodern Theology and Social Construction," in *Social Constructionism and Theology,* ed. C. A. M. Hermans et al. (Boston: Brill, 2002), pp. 93-94.

[17]Ibid., p. 94.

[18]Martin Luther King Jr., *I Have a Dream: Writing and Speeches,* ed. James M. Washington (New York: HarperSanFrancisco, 1992), p. 82.

[19]Gerard Loughlin, *Telling God's Story: Bible, Church and Narrative Theology* (Cambridge: Cambridge University Press, 1996), p. 23.

[20]Grenz and Franke, *Beyond Foundationalism,* p. 268.

[21]Ibid.

[22]Kenda Dean, *Practicing Passion: Youth and the Quest for a Passionate Church* (Grand Rapids: Eerdmans, 2004), pp. 63, 86.

[23]George W. Stroup emphasized his concern in the 1980s that "the crisis in the church is a deep-seated confusion about Christian identity," which is further illustrated when

neither the language of Christian faith nor the participation in the Christian community play a prominent role in many Christians' identity narratives. *The Promise of Narrative Theology: Recovering the Gospel in the Church* (Atlanta: John Knox Press, 1981), pp. 24-36.

[24]Marcus Borg and John Dominic Crossan, *The First Paul: Reclaiming the Radical Visionary Behind the Church's Conservative Icon* (New York: HarperOne, 2009), p. 130.

[25]Ibid., p. 137.

[26]Ibid., pp. 185-86.

[27]Ibid., p. 205.

[28]King, *I Have a Dream,* pp. 30-31.

[29]Ray Anderson, *The Soul of Ministry: Forming Leaders for God's People* (Louisville: Westminster John Knox, 1997), p. 139.

[30]Desmond Tutu and Douglas Carlton Abrams, *God's Dream* (Cambridge: Candlewick Press, 2008).

[31]In the Gospels, Jesus rebukes the disciples and says, "Do not hinder the children" (Mt 19:4). It would be good if we heeded Jesus' understanding of children and their place in society. Today youth are constrained by adults, and they are not given responsibilities as adults.

[32]Rabbi Haim of Romshishok tells a story about a pot and long spoons, and I was influenced by his story as a teenager.

Chapter 12: Relational Responsibility

[1]Richard M. Gula, *The Good Life: Where Morality and Spirituality Converge* (New York: Paulist Press, 1999), p. 52.

[2]I would like to suggest that the love of God that we follow in Christ also moves us beyond our definitions of responsibility that include metaphors such as duty, accountability, obligation, control and so on. The kind of responsibility that the church is to operate from is one of love. Our metaphors change to encouraging, motivating, accepting and so on. Therefore the relational responsibility that I am advocating is not one of duty, service or paycheck; it is because of the love we see and have experienced in Jesus. Our actions toward others overflow from this love.

[3]Stephen Madigan, "Counterviewing Injurious Speech Acts: Destabilising Eight Conversational Habits of Highly Effective Problems," *The International Journal of Narrative Therapy and Community Work* 1 (2003).

[4]This list is a conglomeration of stories told by high school teenagers that I have known through youth ministry. I do not believe their perception is reality, but it is *their* reality, which needs to be taken seriously and sought to be understood through their eyes if change is to take place.

[5]Jennifer C. Freeman, David Epston and Dean Lobovits, *Playful Approaches to Serious Problems: Narrative Therapy with Children and Their Families*, ed. David Epston Dean Lobovits and Jennifer Freeman (New York: Norton, 1997), p. 3.

[6]I am in no way suggesting that youth will have problem-free lives. The approach I am proposing involves practical ways to help our youth overcome their problem-saturated

stories, which complicate their life story and make difficult situations in life even more paralyzing.

[7]Albert Nolan, *Jesus Today: A Spirituality of Radical Freedom* (Maryknoll, NY: Orbis, 2006), p. 158.

[8]Pierre Bourdieu, *Distinction: A Social Critique of the Judgment of Taste*, trans. Richard Nice (Cambridge, MA: Harvard University Press, 1984), p. 468.

[9]Michel Foucault, *Power/Knowledge: Selected Interviews and Other Writings*, ed. Colin Gordon, trans. Colin Gordon et al. (New York: Pantheon Books, 1980), p. 106.

Conclusion

[1]I intentionally use the words *biblical story* and not *Bible* here. If all of the Bibles were to disappear, the biblical story would still exist. The biblical story ceases only when it is no longer shared.

Subject Index

Author Index

Scripture Index

IVP PRAXIS

EQUIPPING LEADERS FOR MINISTRY

"...TO EQUIP HIS PEOPLE FOR WORKS OF SERVICE,

SO THAT THE BODY OF CHRIST MAY BE BUILT UP."

EPHESIANS 4:12

God has called us to ministry. But it's not enough to have a vision for ministry if you don't have the practical skills for it. Nor is it enough to do the work of ministry if what you do is headed in the wrong direction. We need both vision *and* expertise for effective ministry. We need *praxis*.

Praxis puts theory into practice. It brings cutting-edge ministry expertise from visionary practitioners. You'll find sound biblical and theological foundations for ministry in the real world, with concrete examples for effective action and pastoral ministry. Praxis books are more than the "how to" – they're also the "why to." And because *being* is every bit as important as *doing*, Praxis attends to the inner life of the leader as well as the outer work of ministry. Feed your soul, and feed your ministry.

If you are called to ministry, you know you can't do it on your own. Let Praxis provide the companions you need to equip God's people for life in the kingdom.

www.ivpress.com/praxis